# The Master Keys

## A Painter's Treatise on the Pictorial Technique of Oil Painting

---

## Franklin H. Redelius

### Edited by Margaret Cunningham Doyle

iUniverse, Inc.

New York Bloomington

**The Master Keys**
**A Painter's Treatise on the Pictorial Technique of Oil Painting**

*iUniverse books may be ordered through booksellers or by contacting:*
*iUniverse*
*1663 Liberty Drive*
*Bloomington, IN 47403*
*www.iuniverse.com*
*1-800-Authors (1-800-288-4677)*

*ISBN: 978-1-4401-2195-1 (sc)*
*ISBN: 978-1-4401-2197-5 (dj)*
*ISBN: 978-1-4401-2196-8 (ebook)*

*Cover:*
Hieronymus Bosch,
*The Death of a Miser,*
National Gallery, Washington. D.C.

*Printed in the United States of America*
*iUniverse rev. date: 12/02/2009*

*Dedicated in loving memory of my wife, Mary Gray, who understood the agony of a painter turned writer*

# Acknowledgment

I wish to express my deepest appreciation to the poet, Margaret Cunningham Doyle, for her skilled and sensitive editing. She spent countless hours bringing this book to fruition. I also am grateful to Gerald F. Doyle, my friend, fellow artist, and student of Jacques Maroger, for his encouragement throughout this process and his unstinting acts of kindness. Other members of the Doyle family also worked to make this book possible, including Elisa Braver, Judy Doyle, and Kevin Doyle. Claire Joyce provided expert assistance with the formatting and cover design. I wish to acknowledge the artists, Robert White of Winchester, Virginia and Catena Lemonakis-Gielner of Baltimore, Maryland, for procuring important documents for my research. Special thanks is owed to another friend and fellow artist, the late Melvin O. Miller, for his tireless efforts in acting as my secretary in writing to libraries, museums, and companies concerning the purchase of superior elements necessary to our craft. I am grateful to the late H. Gluck of Chantry House Steyning, Sussex, England, who successfully persuaded art supply dealers to stock cold pressed linseed oil.

# Contents

*Acknowledgment* ......................................................... *vii*

*Foreword* ................................................................. *xiii*

*Introduction* ............................................................. *xv*

*Book One* ................................................................ *xix*

FIRST KEY: JAN VAN EYCK (C.1385–1441)—THE GATHERING OF
EVIDENCE ...................................................................... 1

    The Vasari Statement / An Alternate Theory /
    Consideration of Oil—The Treatise of Filarete /
    Dioscorides —Source of Reason / The Gesuati Friars—
    Of Purified Oil / The Varnish of Jan van Eyck—A
    Resin Considered / Preparation of Jan van Eyck's
    Improved Varnish / The Optical Prime Problem and
    Resolve / Historical Evidence / The Grinding Element
    and Pictorial Vehicle of Jan van Eyck / The Palette
    Preparation of Jan van Eyck / The Diluent: A Measured
    Means / Pictorial Procedure—The Underdrawing /
    Painting Technique / In Summation

SECOND KEY: ANTONELLO DA MESSINA (C. 1430–1479)—INVENTOR
UNHERALDED ................................................................. 27

    Maroger and the Oglio Cotto / Maroger's Revision of
    the Oglio Cotto / Theory of Origin / A Gathering of
    Thoughts—The Lead-paste Medium of Antonello da
    Messina / Order of Concern-Antonello's Optical Prime,
    Pictorial Vehicle, Palette Preparation, and Technique /
    Diluent Without Option / A Technique Disseminated
    / Limitations-Consideration of The San Cassiano
    Altarpiece / Dissemination of Antonello's Lead-Paste
    Medium in Northern Europe—Consideration of Durer's
    Salvatore Mundi / In Summation

THIRD KEY: LEONARDO DA VINCI (1452–1519)—BRIDGE BETWEEN
STYLES ................................................................................43

A Gleaning of Evidence / The Lead-Wax Medium
of Leonardo da Vinci / Leonardo's Optical Prime
and Pictorial Vehicle / Consideration of Grounds and
the Application of the Optical Prime / The Palette
Preparation of Leonardo da Vinci and the Introduction
of an Auxiliary Diluent / Trial by Employment and the
Picture Varnish of Leonardo da Vinci / In Summation

FOURTH KEY: GIORGIONE DA CASTELFRANCO (1475–1510)—THE
LIGHT OF VENICE ................................................................53

The Contribution of Giorgione da Castelfranco / A
Founding Principle / Maroger and the Black Oil of
Giorgione / New Thoughts on an Old Theme / A
Matter of Clarification / Giorgione's Venetian Medium
and Pictorial Vehicle / New Visions—Giorgione's Color
Preparation and the White Lead Paste / A Replacement
Diluent / Theory and Resolve of Giorgione's Optical
Prime / The Venetian Technique and Panel / Oil
and Pigment Ground and Optical Prime of Canvas
/ Gesso Ground and the Optical Prime of Canvas /
Consideration of style / A Venetian Tragedy

FIFTH KEY: JAN BRUEGEL THE ELDER (1568–1625)—FLEMISH
LUMIÉRE ..............................................................................79

The Golden Threads / The Black Oil of Anthony van
Dyck / Flemish Medium: Parent Structure of the 17th
Century Flemish and Dutch Pictorial Techniques / Peter
Paul Rubens: Indication of Strength / Mastic Varnish
and the Medium of Peter Paul Rubens / The Ground
and Striated Optical Primes of Panel / The Preparation
of Canvas—Preferred Support of Anthony van Dyck
/ Order of Concern and the Alla Prime Sketches and
Studies / Setting-up of Palette: Preparation of the Paint /
The Diluent "Essential Oil Of Venice Turpentine" / On
Painting "Finished In Every Detail"

THE DUTCH ADDENDUM ....................................................... 122
    Variation on a Theme / Pictures, Pride, and Pronck /
    Resurrected Phoenix

RANDOM THOUGHTS ............................................................. 132
    Theories Revisited

*Book Two* ................................................................... *139*

THE MATERIALS ................................................................. 141

PRE-KEY DIRECTIVES .......................................................... 148

OBSERVATIONS AND KEY DIRECTIVES ................................. 151

FIRST KEY DIRECTIVES: JAN VAN EYCK AND THE XV CENTURY
FLEMISH PICTORIAL TECHNIQUE ........................................ 152
    Selective Thoughts Concerning the XV Century Eyckian
    Technique / Purification of Linseed Oil—Directive I /
    The Liquid Varnish of Jan Van Eyck—Directive II / The
    Optical Prime—Directive III / Jan Van Eyck's Varnish
    Pomade Medium and Pictorial Vehicle—Directive IV / A
    Matter of Paint and the Reasoning for the Diluent

SECOND KEY DIRECTIVES: ANTONELLO DA MESSINA AND THE XV
CENTURY ITALIANS .......................................................... 166
    Regarding the Contribution of Antonello da Messina
    / The Lead-paste Medium of Antonello da Messina—
    Directive I / Antonello's Picorial Vehicle and the Optical
    Prime—Directive II / The Optical Prime of Panel—
    Another Method: Variation of Theme / Preparation of
    the Paints and Setting the Palette / The Diluent / The
    Technique of Antonello da Messina and the Northern
    Painters' Use of Canvas

THIRD KEY DIRECTIVES: LEONARDAO DA VINCI—BRIDGE BETWEEN
STYLES ........................................................................... 174
    Leonardo da Vinci in Measured Step / The Lead-wax
    Medium—Directive I / Leonardo's Optical Prime and
    Pictorial Vehicle Structure—Directive II / Application of
    the Optical Prime / Preparation of Leonardo's Palette
    and the First True Diluent—Directive III / Leonardo's
    Mastic Picture Varnish—Directive IV

FOURTH KEY DIRECTIVES: GIORGIO DA CASTELFRANCO AND THE XVI
CENTURY VENETIANS ............................................................................ 182
    Thoughts on the Venetian Technique / Giorgione's
    Venetian Lead-wax Medium—Directive I / The Black
    Oil of Giorgione—Directive II / The Pictorial Vehicle—
    Directive III / Preparation of the White Lead-paste—
    Directive IV / Preparation of the Paints—Directives
    V and VI / The Essential Oil of Venice Turpentine
    and the XVI Century Venetians—Directive VII / The
    Optical Prime of Panel—Directive VIII / XVI Century
    Venetian Grounds and the Optical Prime of Canvas—
    Directives IX and X

FIFTH KEY DIRECTIVES: JAN 'VELVET" BRUEGEL AND THE XVII
CENTURY FLEMISH ............................................................................ 201
    The Elder Jan Bruegel Flemish Lumiere / The Black
    Drying Oil of Anthony Van Dyck—Directive I / XVII
    Century Flemish Varnish / The XVII Century Flemish
    Medium—Directive II / The Flemish Pictorial Vehicles /
    Rubens' Sun-thickened Oil Varnish

*Source Notes* ........................................................ *217*
*Bibliography* ........................................................ *227*
*Index of Painters* ............................................... *241*

# Foreword

Jacques Maroger (1884—1962), my master for more than a decade, stated in his book, *The Secret Formulas and Techniques of the Masters*, "...if time should not prove me to be entirely right in all my conclusions, I know that the essential principles discovered will at least provide a proper basis for further adaptation and discovery on the same lines."[1] By the license granted in Maroger's statement, I deem it proper, indeed imperative, to offer in the following pages my own discoveries based on those "same lines."

In time, Maroger realized many of his proposals in *The Secret Formulas* were incorrect, and before his death in 1962 he dictated to me a brief but poorly organized revision of that work. His wish was that the revision be put in "better order" and published. This was not to be, since during my attempts to prove by trial application the various proposals contained in his work, negative response became the rule rather than the exception. Reluctantly, I was forced to conclude that Maroger has erred in the revision, and that his last effort was born of frustration and desperation—a grasping at straws which, if published, would serve only to minimize the research value of his first work.

In the ensuing years of accumulating knowledge and painterly experience, I became aware of still more error in Maroger's *Secret Formulas*—errors he had not suspected. The first, the blighted seed of his entire research, was his belief the *Strausburg Manuscript*, (an early 15th Century document of unknown authorship) contained an "interesting clue" to Jan van Eyck's contribution to the pictorial technique of oil painting, namely a new and improved oil based varnish.[2] Visual assessment of 15th Century painting and trial application of Maroger's theory do not support his belief.

The interesting clue Maroger referred to is an element called "oleum preciosem," which is no more than a superlative for a fat, thickened, linseed or walnut oil introduced sometime in the 13th Century; perhaps even as early as the 8th Century. The additives of calcined bone dust, pumice powder, and zinc vitriol recommended by the manuscript's author would do nothing to alter the fat quality of the oil.[3]

The challenge to determine the "true" varnish of Jan van Eyck spurred the forthcoming research. This, it was decided, would be the first priority, since I was convinced that all master techniques stemmed from van Eyck's contribution to oil painting and could not be resolved until the improved varnish had been identified.

As this research progressed and my assertive self grew, I recalled Maroger's words: "Remember, my boy, it is no longer Maroger, it is the medium." His words, spoken prior to the coma that eased him into death, relinquished to me the role of researcher—a legacy that, though unwanted, was accepted nevertheless.

F.H.R.

# Introduction

Although in agreement with the late conservator David Rosen on many issues concerning the restoration of paintings broached in his article "Preservation Versus Restoration," I vehemently disagree with his observation, "We have come to realize that no living person can duplicate the painted surface of the masters."[1]

The painted surfaces of the masters' works were dependent upon technical innovations that could only be arrived at through a process of reasoning. Such reasoning is in the province of nature's teaching, and as we know, what nature will teach to one, she will also teach to another.

Unlike the majority of art historians, picture cleaners, and paint chemists, artists are craftsmen. Their craft is their means of self-expression and livelihood. Thus the artist approaches painting realistically knowing that the make-up of a paint structure is revealed for the most part by the manner in which that structure performs. Therefore, paintings that have retained their freshness over hundreds of years must owe their quality to other than the "oil-simple" pictorial vehicles and practices generally employed in our time. Never could a thoughtful painter believe that the precious transparent qualities and brilliant colours we enjoy in 15th Century oil painting were merely the result of time or, as naively suggested by Emile Renders, by polishing the painted surface with an agate.[2]

Painters also know that desire alone cannot enforce style. They would be the first to agree that the technical methods employed by Rubens and Rembrandt could not have been identical with those employed by van Eyck. Nor could the technical methods of Titian and Tintoretto be identical with those employed by Antonello da Messina.

Painterly response, an element which none but the painter can identify, determines style. Through awareness of that intangible element, the painter equates brilliance and embodied transparency with varnishes and unctuous compounds. Just as the need for a prearranged underdrawing, coupled with a laminated style, would be equated with a limited pictorial vehicle, so playful invention would be associated with a more immediately responsive and tractable pictorial vehicle. And immediacy, coupled with tractability, bring to mind siccative grasp which would logically be equated with accelerated drying and drying agents. This considered, it may be said that most painters speak a common language even though they may not agree on its interpretation. They would all agree, however, that things that are painterly are in the domain of the painter's science. A science based not merely on theory, but one that demands tactile and visual response. Thus, the material and technical problems faced by the masters of the past also face the painters of today who would emulate their style.

Painting is not a vagabond's craft. It demands organization and stability. From the 15th through the 17th Centuries, painters studied past techniques in order to evaluate the possibility of improvement that it must be realized was attained by a process of logical progression. Therefore, many of the elements that, by proper analysis, could be identified in the paint film of a painting by Jan van Eyck, the inventor of the first successful system of oil painting, could also be identified in the paint film of a painting by Tiepolo, the last of the important "Old-Masters." To explain the logical progression from one technique to another, this study is divided into Keys. Each Key deals with a major step forward in technique and proposes the master to whom credit should be given.

As for the evidence on which various trials and proposals contained in this work are based, there have been no new discoveries made of heretofore unknown source documents that state unequivocally the "secrets" of the masters. Instead, the offering about to be made involves new evaluations of evidence obtained from documents already known and available to all who care to study them. It should be noted when rationalizing the meaning of source or near source evidence, such as offered by Theodore de Mayerne (1573—1655)[3], it is as though we entered a room in time to hear the answer to a unheard question, but left the room before the answer was qualified. These in-progress and partial conversations must not be thought of as mere literary curiosities. They are best interpreted and their nuances of meaning understood, by those who practice the craft of painting. Extant written evidence of the masters' techniques, are all too rare, and the advice of this author is to assiduously heed those precious recordings. What must be realized by all who would involve themselves in technical interests pursuant to the masters' techniques, is that any difficulty experienced in the application of those extant evidences often rests not with the advice found in those evidences, but with the lack of proper comprehension on the part of the investigator.

To my master, Jacques Maroger, is owed an inestimable debt, not only for the example of his dedication, but for the following salient points of his research:

1.  All master schools of oil painting predicated their pictorial techniques on the use of pomade-like or gelatinous mediums.
2.  Contrary to popular belief, Antonello da Messina was an inventor and a major contributor to the advancement of oil painting technique.
3.  Antonello da Messina is to be recognized for the use of lead as a basic material in the preparation of cooked drying oils.
4.  Beginning with Antonello da Messina, all master techniques employed, in one form or another, lead-charged preparations of mediums and pictorial vehicles.
5.  Lead-charged mediums and oils were optically blackened by cooking.
6.  Beeswax was an essential element employed in the technique of both Leonardo da Vinci and the16th Century Venetians.

7. The transparent, striated-primes so often noted in 17th Century Flemish panel paintings were of an oleoresinous nature.

This is a work primarily for painters, chemists, and lay persons interested in the pictorial techniques of the masters. It is an empirical study, strengthened by science and theory, concerned with the craft of painting, and resolved as only such a work could be by a practicing painter.

In the dissemination of the findings, only those theories, formulas, and directives that are positive in value will be recorded. The various trials and error, although at times interesting, were more often frustrating—personal travail, the details of which would stuff this writing with extraneous information. To paraphrase the words of my master, if someday I should be proved not entirely right in all my conclusions, I at least know that I have significantly advanced the legacy bequeathed me.

# Book One

# The First Key
## Jan van Eyck (c. 1385—1441)
## The Gathering of Evidence

Although intrigued with the various questions involving the oeuvre and kinship of Hubert and Jan van Eyck, my primary concern is with such things as are painterly, an area wherein my particular qualifications may best be realized. The problem of identity I leave to the art historian. Nevertheless, I am personally persuaded that Jan van Eyck was the inventor of the first successful system of oil painting and was the sole creator of *The Ghent Altarpiece*.

This research begins with Jan van Eyck's contribution to the pictorial technique of oil painting, and deals with the problems of roots, pictorial elements, preparation of materials, and technique. Among other references, consideration will be given to both the oft-quoted statement of Giorgio Vasari (1511—1574) which is contained in his life of Antonello da Messina, concerning the theoretical and material nature of Jan van Eyck's contribution, and to the 11th Century treatise of Theophilus Presbyter, wherein is found the earliest mention of oil paintings technique.

The decision to deal with the treatise of Theophilus was reached during an attempt to reconstruct the techniques recorded by that ancient craftsman, believing they would be rejected from this research. Instead, there were values found that could not be dismissed. This was ironic, for it is the directives of Theophilus concerning painting with colors ground in linseed oil that are most often cited by the literati to chide Vasari, in their mistaken belief that he credited Jan van Eyck with the "invention" of that practice. Thus began the tempest of trivia, repetition of which served only to cloud and confuse the rewarding indication found in the treatise of Theophilus and the statement of Vasari.

## The Vasari Statement

Though not the earliest writer to mention Jan van Eyck in connection with a new technique of oil painting. Vasari was the first to proclaim Jan as the inventor of an improved method. In preamble, we are informed by Vasari that some Italian painters sought in vain to change the method of egg tempera painting to one wherein oil would act as the primary fluid element "always without any useful result. " Continuing, Vasari states:

> A similar wish was at the same time felt by many of the
> elevated minds devoted to painting beyond the confines
> of Italy; by the painters of France, that is to say, of Spain,
> of Germany, and other countries. It happened, therefore,
> when matters stood at this pass, that Giovanni da Bruggia
> (Jan van Eyck) working in Flanders, and much esteemed
> in those parts for the great skill which he had acquired
> in his calling, set himself to try different sorts of colours;
> and being a man who delighted in alchemy, he laboured
> much in the preparation of various oils for varnishes and
> other things, as is the manner of men of inventive minds
> such as he was. Now, it happened upon a time, that after
> having given extreme labour to the completion of a certain
> picture, and with great diligence brought it to a successful
> issue, he gave it the varnish and set it to dry in the sun,
> as is the custom. But, whether because the heat was too

violent, or that the wood was badly joined, or insuffiently seasoned,the picture gave way at the joinings, opening in a very deplorable manner. Thereupon, Giovanni, perceiving the mischief done to his work by the heat of the sun determined to proceed in such a manner that the same thing should never again injure his work in like manner. And as he was no less embarrassed by his varnishes than by the process of tempera painting, he turned his thoughts to the discovery of some sort of varnish that would dry in the shadow, to the end that he need not expose his pictures to the sun. Accordingly, after having made many experiments on substances, pure and mixed, he finally discovered that linseed oil and oil of nut dried more readily than any other of all that he had tried. Having boiled these oils therefore with other mixtures, he thus obtained the varnish which he, or rather all the painters of the world had for long desired. He made experiments with many other substances, but finally decided that mixing the colours with these oils, gave a degree of firmness to the work which not only secured it against all injury from water when once dried, but also imparted so much life to the colours, that they exhibited a sufficient lustre in themselves without the aid of varnish, and what appeared to him more extraordinary than all besides was, that the colours thus treated were much more easily united and blent than when in tempera. Rejoicing greatly over this invention, as it was reasonable that he should do, Giovanni then commenced a multitude of paintings with which he filled all those parts, to the great delight of all who beheld them as well as with very large gain to himself; his experience increasing from day to day, and his pictures constantly attaining to a higher degree of perfection.[1]

Concerning specific materials, preparation, and pictorial procedure, Vasari gives little of substance in the above statement. He does tell us of Jan's inventive and scientific nature; his search for and development of a superior varnish; and that oils were prepared by a labored process. Although greater clarification could be desired, Vasari also informs that the improved varnish was the element finally decided upon by van Eyck for mixing his colours: "mixing" being an ambiguous connotation for grinding element and tempering vehicle. Vasari's simplistic term "these oils" used to designate that element is unfortunate, but understandable. Oil after all, was the only fluid element in van Eyck's improved fifteenth15[th] century varnish, and its embodiment with resin did not change that fact.

That a simple raw linseed or nut oil could not have been the mixing element Vasari meant is readily realized in the attributes he credits to that element, attributes which are not applicable to those weak and wanting vehicles. Vasari was using the simplistic designation in order to stress the difference between an oil technique and the technique of egg tempera painting. Significantly, Vasari does not mention a superficial varnish, informing instead that the lustrous quality of van Eyck's paints eliminated the necessity for such a coating, indicating that van Eyck's pictorial vehicle was of an oleoresinous nature.

The most disturbing of Vasari's proposals is in the section defining a background reasoning for van Eyck's search of an improved varnish beginning "Now it happened upon a time" and concluding "to the end that he need not expose his pictures to the sun." In this section, which will be referred to as the "Split-Panel Theory," Vasari implies that Jan van Eyck began his search in his desire to develop a better surface varnish for tempera painting, and having succeeded, all subsequent results relating to an improved oil technique were mere happenstance. This is unacceptable, suggesting instead that Vasari's simplistic reasoning is but a convenient trapping, a play of words in lieu of facts, which may or may not have been known to that Florentine artist-writer.

## An Alternate Theory

To better present the reasoning of van Eyck's invention, an alternate theory to Vasari's Split-Panel Theory is proposed, based on selected directives from the *Treatise of Theophilus*.

In his chapters on painting, Theophilus describes two methods of preparation for an element called *varnish gluten*. The varnish consisted of a hard or semi-hard resin (one of the copals or sandarac) cooked with raw linseed oil until melted and the oil based thickened. Both methods were commonly known to painters at the time of Jan van Eyck, since they were similar to those used for the preparation of *vernice liquida*, the varnish employed by Northern and Italian painters from the time of the 13th Century. There was, however, a major difference in the proportions of Theophilus' *varnish gluten*. Whereas the common *vernice liquida* was composed of three parts linseed oil to one part sandarac resin[2], Theophilus directs for the *varnish gluten*: "And take care in this, that in weight there are two parts of oil and a third part of gum."[3]

Van Eyck would have recognized the potential value of this leaner varnish, especially after observing Theophilus' directive "Of Tin Leaf," concerning a decorative process employing the varnish as a liaison prime. Theophilus describes the battening and smoothing of tin into thin leaves, and directs they be attached with wax to wood "so that they cannot be moved," adding, "superpose with your hand the before-mentioned *varnish gluten*, and you will dry them in the sun." Theophilus recommends staining the varnished tin leaves with a saffron solution and concludes:

> ...you will again attach them to the wooden tablet, varnishing them over with gluten as before, and when they are dry, you have ready tin leaves, which you may place upon your work according to your wish with a skin-glue. And then take the colours which you wish to lay on grinding them carefully with linseed oil, without water, and make tints for faces, and for draperies, as you before made with water, and you will vary beasts, or birds, or leaves in their colours, as it may please you.[4]

Applying the above directive, van Eyck would have been intrigued by the response of the linseed oil-ground colors laid over the oleoresinous coating. However, when diluted with additional linseed oil as was realized through trials, the colors ran and could not be made adequately transparent. Also, because of their raw oil tempering, the colors appeared mottled and sullen when dry. In addition, the *varnish gluten* was excessively dark and too thick to be used for "ordinary purposes." Despite the problems, there were sufficient values in Theophilus' directive to spur van Eyck's investigation.

Thus an Alternate Theory, a replacement for Vasari's Split Panel Theory, can be deduced. Having tried the decorative practice recorded by Theophilus, Jan would have been inspired by the principles offered, and would have sought to make the primitive materials and decorative technique more sophisticated and applicable to works of a studied nature.

Jan would have realized the *varnish gluten* was too thick and dark to be employed in fine works on white gesso panels. He would have searched for a way to lighten both the color and body of the varnish, and to improve its drying power so that he need not endanger his panels by exposing them to the heat of the sun.

There was also the problem of surface shine. Since all fixed-oil varnishes were known to yellow, it was necessary to devise a means whereby the colors would dry with brilliance and imperviousness in order to insure freedom of the painted surface from the application of a superficial varnish coating. Jan would have known that raw oil was his primary problem, and held its purification uppermost in his search.

Aided by the logic of the above Alternate Theory, we will proceed to the probable reasoning of Jan van Eyck. In order to avoid the pitfall of arrogance, where it is assumed an advanced time frame is an automatic passport to advanced knowledge, this investigation and its resulting values will be assessed, not in the light of our present time, but in the time of that of Jan van Eyck, and the imperfect pictorial system of oil painting which he sought to change.

## Consideration of Oil—The Treatise of Filarete

Since spirit of turpentine did not come into pictorial use until late in the 15th Century, and not commonly so until the 16th Century, the basic fluid element in Jan van Eyck's technique was necessarily a fixed-oil. Antonio de Piero Averlino (c.1400—c.1469), an Italian architect and sculptor, better known as Filarete, in his *Treatise on Architecture* links the names of Jan van Eyck and Rogier van der Weyden (c.1388—1464) with a newly instituted system of oil painting, and a quicker method to lighten the dark color of raw linseed oil. The time of Filarete's *Treatise*, composed between 1461 and 1464, is important since it follows Rogier van der Weyden's visit to Italy in 1450, "the year of the Jubilee,"[5] and pre-dates the alleged dissemination of Flemish methods to Italian painters by Antonello da Messina in 1475.

During Rogier's visit, he most certainly would have communicated to Italian painters the various contributions emanating from the North. Unfortunately the information in Filarete's *Treatise* is limited, and probably obtained from a second or third hand source. It is ambiguous and tells us nothing of substance concerning what was, no doubt, a new procedure for the purification of linseed oil. Nevertheless, it is another thread that, in combination with others, weaves a fabric of increasing strength and bond. A section of Filarete's *Treatise*, composed in question and answer form, begins with discussion of painting on walls and digresses when adding:

> '...This you have to do with tempera and also in oil. You can mix all these colors [in oil] but this is another practice and another mode; it is beautiful for anyone who knows how to do it. In Germany they work well in this technique, especially Jan van Eyck and Roger van der Weyden, who have, both worked excellently in these oil colours.'
> 'Tell me how one works in oil. What oil is it?'
> 'It is linseed oil.'
> 'Isn't it very dark?'
> 'Yes, but it can be lightened, I do not know how except that it is put in an amoretto. Let it stand for a good time and it will clarify. It is true that they say there is another way to do it quicker.'[6]

Lacking knowledge of the quicker method, Filarete concludes the query abruptly, stating, "Let us leave this"—an unfortunate decision for those who follow in history.

Although it would have been possible for Filarete to acquire additional knowledge of the method in question, this was not to be. Before proceeding to what the quicker method may have entailed the required ends of that method will be considered.

Holding to the Alternate Theory and van Eyck's search for an improved *varnish gluten*, ease of spreading was undoubtedly one of the primary requisites. Consequently, the premise cannot be accepted that van Eyck, in order to assure fluidity for his improved varnish, would have considered any condition other than oil in its thinnest state.

There was also the need for improved drying power, geared more to quality than to rapid drying. If metallic dryers were not employed in Jan's varnish structure, the improved drying power must have been consequential—as was the lessening of the oil's color—to the very process devised by Jan for the purification of his oil. It should also be noted that although Vasari offers both linseed and walnut oil as seemingly interchangeable in van Eyck's technique, Filarete, who wrote in a closer time proximity to the invention, states unequivocally that linseed oil was employed in what was obviously a new technique of oil painting. Hence, the search for van Eyck's process of purification was aided by the predetermination that linseed oil would be the preferred oil. In addition, the oil portion of Jan's improved varnish was thin in body, light in color, and increased in drying power.

## Dioscorides—Source of Reason

Fortunately, there was no need to rely solely on the meager information offered by Vasari and Filarete. Evidence preserved by the grace of ancient recorders allows the privilege of self-logic, applicable to the problem at hand. The first such evidence occurs in an observation made by the ancient Greek physician, Dioscorides (1st Century A.D.) and represents the basis on which van Eyck reasoned his successful method for purification of drying oils.

Dioscorides' observation was brought to this writer's attention by way of Sir Charles Lock Eastlakes's invaluable and engaging reference work *Materials for a History of Oil Painting* wherein he stated:

> Speaking of the juice expressed from the seed of the black poppy, Dioscorides observes that it is easily diluted (forms an emulsion) with water; that when exposed to the sun the oil becomes separated from the mucilage, and then burns with a very clear flame.[7]

Later in his work Eastlake notes that the writings of Dioscorides were familiar to the early painters or to their teachers. Almost certainly Jan van Eyck had knowledge of Dioscorides' observation, and reasoned that if poppy oil could be freed of chartable matter, could not all vegetable oils be so treated? And would not this undesirable matter, which apparently is an attractor of water, also be attracted to water? Jan may have reasoned that the removal of such aqua-loving antagonists from the base oil would reduce the oil's affinity for moisture, and thereby improve its drying power.

## The Gesuati Friars—of Purified Oil

No directives for purifying oil are found in writings emanating from 15th Century Flanders, the century and place where, it is herein proposed, this knowledge was fully developed and instituted into pictorial technique. This is not surprising, since the method was originally taught in the oral and visual tradition of atelier training. Ateliers were craft shops, not merely schools, and technical methods thus taught were considered so perfect that any change was unthinkable, as would have been the thought that one day the methods held indispensable to the craft of painting would be confused or lost. Fortunately, dissemination of the methods extended to lands beyond the North.

Because of the pressure of time and difference of tongue, visual and oral directives given by Flemings to painters of Italy were often limited. As a consequence, the written word was necessary for clarity. The following directive has survived by its inclusion in the 16th Century *Secrets of the Reverendo Don*

*Allessio.* It is, in all probability, an elaboration of a method originally demonstrated, or orally communicated by Rogier van der Weyden in 1450, possibly in Florence, to an assembly of painters and interested friars who, as Eastlake noted, were often the manufacturers of the painters' materials. The directive reads:

> Take fine clear linseed oil of a golden colour in the quantity required; put it in a horn or in a horn-shaped [cone-shaped] glass, having an orifice with a stopper at the point below. Add water, and with a stick stir and mix the oil and water effectually; then, after allowing the fluids to settle, unstop the orifice and let the water run off. Add more, and repeat the operation seven or eight times, or till you find that the water, at its exit, is as clear as when it was poured in: thus the oil is purified. It is then to be kept in glass bottles for use....[8]

Referring to other preparations and procedures given in his *Secrets*, Don Alessio adds, "...observe that whenever you find oil mentioned, this purified oil is meant...," a statement which shall be reiterated in the Directives Section of this present work.

Until now, with respect to pictorial technique, no one to my knowledge has declared Jan van Eyck the inventor or innovator of this purification process. Nevertheless, logic dictates that to achieve a successful system of oil painting, particularly when resin is involved, the base element, namely oil, must be freed of impurities. The system introduced by van Eyck was obviously the first successful technique of oil painting. Therefore, the purification of oil by water washing began with him, and should be recognized as one of Jan's most important contributions. That this method of purification is tedious is not to be denied, nor are the resulting rewards to be underrated, for without that process van Eyck's greatest technical and visual achievements could not have been realized.

## *The Varnish of Jan van Eyck—A Resin Considered*

The premise resting most comfortably with this writer is that once van Eyck had the proper means to purify oil, all else involving the preparation of his improved fixed-oil varnish fell readily in place. In essence, all that remained to be decided was the choice of a resin, and a more rewarding method of combining the vitreous and embodying element with the oil base.

The resin chosen by Jan was no doubt mastic, one of the oldest known soft resins. The obvious reason for this choice was its strength; [the term "soft" does not mean weak] elasticity, light color, and low melting point, which require no greater heat than provided by boiling water.

It might he questioned why in the early history of varnish making was not mastic preferred over other resins? The answer is relatively simple: unlike hard resin, mastic, due to its gummy quality dries poorly when combined with mucilage and other aqua-loving ingredients present in raw state oils. This is compounded when such oils are thickened, since nearly all the gummy matter is held in suspension, owing to the heavy, viscous body of the oil. Such a combination results in a virtually non-drying varnish because the greater the ratios of mastic resin to oil, the greater the problem of drying.

It might also be questioned why mastic was not simply combined with oil in its thinnest state—perhaps an oil accelerated in drying by the use of white lead or litharge, a process similar to that described by Eraclius in the 12th or 13th Century.[9] This could not have succeeded. When lead is present in oil, owing to what in herein termed the lead-resin suspension principle, the melted mastic fixes in suspension when the oil has cooled, forming a cloudy non-fluid compound. In that event, why could not the oil-based mastic varnish be prepared without a drying agent, and when clarified by the deposit of the mastic debris, then a dryer added? This too could not have succeeded, since a similar non-fluid compound forms, and drying of the varnish is retarded by an intake of moisture via the aqua-loving ingredients present in the nonpurified oil base.

Fortunately, these problems faced by Jan van Eyck were resolved through his purification of oil, insuring in the history of master techniques the role of mastic as the "painters' resin."

## *Preparation of Jan van Eyck's Improved Varnish*

Jan van Eyck's method for the preparation of his superior varnish, though simplistic, may have been new in the history of varnish making. In the absence of historical reference, the following hypothesis is offered.

A device was arranged—somewhat like our double boiler—using two glazed earthenware pots. The larger pot, containing water, was placed on the fire to boil. The smaller pot into which was measured, by weight, two parts purified oil and one part pulverized mastic resin, was rested over the larger pot and the ingredients stirred until the resin melted and was incorporated with the oil. Van Eyck would not have feared overcooking this compound since the boiling water would prevent the resin from being carbonized and the oil from becoming thick.

When finished, the varnish was removed from the heat and strained into a glass container. The cloudy mixture was then well stopped and rested. When clear, a process requiring from weeks to months, the varnish was but slightly hued, and tilting the container revealed a transparent film rewarding in body, yet sufficiently fluid and as bright as crystal.

## *The* Optical Prime—*Problem and Resolve*

In furtherance of the logic provided by the Alternate Theory, van Eyck, having developed his improved varnish, would next have considered its use as a prime, to act as an optical liaison for the advantage of what he believed would be the oil-simple colors worked over it.

That, indeed, an *optical prime* was used by van Eyck and others who followed his lead, is revealed in several sources, the most explicit of which is Carel van Mander's (1548—1606) *Schilderboeck* of 1604. Writing of his artistic kin—Jan van Eyck, Albrecht Dürer, Pieter Bruegel, and Lucas Van Leyden—van

Mander refers to the thick, smooth white grounds of their panels. While neglecting to mention a necessary absorption-breaking coat of jellied glue size, he describes the preparation of the underdrawing, and the application of a thin prime coat through which the underdrawing was clearly visible. The marginal note reads: "They drew their things on the white ground and then put over it an oil-like priming."[10]

Returning to the immediate problem, van Eyck may have believed all that need be done was to brush spread his varnish thinly over the ink underdrawing. Had he employed that reasoning, he would have realized the following deficiency: because of its viscous fluid body the varnish when spread with the brush, puddled and crept unevenly over the face of the panel. Also due to the inordinate length of time required for the varnish to dry, portions of the oil base were coaxed through the meager glue size, thereby spotting the white gesso ground and matting the desired equitable shine.

Jan would have reasoned that the failure of the priming process was related to the uncontrolled fluid structure of the varnish, and to the length of time required for it to dry. Thus the problem he faced was three-fold: how to maintain the viscous body of the varnish, and at the same time make it sufficiently buoyant to be thinly and cohesively brush spread over the panel as well as how to increase the drying power of the varnish so as to lock-up the oil content before it could be coaxed through the meager glue size.

The solution to Jan's problem was conveniently at hand. Litharge, a yellow oxide of lead, had been known since antiquity as a dryer of oleaginous preparations. It was used in the 14th Century as both a drying and "setting" ingredient in thickened oil, and oleoresinous sizes which were employed for the application of gold leaf. In all probability it had been tried and necessarily rejected by Jan in the initial preparation of his purified oil and improved varnish.

The manner in which litharge functioned in van Eyck's *optical prime* structure was based on the simplest rationale. Its purpose was to "set" and thereby prevent the creeping of the varnish, *i.e.* the lead-resin suspension principle. Also, it would promote drying of the varnish within twenty-four hours. The mode of employment was as basic as the following preparation. A portion of van Eyck's improved varnish was placed upon the stone, then a small amount of dry litharge was immixed with a palette knife. This rendered the clear varnish yellow in color.

In a few minutes a buoyant pomade was formed and when this preparation was spread over the glue isolated gesso panel, an interesting tactile response was felt under the brush, due to the rapid intake of oxygen into the oleoresinous preparation. Since it is the litharge which imparts the color to the pomade, and also induces the rapid intake of oxygen, both the color and the drying time of the pomade is in direct accord with the amount of litharge used.

During this research and test preparations of this process, it was realized the variance of color may possibly be linked with evidence existing from the 15th Century.

## Historical Evidence

Once again we return to Filarete's 15th Century *Treatise on Architecture*. You will recall that Filarete's knowledge of oil painting was obtained second or third hand. This, and the fact that he was not a painter, could explain why he erroneously juxtaposed the execution of an ink underdrawing and the application of an *optical prime* coat, as you will note in his directive:

> First the wood [should be] gessoed and well polished and then you give it a coat of glue. Then [give it] a coat of a color ground in oil if it is white and good or if it is any other color. It is not important what color it is. Make the drawing of your plane with finest lines in the way that was told you before.[11]

By his terms "color ground in oil" and "It is not important what color it is," Filarete implies the prime coat used in 15th Century painting was an opaque mixture of pigments ground in an oil-simple vehicle. To the contrary, very often in 15th Century oil paintings the white gesso ground of panel and the underdrawing are clearly visible through the various coats of paint, particularly the areas where lighter colors predominate. It is obvious that Filarete's words cannot be taken at face value. It is suggested instead he is referring to the litharge added to van Eyck's improved varnish and to the various degrees of color added resulting from that mixture in direct accord to the amount of litharge employed.

More likely, Rogier van der Weyden, who first communicated the Eyckian preparation of the *optical prime* to the Italians, explained to his audience that to a portion of the improved *liquid varnish*, a. small amount litharge was added. Depending on the amount of litharge added, the color of the resulting prime structure (which was to be applied over an ink underdrawing) ranged from the lightest tint to varying degrees of yellow. Rogier assured his audience that when the lightest tint (termed "white" by Filarete) was good provided it contained sufficient litharge to "set" the *liquid varnish*, and insure rapid drying of the prime coat; but that the colour of the prime was not important, for once it was spread the color soon dissipated, leaving little or no trace.

## The Grinding Element and Pictorial Vehicle of Jan van Eyck

Inspired by the directives of Theophilus, Jan van Eyck in his early trials ground his colors in the purified raw oil. However, from the evidence in van Eyck's paintings and Vasari's description of the inherent power of Jan's grinding vehicle, one may conclude—as earlier theorized that Jan rejected the purified raw oil in favor of his improved *liquid varnish*. Although the *liquid varnish* was a fat varnish, it possessed body and was brilliant in quality with certain of its fat quality displaced by the lean resin; whereas raw oil was weak in body and unacceptably fat-saturating.

The problem faced by van Eyck concerning the structuring of his pictorial vehicle was basically the same as that of his *optical prime*: how to "set" the viscous *liquid varnish* and prevent it from uncontrolled running. Surely the potential of the priming pomade to act as a tempering and transparentizing pictorial vehicle did not escape van Eyck's reasoning. However, litharge, so useful to the structuring of the *optical prime*, could not be successfully utilized in the preparation of van Eyck's pictorial vehicle. Although van Eyck may have attempted the use of litharge, the less than sophisticated mode of its employment may have posed more problems than Jan believed could be solved. These problems were to be resolved through the efforts of another man, at a later time, in a land distant from Flanders.

Fortunately, the basic means for resolving the problem of pictorial vehicle was readily at hand. It has been suggested that Jan's early training was as a glass painter. Whether or not he actually practiced that technique is uncertain. However, we are certain that during his atelier training he was taught the technical devices employed in that system of painting. Jan knew how varnishes were applied to glass and fixed from flow; a practice akin to a directive given in the 14th Century Venetian Manuscript, translated as follows: "Take yolk of egg and *vernice liquida* equal quantities, incorporate them well, and apply the mixture, as a coating, with the brush. It is proof against water and everything else."[12]

With the thought of employing such a method, Van Eyck would no doubt have realized its value was primarily in the stabilization principle. His objective, a buoyant, ductile structure that would yield and spread thinly under the brush, restructuring upon cessation of that pressure. A structural strength, able to tolerate a degree of fluid dilution of the paints used in the execution of details (a subject yet to be considered).

It is in the interest of Van Eyck's pictorial vehicle that we offer the following proposal.

To a one part measure of yolk of egg, immix with the knife— bit by bit—one equal part measure of Van Eyck's *liquid varnish*, until the ingredients are fully emulsified. Then to this "set" structure, incorporate yet another two equal part measures of *liquid varnish* one at a time, also bit by bit: for a ratio total of 3 parts *liquid varnish* to one part egg yolk. The ever-increasing softened structure resulting in a puddle emulsion which when dropped from the blade of the knife holds at the point of flow. Hereafter a preparation to be referred to as the *varnish pomade.*

When brush-spread, the tactile and visual rewards of this pomade are gratifying. Though easily spread, the pomade has body and an interesting resistance to the stroke of the brush. In effect, this lustrous blond pomade is a transparent paint which, in kind to the litharge enforced *optical prime* pomade, retains its pristine clarity, without the oil base yellowing; which cannot be said of the oil based varnish when painted on a panel in a liquid state.

Due to the water content and antioxidants present in the yolk of egg, the time and quality of drying of the *varnish pomade* is not as convenient as might be desired. However, this was a drawback which could be tolerated, especially since the paints with which the pomade would be used, were to be worked over a dry, non-absorbent surface—namely, the *optical prime.* In addition, many of the pigments were themselves of a drying nature, and aided, thereby, to the drying of the pictorial vehicle–a process which will soon become clear in the following discussion.

## The Palette Preparation of Jan van Eyck

In the light of the above reasoning, Jan van Eyck's palette was prepared as follows: using the improved *liquid varnish*, van Eyck used his knife to grind his pigments, each in turn, into tightly compacted globoids, which were then tempered to ductility with no less than an equal portion of the *varnish pomade.* Along with the prepared colors, a portion of the *varnish pomade* was also placed on the palette to act as a transparent vehicle, to be added with the brush to the paints, when needed during the course of the painting.

Employing the prepared colors on his optically primed test panel, van Eyck was immediately aware of the rewards. Unlike

17

the egg tempera technique where colors dry too rapidly, requiring laborious rendering, van Eyck's colors could be spread broadly and with ease, rivaling by their transparent brilliance those of glass painting.

The white lead paint, however, though ductile when placed on the palette soon became awkwardly stiff. Cognizant of the suspension which occurs between lead and resin, van Eyck may have anticipated this result and believed it could be remedied merely by the pressure of the brush. Unfortunately, the suspension of the white lead paint was much too resistive and, since it was unattractive when spread thickly, required transparentizing with brush additives of the *varnish pomade* in order to improve its quality and facilitate spreading. Obviously, since opacity is the quality generally sought for in white, van Eyck's method of applying white lead paint in thin, semi-transparent layers was not one of choice but one of concession.

## The Diluent: A Measured Means

As witnessed in virtually all of Van Eyck's paintings, it is obvious that there was a rich and rewarding fluid element involved in the execution of minutiae. Detailed accents within masses of Knights, Holy Pilgrims and Hermits, saints, as well as tragic sinners gathered under the outstretched wings of Death as they fall into Hell: objects such as the rendering of bejeweled, golden repousse crowns and gem studded mitres and staffs; gold threaded, embossed designs on robes and decorative hangings; intricate bases and capitals of marble columns. There are also those stratified sedimentary rocks and mounds; magical distant vistas with jewel like turrets and belfries scatter throughout crowded cities; flower studded green fields and exotic, fruit laden trees.

Regarding the material make-up of a vehicle used in such as the above, there was but one acceptable element–Jan's newly devised *liquid varnish*. The very same oil-superior, resin enforced element used in conjunction with litharge to form the *optical prime*. And, when emulsified with yolk of egg, was the element used to form the *varnish pomade* pictorial vehicle. That oleo-resinous preparation used in the structuring of the *liquid varnish* compacted pigments into paint form, spreading agent and the means by which to achieve transparency and translucency. By its use, paint films were assured both protectivity and longevity. Little wonder that Vasari—a painter—credited, and we as painters agree, Jan Van Eyck (and the mythical brother Hubert) the "invention of painting in oil" (Vasari Vol. 5 p. 458). Not with the first use of oil in painting, but with the first successful system wherein oil was employed as the basic fluid element involved in that system.

Concerning the manner in which the *liquid varnish* was employed, it is essential that our readers do not think of that diluent as the spreading and transparentizing element—that was the duty and the function of the *varnish pomade* pictorial vehicle, housed on the palette along with the paints. Instead, the *liquid varnish* diluent, was kept in a cup or bottle on the cross bar of the easel on which the painting rested or on a nearby stand or table.

In the employment of the diluent, the brush was but slightly immersed into the *liquid varnish* and then immixed into the desired paints and, if necessary that the paint be made translucent, a small amount of the *varnish pomade* is to be added. Otherwise, the effect was no more a softening of the paints, sufficient so that the paint may be picked-up with the tip of a sable brush and, in certain cases when diffused lights were desired, laid down onto a wet paint film. Where, however, crisp and sharper highlights are desired, the softened paints are to be rendered or laid down, over a dry film. In those cases, the fact that the paints did not run or creep from the appointed placement is owed more to the structurally bound paint globules than to the *varnish pomade* pictorial vehicle.

As with all technical chores, repeated practice lends to understanding, and by understanding, perfection may be achieved.

## Pictorial Procedure—The Underdrawing

In 15th Century oil painting, as in the tempera technique which it would replace, the underdrawing was mandatory. It was the skeletal framework and equally as essential to the finished work as were the coats of real paint. Never should the underdrawing be referred to as a "mere" preparation.

As indicated in the following quotation from Carel van Mander, underdrawings were rendered with care and delicacy. Referring to Jan van Eyck, and others, he states:

> They also employed cartoons which they transferred upon that fine even white layer; these they were in the habit of tracing through after having rubbed something black on the reverse, and then they redrew the design neatly with black chalks or pencils. But the loveliest thing was that several of them took some finely ground charcoal, mixed with water (or even dry), and modeled their forms very meticulously and properly....[13]

Van Eyck's underdrawings, executed in bistre-ink, rather than charcoal, were often meticulously rendered, as evidenced in his *St. Barbara*, Antwerp, Kon. Museum Voor Shone Kunsten. The completed drawing is free of oil color, revealing only blue-to-ochre sky coloring executed in tempera. This coloring was intended to depress the brilliance of the white gesso ground that would otherwise glare through the transparent oleoresinous colors to be painted over it. This light-depressing device would not have been used in other areas of the painting. It is through this tempera device, witnessed in the *St. Barbara*, that we understand why that precious work remains unfinished.

Van Eyck either failed to adequately temper with egg the pigments used for his sky colors, or had not allowed sufficient time for the egg-bound colors to dry before applying the *optical prime* of litharge enforced *liquid varnish*. In either case, portions of the prime structure would have impregnated the absorbent areas of color, staining and discoloring them, as may be seen to this day. Any attempt at correction would have ruined the initial design.

If this theory is correct, the *St. Barbara* panel still retains its litharge charged oleoresinous prime coat, and would be an ideal subject for microchemical analysis which should reveal the presence of linseed oil, mastic resin, and lead.

It has been wrongly suggested by Panofsky that the delicate lines of the *St. Barbara* would have been obliterated by the application of the first and thinnest coat of paint.[14] Had the painting proceeded, the drawing would have remained visible to van Eyck's eyes throughout the various coats of paint. To the eyes of the average technically uninvolved viewer, however, the drawing would have been diminished and obscured by the manipulation of the final glazes.

For van Eyck, meticulously rendered underdrawings which acted as an additional source of form for the finished painting were the rule rather than the exception, particularly in subjects of small dimension. They were employed in *The Madonna of the Fountain*, Antwerp, Kon. Museum Voor Schone Kunsten. This work also displays under the oleoresinous sky coloring the successful employment of the light depressing tempera device: the tempera color layer easily discernable with the naked eye. Meticulous underdrawings were also used in *The Portrait of Jan de Leeuw*, Vienna, Kunsthistorisches Museum; *The Three Marys at the Sepulchre*, Rotterdam, Boymans-van Beuningen Museum; certain panels of *The Adoration of the Sacred Lamb*, Ghent, St. Bavo's Cathedral; *Boudoin de Lannoy, Madonna in a Church*, and *Crucifixion*, all in Berlin Staalich Museum; *Man in a Red Turban*, London, National Gallery; *Stigmata of St. Francis*, Philadelphia Museum of Art; *Calvary* and *Last Judgment* panels, New York, Metropolitan Museum; *The Annunciation*, Washington, D.C., National Gallery; and others.

Occasionally van Eyck employed a simple ink-line underdrawing. Such a drawing is clearly visible under the two-sitting rendering of his unfinished *Portrait of Cardinal Nicholas Albergati*, Vienna, Kunsthistorisches Museum. The simple line drawing is also visible—under scrutiny—in the head of the Canon in *The Virgin and Canon van der Paele*, Bruges, Shone Kunsten Museum; *The Portrait of Giovanni Arnolfini*, Berlin, Staaliche Museum; *The Arnolfini Wedding Portrait*, London,

National Gallery; and in *Adam and Eve* and certain other large subjects in *The Adoration of the Sacred Lamb.*

Whether meticulously rendered or simple ink-line, Jan's underdrawings were always transferred from a previous rendered master design, often executed in silver point on prepared paper or parchment. From the beginning of the painting until its finish, it is certain that the master design was kept in view and constantly consulted.

## Painting Technique

Earlier in this chapter Filarette's directive concerning the ink underdrawing and application of the *optical prime* was discussed. By properly arranging his sentences Filarete's directive reads:

> Make the drawing of your plane with the finest lines in a way that was told you before. Then [give it] a coat of color ground in oil if it is white and good or if it is any other color. It is not important what color it is.

Describing the actual painting procedure Filarete continues:

> Then make the areas on top of this. Then [go over it] as you want with a shadow of white. That is give form to your figures, building, animals, or trees, or whatever you want with this white. It should be well ground, as should all the other colors. Each time let them dry well so that they can bind themselves together. When you have given a coat of white to the forms of all things that you want to do on this panel, go over it with the colors that you want to use for shadows and then with a light coat of the color that you want to clothe them in. When your shadows are dry, you can return, heightening with white and other colors that go well with what you have given your figures.[15]

Filarete directs the above technique be used "with every thing you paint," whether on "gessoed panel" or "wall." With his usual abruptness where oil painting is concerned, he adds: "You understood enough about how to apply colors with oil. Practice will make you master of it."

We note Filarete describes five distinct layers of paint, each of which must dry well before another is applied, a point to be well taken. Unfortunately, there is no mention of the pictorial vehicle, and only scant reference to the preparation of the colors. We can only hope the various proposals offered in this work will satisfactorily supplement Filarete's lack of particulars.

In analysis of the above procedure, the first layer of paint may be termed "flat painting." It involves a thin, transparent or semi-transparent coating rendered smooth, without attempting form, in the areas indicated by the underdrawing. This laying-in of color acted as a full bodied *imprimatura*, so to speak, wherein the paint was made sufficiently transparent with brush additives of *varnish pomade* to reveal the underdrawing and primary light source of panel where desired. Thus, the greater the degree of form rendered in the underdrawing, the greater the illusion of form in the flat painting. The only sections of the painting that may be executed without regard for transparency are the areas of dark background, where no underdrawing was used and the light source of the panel need not be preserved.

Backgrounds were painted first and allowed to dry. This was followed by painting draperies, requiring the filling-in of their delineated area with a transparent, or but slightly whitened red, blue, or green paint, in accord with the material being painted. Next, flesh and stone colors were gradated with white to create an all-over middle tone, and painted carefully in their areas. It should be stressed that each of these areas was allowed to dry before beginning another, in order to avoid blurring the edges with the surrounding colors—sharpness of edges, for reasons of quality, preferable to an immixed softness. The manner of the application is best described by Carel van Mander: "They laid on their colors beautifully, neatly, and pleasingly, and they never heaped them on their panels." Such a manner of application will lend not only to the beauty of the coloring, but will also aid greatly in the drying of the paint film.

The second layer of paint may be called "form defining." In this sitting white or light tones were used to add form to the all-over middle tones and tints of the flat painting. The paint was kept thin and transparent to preserve the reflective light of the white gesso ground. In the purest technique, true opacity was acceptable only in areas where glazes of strong color would later be applied, and where solidity of the underlying form-defining paint displays best the object painted.

In the third layer of paint, which will be termed "shadow rendering," shadow areas were determined by the visible under-drawing and from the master design executed on paper. Flesh tones were deepened with burnt umber and reds to create the shadow areas of the flesh. Heavy loading of the paint was carefully avoided and, rather than add opaque paint when a reflected light or intermediate tone was desired, brush additives of *varnish pomade* were used to transparentize the darker paint and reveal the underlying light source. The intensity and solidity of the shadow tones were increased gradually; their ultimate force was established in subsequent sittings.

The fourth layer of paint is in effect a "veiling." In this sitting, overly delineated forms of flesh, fabric, foliage, and other accessories were unified with glazes of flesh tint or pure color, disguising the laminated process employed in the earlier sittings, and placing the various objects in the desired plane of vision or aerial plane.

By this veiling, the form-defining earlier sittings seemed to pulsate through the glazes and half-pastes of color. Thus were the conscientious efforts of the painter rewarded. In effect, the veiling was an epidermis that created an illusion of atmosphere and added equitable shine to the pictorial finish.

In the fifth and final paint layer, "embellishment," the minute details were rendered to advantage the objects portrayed. Crisp highlights and contrasting accents of light and dark added sparkle and depth to carvings, baldachins, gold and silver ornaments, pearls and brightly colored gems. Accents between the lips made them appear parted, and embellishment of eyebrow, lashes, and strands of hair and fur added over the half-pastes and glazes of the veiling sitting, lent buoyancy to the bolder underlying form. Subtle nuances created the illusion of nap to velvets and brocades, and delicate glazes of carnation tint lent warmth to the fleshy blood areas.

Although van Eyck utilized embellishment extensively, he was always cognizant of his painting as an integral whole, having perceived it in his mind's eye as a finished unit from the very outset of the pictorial process. He was also aware of the need for selectivity in determining where minutiae would enliven rather than disturb the painted plane.

Yet another point to be noted with regard to Filarete's discourse on oil painting technique concerns his remarks that allude to a less than perfect drying of the paints. He notes that each coat of paint should "dry well so that they can bind themselves together." This implies an extended drying time, and the term "bind themselves together" refers to the change of quality which occurs in the paint film once the moisture content of the yolk of egg has completely evaporated leaving the colors more enameled in quality than when they were first applied.

In concluding this analysis, it is interesting to note that Filarete made no mention of a superficial varnish, which reinforces Vasari's observation. It should be concluded therefore that the ultimate shine of van Eyck's paintings was guaranteed by the pictorial vehicle, and the process by which the paints were applied.

## In Summation

Looking ahead to later schools of master painting, the most significant contributions made by Jan van Eyck, other than his pictorial works, are the following elemental principles and practices:

1. Purification of oil by water washing.
2. Development of a superior oleoresin varnish and institution of mastic as the painter's resin.
3. Use of varnish as a primary pictorial element in easel painting.

4. The visual advantage and necessary structural formation of the *optical prime.*
5. The advantage of a suspended or pomade-like pictorial vehicle, as opposed to a simple fluid.
6. Rejection of an oil based varnish as a protective cosmetic coating over the surface of oil paintings.

By his invention, Jan van Eyck changed pictorial technique for all time. His technique flourished in the North, and among the followers of his methods, in addition to Rogier van der Weyden, were Robert Campin (c. 1378—1444), Petrus Christus (active c.1442—c.1472), Dirk Bouts (d. 1475), Hugo van der Goes (active c.1467—1482), and Hans Memling (c.1430—1494).

In Italy, the story was somewhat different. Many Italian painters were reluctant to employ the Eyckian method of painting disseminated by Rogier van der Weyden. Perhaps, as Maroger suggested, they may have feared the use of egg yolk within the oil technique. Also, they may have found it difficult to equate the meticulous style of the Flemings to their own bolder artistic concept. Whatever their reasons, the truth is that oil painting executed by Italian painters during the last quarter of the 15th Century, and generally believed to have been painted in the Flemish technique, were similar only in their manner of application. In material composition they differed significantly.

Thus we are brought to the threshold of the Second Master Key: a search that will take us first to Sicily, and to a painter who, save for Maroger, has been denied his rightful role in the history of pictorial technique.

## The Second Key
## Antonello da Messina (c. 1430— 1479)
## Inventor Unheralded

Of the seven salient points Jacques Maroger offered through his research, four involved the Sicilian painter Antonello da Messina. Maroger was among the few to break with the tradition established in the 16th Century when Giorgio Vasari erroneously assigned to Antonello the role of a teacher who disseminated the Northern technique of oil painting to Italian painters, "making known, "Vasari said, "the new method of colouring."[1]

In opposition to Vasari's oft-repeated theory, Maroger declared Antonello an inventor who, by his introduction of lead into the cooking of oil, made an important advancement in the technique of oil painting. To emphasize the role of Antonello as inventor, Maroger refers to the message implied in Antonello's epitaph which reads: "not only was he revered for the excellence of his pictures, but also because he was the first who gave splendor and permanence to Italian painting, by mixing colors in oil."[2]

Realizing that epitaphs are written to inform the living, as well as to commemorate the dead, we can scarcely believe such words of praise would have been lavished on Antonello had he not advanced the technique of oil painting. Eastlake lends still greater credence to Maroger's proposal and to the message of the epitaph, in his observations: "Sansovino, without mentioning the epitaph, even remarks that Antonello was the inventor of the process."[3] Sansovino's accreditation to Antonello clearly indicates a process different in some aspects from that of Jan van Eyck.

In addition to the foregoing, and the pictorial chronicle of Antonello's experimental *oeuvre* commencing sometime before 1465 and successfully culminating late in 1474, another source evidence of major importance is a painted inscription on Antonello's *Crucifixion*, Antwerp, Kon. Museum Voor Shone Kunsten, dated 1475, which states: "Antonelius Messaneus Me O° Pinxt."[4] The abbreviation O° stands for "oleo" and, by its use, Antonello is proclaiming to all who understand his cryptic message the employment of an oleaginous preparation designed as a replacement for egg yolk. With respect to the exact nature of the replacement, no further proposals should be made without first considering Maroger's rationale of Antonello's technical advancement.

## Maroger and the Oglio Cotto

Without fully realizing the uniqueness of his own proposals, and seemingly unaware of Antonello's cryptic message, Maroger in commenting on Antonello's role in the history of oil painting wrote:

> So far as we can tell, it was Antonello da Messina... who introduced the next radical change. It was he, it seems, who discarded the last vestiges of the methods and materials of the tempera painters, and produced the first medium for painting with a technique based entirely on the use of oil.[5]

In his quest for the actual change made by Antonello, Maroger singled out a preparation described by J.F.L. Mérimée (1757—1836) in *Art of Painting in Oil and in Fresco*. Of this preparation, Mérimée notes: "I have found it employed in Italy; and as no person can account for its invention, I presume that it must be very ancient." He then describes it as follows:

> It resembles honey in consistency, and is named *oglio cotto* (baked oil): it is merely nut oil, baked before a slow fire, and holding into solution as much litharge as it will retain. In using this preparation, the usual method is to mix it with common varnish; this produces a sort of pomade, in which is combined the greater part of the qualities required in varnish which is to be used with colour. This varnish flows under the pencil like oil, and yet on the palette it holds its place like the colours. This quality is valuable for transparency: no matter how liquid the colours may be that are made by this mixture, they can be freely used, without the danger of separating or spreading beyond the spot where they are placed by the pencil. ...Whenever this oil loses its fluidity it is owing to the varnish with which it must be combined; for the volatile oil of the latter constantly evaporates, and the colour, becoming too thick for use, restrains the freedom of the pencil.[6]

Regarding exact proportions and preparation Mérimée later states:

> It is prepared by incorporating, over a slow fire, two parts of linseed or nut oil, with one part of litharge, ground as fine as possible. The mixture must be frequently stirred with a spatula, to quicken the operation. The combination is completed in a longer, or shorter period according to the quantity of the materials employed. This is ascertained by dropping a small quantity of it on a flag, or other cold surface, when it fixes in cooling, like tallow, the operation is rightly done; if not then it is clear that the process has been stopped too soon.[7]

Persuaded by Mérimée's assumption of the antiquity of *oglio cotto*, Maroger associated that element with the technical achievement of Antonello da Messina. In his attempt to reason the association, however, Maroger ignored Mérimée's mention of the use of varnish. It is possible, of course, that Maroger had tried the varnish additive in the manner described by Mérimée and, failing to grasp the principle involved, the resulting thickness of the colors convinced him the element should be dismissed from further consideration.

## Maroger's Revision of the Oglio Cotto

In his rationale of Mérimée's directive, Maroger continued to attach importance to the *oglio cotto* as an independent vehicle, dismissing all thought of a continued oleoresinous preparation. The error in this reasoning was Maroger's failure to correctly identify the varnish of Jan van Eyck. As a consequence, he did not realize the value of a varnish addition to the heavily leaded *oglio cotto*, a preparation involving the suspension which occurs between lead and mastic varnish. Nevertheless, Maroger's preoccupation with the *oglio cotto* led to one of his major contributions.

Unlike the directive of Mérimée's, where litharge is simply mixed with oil and heated until it stands in solution, Maroger recommended a constant stirring of the *oglio cotto* until the litharge had entirely dissolved in the oil, commenting, "Cooking the oil in this way gave it a color as dark as that of coffee."[8] In this proposed method Maroger was correct, since only by completely dissolving the litharge and turning the oil black is the *oglio cotto* made homogenous and optically charged.

Maroger, who was the first researcher to associate Mérimée's directive with the technique of Antonello da Messina, believed that when the *oglio cotto* proportioned as directed by Mérimée, due to its darkness and thickness, it was an unusable compound and proceeded to weaken the structure with additional oil.[9]

The result was a preparation offering limited tactile and optical rewards. In his distortion of the *oglio cotto*, there arose for me a Phoenix—a possible link between the *oglio cotto* preparation of the 15th Century Sicilian painter, Antonello da Messina and a far more ancient *oglio cotto.*

## Theory of Origin

Although Antonello da Messina, through his knowledge of the Flemish method of oil painting, would have known of the use of litharge in van Eyck's *optical prime* structure, he must have had a more sophisticated source of inspiration for his *oglio cotto.*

It has been said of Antonello that "his works must be considered in an Italian rather that a Sicilian context."[10] In visual assessment of Antonello's painting, I would agree. However, when determining the material aspect of his art and contribution, the opposite would be true, and geography may have granted him certain advantages.

During Sicily's long and turbulent history, Greek culture once flourished there, and in that ancient soil, it is believed, rest the earthly remains of Aristotle. Could it have been that in the cloisters on that isle, there was known through traditional practice or ancient recording, a formula for what the elder Pliny (23—79 A.D.) called *atramentum*, reasonably translated "black varnish"? Pliny wrote of the ancient Greek painter, Apelles (400 B.C.):

> His inventions in the art of painting have been useful to all other painters as well, but there was one which nobody was able to imitate: when his works were finished he used to cover them over with a black varnish of such thinness that its very presence, while its reflexion threw up the brilliance of all colours and preserved them from dust and dirt, was only visible to anyone who looked at it close up, but also employing great calculation of lights, so that the brilliance of the colours should not offend the sight when people looked at them as if through muscovy-glass and so that the same device from a distance might invisibly give sombreness to colours that were too brilliant.[11]

Of particular interest, when reasoned in the light of the above statement, is the report by Galen (131—200 A.D.) that linseed oil could be coagulated by the use of lead oxides.[12] Coagulation of linseed oil and lead oxides, it must be stressed, is possible only by cooking. In which case, Galen's report, together with Pliny's observation, indicate a principle applicable to Antonello's *oglio cotto.*

In all probability, Antonello's trial preparation for his *oglio cotto* stemmed from Apelles' less embodied *atramentum* and progressed to the strongest leaded oil. This would account for the advancement from the damaged paint film of his signed and dated *Salvatore Mundi* of 1465, London, National Gallery to the fully achieved technique of his Antwerp *Crucifixion* of 1475.

Through trials it was found that when the strength of Antonello's *oglio cotto* is reduced by using eight parts oil to one part litharge, and cooked over a moderate fire, constantly stirring until black, the result is a transparent "lead-varnish." Painted on a test panel, and thinned and made cohesive with the palm of hand, this siccative but tractable amber-toned varnish becomes light in color, offering all the optical advantages attributed by Pliny to the "atramentum of Apelles."

## A Gathering of Thoughts—The Lead-Paste Medium of Antonello da Messina

Convinced that the proportions of the *oglio cotto* (which Mérimée noted in use and recorded in the 19th Century) originated in the 15th Century, a theory was formulated on which to base a reconstruction of Antonello's medium and pictorial vehicle. Three principles predominated:

1. Spirit of turpentine was not employed by painters at the time of Antonello's successful resolve.
2. Maroger had correctly devised the method for cooking the *oglio cotto* recorded by Mérimée.

3.  While at the time of Mérimée's sojourn, when only remnants of the grand Italian techniques remained, Italian painters were using spirit of turpentine based mastic varnish combined in some form with the *og1io cotto, whereas Antonello da Massina would have employed the fixed-oil based mastic varnish devised by Jan van Eyck.*

In effect, when combining van Eyck's oil based mastic varnish with a still hot, heavily leaded *oglio cotto*, the dark color of the *oglio cotto* is diminished, and its restrictive body made sufficiently fluid for decanting. Because of the suspension which occurs between leaded oils and mastic varnish, the combination, when cool, forms a viscous paste-like medium. Such a structure, I realized, would require fluid extension with knife additives of van Eyck's *liquid varnish* and owing to the lead-resin suspension would "reset" to a controlled pictorial vehicle.

Aided by the thought of the material being sought, namely an oleoresin, lead-charged replacement for the yolk of egg, all that remained to be determined was the exact proportions for the combination of the *liquid varnish* and the *oglio cotto*.

As in all cases, the decision regarding proportions was accomplished through trials, requiring only that the successful trial be recorded as follows:

The *oglio cotto*, prepared with one part litharge and two parts oil, both measured by weight, was cooked over a moderately high flame and stirred until the litharge was completely dissolved and the ingredients dark as coffee. While the concoction rested over the fire, a pre-weighed portion of van Eyck's *liquid varnish*, equal to the oil portion of the *oglio cotto*, was added and stirred until the two elements were homogeneous. The mixture was then removed from the fire, and while still quite warm was decanted and well capped.

After several days a bit of the congealed lead-paste medium was taken with the knife and test ground on the stone. Although darkly amber hued, it proved to be both transparent and brilliant while its viscous body offered an interesting, resistive tactile response under the pressure of the knife. All of these qualities encouraged supposition as to how this medium would function.

## Order of Concern—Antonello's Optical Prime, Pictorial Vehicle, Palette Preparation, and Technique

Visually, 15<sup>th</sup> Century Italian oil painting is much like its Flemish counterpart. Numerous examples of paintings in various stages of rendering reveal a preliminary underdrawing, laminated style of rendering, and utilization of an underlying light source.

The first concern was the preparation of *Antonello's optical prime* structure. Owing to the siccative nature of Antonello's lead-paste medium, the Eyckian practice of adding dry litharge to his varnish in order to form the prime structure was no longer required. Since the lead-paste medium was a determined and sophisticated mechanical substitute for egg yolk, the natural emulsifier, it seemed logical to believe that the extension of the lead-paste medium, employing van Eyck's *liquid varnish* would also be of determined proportion. After trials, it was decided that, in similar proportion as that employed by van Eyck, three parts of van Eyck's *liquid varnish* were required to sufficiently extend one part of the dark, thick lead-paste medium.

When immixing the two elements, a viscous fluid unguent was formed. However, in a short time following that immixture, the unguent—by virtue of the principle of lead-resin suspension—became a fixed pomade. When brush spreading this pomade thinly over the ink underdrawing as an optical-prime, it proved sufficiently tractable, yet interestingly resistive. Visually the pomade was somewhat darker than the optical-prime structure of Jan van Eyck. However, in less than the twelve or so hours required for the prime to dry, its amber tint diminished to no more than an optically enriched, lucid hue.

As to the preparation of Antonello's pictorial vehicle, it was identical to that of the above noted optical-prime structure.

The palette preparation was also similar to van Eyck's. The colors, including white lead were each in turn ground with *liquid varnish* into tightly compacted globules which were then tempered to ductibility with no less than an equal portion of the pictorial vehicle. Along with the prepared paints, a portion of the pictorial vehicle itself was placed on the palette to act as a transparent vehicle to be added to the paints with the brush as needed during the course of the painting.

In trial usage, the success of Antonello's palette was immediately realized. Compared to Jan van Eyck's egg-bound *varnish pomade*, Antonello's pictorial vehicle proved measurably more rewarding. The drying of the paint film was greatly accelerated, allowing for faster reworking and no longer did the quality of the paint film have to wait for the evaporation of water contained in the yolk of the egg in order to achieve its most perfect quality.

Although van Eyck's laminated method of application was followed, Antonello's lead-enforced vehicle offered somewhat greater tactile rewards, requiring—by conscious consideration—fewer sittings for a perfect pictorial finish. Also, by its intrinsic power, the leaded vehicle enhanced the optical value of the colors. No less rewarding was the fact that although the white lead paint structure of Antonello's palette was of a highly vitreous nature, because of the fatter *oglio cotto* portion of Antonello's pictorial vehicle, no longer did the white lead paint stratify but instead remained comfortably ductile and easily taken with the brush. As with all new procedures, time and familiarity lent increasing insight to the response of Antonello's palette.

## Diluent Without Option

As van Eyck found raw oil an unacceptable diluent, so did Antonello da Messina. This left but one fluid element able to act in that capacity, namely, the *improved liquid varnish* of Jan van Eyck. The Eyckian technique requires care be taken so as not to overutilize the amount of fluid *liquid varnish* because there were less perfect means to fix it from flow. It was reserved for the smallest detail work. Antonello, by way of his *lead-paste* medium was less restricted, owing to the structuring principle of lead resin suspension, holding or fixing the fluid *liquid varnish* diluent at a point of fixed suspension. This allows, thereby, for a greater use of the diluent, determined by the needs and wants of the individual painter.

## A Technique Disseminated

The masters who employed Antonello's lead-paste medium ranged far and wide from the Isle of Sicily where that element was first devised. It is documented that Antonello was present in Venice in 1475. Just as it has been speculated that Rogier van der Weyden visited Florence on his way to, or from, Rome in I450[13], it is herein speculated that Antonello da Messina, on his way to Venice, first stopped in Florence where he communicated his technique to the atelier of the brothers Antonio (1429—1498) and Piero (1443—1496) Pollaiuolo. We must remember the brothers would have known of the improved Flemish technique and no doubt possessed quantities of washed oil and Jan van Eyck's *liquid varnish*. It is quite possible they executed small works in the Flemish technique and (as I also speculate for Verocchio and Botticelli) they may have finished their tempera paintings with half-pastes and colored glazes, employing van Eyck's medium and, as one, pictorial vehicle.

With the materials of the oil technique readily at hand, Antonello required no more than a visit of about a week to instruct the Florentine brothers and their colleagues in the cooking of the *oglio cotto* preparation of the lead-paste medium; technical application of the *optical prime* coating over a finished underdrawing; and the various sittings required to complete the painting.

That such a studio gathering could have occurred and escaped notice is not surprising. To the painters who were involved in this exciting time of change and aesthetic invention, these affairs were no more than "cookery" or "kitchen work." With respect to the evidence of such a dissemination, it is here suggested, *The Martyrdom of Saint Sebastian*, National Gallery, by Antonio and Piero Pollaiuolo, datable 1475[14], was executed in the technique of Antonello da Messina taught to them by the master himself. In no way did the painters falter, which indicated the lesson for the preparation of Antonello's lead-paste medium was well learned and the technique of its employment properly comprehended.

Another evidence of the early dissemination of Antonello's technique is Piero della Francesca's (c.1410—1492) *Nativity*, London, National Gallery, which was executed in a close time proximity to that of *The Saint Sebastian*. In this unfinished work, evidence of a faltering technique is found, indicating Piero's knowledge may not have been obtained first hand, but was from a second source shortly after the original dissemination.

Analysis of *The Saint Sebastian* or *The Nativity* would yield no evidence of egg yolk in the paint film. The transparent areas of pure color would reveal a relatively large amount of lead, thus confirming that the mode of coloring was not of Eyckian derivation, but was Antonello da Messina's new mode of "oil-coloring."

Most likely, Pietro Perugino (c.1445—1523) used the afore discussed mode of coloring in his oil paintings executed for the cloisters of the Ingesuati. Vasari notes of these paintings:

> These three pictures have suffered considerably. In the shadows and on all the dark parts there are numerous cracks, and this has happened from the circumstance, that when the first color was laid on the ground, it had not perfectly dried before the second (for there are three coats of colour given one over the other) was applied, wherefore, in the gradual drying by time, they have become drawn throughout their thickness, with a force that has sufficed to produce these cracks; a fact that Pietro could not know or anticipate, since it was but in his time that the practice of painting well in oil first commenced.[15]

In the above quotation Vasari refers to three coats of color when five coats would have been required for a perfect finish had Perugino employed the Eykian technique. The ill effects Vasari refers to are to be associated with a moisture content, coupled with a poorly employed leaded vehicle, where the artist had not properly considered the accelerated drying of his paint layers.[16]

## *Limitations—Consideration of The San Cassiano Altarpiece*

Antonello's pictorial vehicle was not ideally suited to *an alla prima* technique. However, when preparing the pictoral vehicle if the lead-paste medium is less extended by immixing a small amount of *liquid varnish* the result is a dark but tractable structure offering greater tactile response. Unfortunately, in Antonello 's technique the *optical prime*, grinding element, and pictorial vehicle were too closely related in their oleoresinous composition, preventing superimposition (wet-into-wet) of the white paint. No less unfortunate were the problems of restricted tractability. Also, owing to the dark color of the pictorial vehicle and the necessity for the white gesso ground to reflect forcefully through the light colors, there were problems of discoloration.

Antonello's attempt to obtain still greater siccative grasp in his pictorial vehicle is witnessed in panels now in the Vienna, Kunsthistorisches Museum, and believed to be fragments of his *San Cassiano Altarpiece*. Our primary interest in these panels is their survival in varying stages of completion. The tensive quality of the paint structure and the dark tonal values of the semi-transparent paint film indicate experimentation. Inasmuch as I believe these fragments are by Antonello's hand and formed part of his famed altarpiece, the story they reveal, other than technique, is much more informative than previously realized. Since the paint film remains relatively free of damage from cleaning and restoration, the following historical conclusions are noted:

Vasari, in his praise of the *San Cassiano Altarpiece* apparently over embellished the facts when he stated, "he [Antonello] gave much time to its completion…. Being finished, it was highly commended for the novelty of its colouring."[17] Obviously,Vasari's descriptive words "completion" and "finished" do not reflect the appearance of the Vienna panels, where heads and hands of the saints on the side wings are no more than the work of a first sitting. And "novelty of the colouring" can only be attributed to Antonello's new method of coloring in oil, not to the darkened tints exhibited in the Vienna panels, which are uncharacteristic of Antonello's paintings.

We note that on March 9, 1476, Galeazzo Maria Sforza wrote to his ambassador in Venice requesting him to send the "pictora Ceciliano," that is, Antonello da Messina to Milan. Also, that Antonello's patron for the commission of the *San Cassiano Altarpiece*, Pietro Bon, consented to Sforza's request with the provision that Antonello return to Venice to complete the altarpiece.[18]

Antonello did leave Venice, for we know from a document that on September 14, 1476, he had already returned to Messina. Whether or not he met with Sforza in Milan is uncertain. We do know that if the Vienna panels are indeed part of the altarpiece, Antonello failed to honor the request of Pietro Bon since the work obviously remains unfinished. Could it be that Antonello feared the experimental nature of his great work would prevent a perfect finish? The answer we may never know.

We can be assured that such a noble invention and bold attempt for an advanced style of rendering elicited praise from Antonello's fellow painters. Perhaps the praise of the altarpiece by painters such as Giovanni Bellini (c. 1430—1516) and Alvise Vivarini (c.1446—c.1502) quieted the discontent of the donor and the clergy of San Cassiano. These accolades which continued to reverberate through the brotherhood of Venetian painters well into the 16th Century led Vasari to assume they referred to a perfect surface finish of the work which in likelihood he had not seen. Be that as it may, the most significant indication noted in the unfinished masterpiece is that by 1476 Antonello was already searching for a means to enlarge upon the pictorial technique and principle which he had succeeded in developing a mere two or three years earlier.

## Dissemination of Antonello's Lead-Paste Medium in Northern Europe—Consideration of Durer's Salvatore Mundi

Unlike van Eyck's technique, which found few followers in Italy, Antonello's innovation to that technique found many followers in the North. Albrecht Dürer was probably the first of the northern painters to adopt the new Italian mode of oil painting, having learned of this method in Venice in 1495. Immediately thereafter, his work was characteristic of that leaded element and, in the hands of this disciplined German, Antonello's medium proved rewarding.

One of Dürer's most technically interesting works executed in the new method, c.1503, is his unfinished *Salvatore Mundi*, now in New York's Metropolitan Museum. To quote the Metropolitan's 1947 catalogue, the painting was "recently freed of sentimental nineteenth-century repainting."[19] The cleaning, which would have necessitated the use of strong solvents revealed Dürer's extremely delicate and meticulously rendered underdrawing. Nevertheless, one would not dispute (as did Panofsky of van Eyck's *St. Barbara*) that the *Salvatore Mundi* was intended to receive subsequential layers of paint.

Notwithstanding the harsh cleaning, the areas of oil color executed by Dürer remain relatively intact. It should be noted that the solvents did not penetrate to the already "crackled" gesso ground. This is particularly important in that it lends considerable support to the theory of a transparent oleoresinous prime structure applied over the finished preliminary drawing and allowed to dry prior to application of the first layer of real paint.

In the *Salvatore Mundi*, the *optical prime* coating is revealed in the unpainted areas of Christ's face. The first layer of real paint is apparent in areas of the globe, the hands and the raised right arm. There are at least two layers of transparent burnt umber in the unfinished mass of Christ's hair, and no less than three layers of color in the blue tunic, red robe, and blackish-green background. This work would be an excellent subject for microchemical analysis to prove, among other things, the misrepresentation of its paint structure as "Tempera and Oil."[20]

Surely, Dürer introduced the Italian technique to other German painters, and with the rapid dissemination of ideas, the Eyckian system of oil painting was eventually abandoned. Some of the most prominent transitional masters were: Mathias Grunewald (c.1460—1528), Lucas Cranach the Elder (1472—1553), and Albrecht Altdorfer (1480—1536).

The earliest dissemination of Antonello's technique to Netherlandish painters was probably by Jacopo dei Barbari (c. 1440/50—1511/1515) who worked north of the Alps after 1500 and within the first decade traveled to the Low Countries. But the principle dissemination was by Netherlandish painters after their return to the North from travels in Italy. Among the prominent Netherlandish painters who adopted Antonello's methods were: Gerard David (1450/60—1523), Jan Gossaert (1478—1533/36), Lucas van Leyden (1494—1533), and the greatest of the 16th Century Flemish painters, Pieter Bruegel the Elder (c. 1525—1569), though by the time Breugel received his training Antonello's technique was well entrenched in Flanders.

Regrettably, in the North and in Italy, the name of Antonello da Messina was not associated with the improved technique, causing his primary role in art history to be buried in obscurity. The reason may have been, as Maroger suggested that:

> The renown of van Eyck was so great that, generally speaking, it eclipsed any other development along the same lines that may have occurred at that time, and legends that arose about such other new techniques all crystalized around his name.[21]

## In Summation

By Antonello da Messina's invention, greater freedoms were granted the painter, and there was an inner warmth offered the colors that was not inherent in the paint of the Flemish. While it was true that because of the highly oleo-vitreous nature of the paint structure and the lack of adequate siccative grasp, it was necessary to employ Antonello's palette in much the same laminated manner as the palette of the 15th Century Flemish, there was an important exception. During the course of the painting, if the artist failed to make the white lead, or the tints where white predominated, adequately translucent, the quality of that denser paint structure was not jeopardized. Owing to the elasticity granted by the *lead-enforced oglio cotto*, the white paint remained ductile on the palette, and enhanced by the inner warmth, no longer depended solely on the mode of rendering to realize its preferred quality. This is not to say that a didactic method of applying white could have been abandoned, and absolute freedom adopted; merely that the painter clever enough to disguise the style of his pictorial rendering could achieve the illusion, if not the letter, of painterly freedom.

We marvel at the handling of the paint in Leonardo da Vinci's *Portrait of Ginevera d'Benci*, (c. 1478), Washington, D.C., National Gallery, a work which, it is herein proposed, was executed—with but little change—in the technique of Antonello da Messina. In this beautifully modelled painting, despite a laminated style, Leonardo applied his law of *sfumatic* rendering. But then, to mention the paintings of Leonardo da Vinci is to close one door and open another. Just as did the medium and method developed by Jan van Eyck want for improvement, so also did Antonello's improvement upon the Flemish contribution want for change.

# Third Key
## Leonardo da Vinci (1452—1519)
## Bridge Between Styles

With respect to the change in Antonello's technique, Maroger observed: "Many artists were engaged in this investigation, and among them was Leonardo da Vinci."[1]

Assuming the earlier proposal for Antonello's dissemination of the technique is valid, Leonardo, an eager youth of twenty-three years and already a master, would have been present at Antonello's atelier gathering in Florence in 1475. There he would have learned the principles concerning that master's improvement to the Flemish system of oil painting. How soon thereafter Leonardo envisioned a change in Antonello's pictorial system is uncertain. What is certain is that by 1481, when Leonardo executed his unfinished *Adoration of the Kings*, Florence, Ufizzi Gallery, change had taken place. Certain aspects of this change are more easily assessed in his *Madonna of the Rocks*, (1483—1485), and such later paintings as the *Mona Lisa, Virgin and Child with St. Anne, St. John the Baptist*, and *Bacchus*, all in Paris, Louvre.

It is obvious that the paint in the above works was tractable and siccatively responsive. Although to obtain a perfect pictorial finish it was necessary for Leonardo to apply his paint in several sittings, his flesh tones were not unduly transparent, nor were his paints applied in a didactic laminated manner. Undoubtedly, the paints of Leonardo's palette—including white lead—were more ductile, and the pictorial vehicle used in their preparation less resinous than those of Antonello da Messina.

With this brief assessment of Leonardo's contribution, let us begin the reconstruction of his methods, supplementing the above theory with tangible evidence.

## A Gleaning of Evidence

How Leonardo viewed and furthered Antonello's invention can only be conjectured. However, there is certain extant evidence that will serve as a substantial fabric on which to design a blueprint of construction.

Referring to Leonardo's literary works, Eastlake stated: "He nowhere mentions dryers."[2] Consequently, there was no mention of a painting medium such as Antonello's heavily leaded compound proposed in that body of work. Leonardo's failure to record the medium is not surprising, since he generally recorded only his own observations and inventions, seldom those of others. Also, because the painters of Leonardo's time would have been aware of Antonello's achievement, he may have deemed its recording unnecessary—this leads us to an interesting possibility. Since purification of oil by water washing was certainly known to all painters prior to the time Leonardo began his notebooks,[3] Leonardo's remarks on that process are most curious. In an observation concerning oil used in painting (the first part unfortunately is missing) he describes what was probably a personally designed device for siphoning and separating walnut oil from a "milky liquid," an apt description of the water remaining after a final washing. Leonardo says of this purified oil, which would have been in its raw and thinnest state, "it will enter the bottle and be as clear as crystal," significantly adding, "and grind your colours with this."[4]

Contrary to the rationale of many of his contemporaries, Leonardo was confident the oil was quite fit for this use, since

44

it was freed of impurities or as he phrased it, "every coarse or viscid part." Continuing his assurance of the purity of the oil, he states:

> You must know that all the oils that have been created in seeds or fruits are quite clear by nature, and the yellow colour you see in them only comes of your not knowing how to draw it out.... The change in oil which occurs in painting proceeds from a certain juice of the nature of a husk which exists in the skin which covers the nut, and this, being crushed along with the nuts and being of a nature much resembling oil, mixes with it; it is of so subtle a nature that it combines with all colours and then comes to the surface, and this it is which makes them change.[5]

Why did Leonardo offer the above supposition regarding the reason for the yellowing of oils—a supposition which Leonardo himself must have questioned in the course of experimentation? Could it be he was justifying to himself the use of oil in its raw and thinnest state, not only for the grinding of colors (a practice rejected by Jan van Eyck and Antonello da Messina) but also for the fluid extension of the heavily leaded medium? Considering the apparent fatty saturation of Leonardo's paint film, which betrays the presence of raw oil, this reasoning appears logical, tempting the belief that Leonardo's rationale was relatively simple.

Since Antonello's *lead paste* medium was of a siccative and embodied nature, composed as it was of two forms of varnish—one resinous and the other metallic—would not that heavy compound be made more tractable if removed from suspension by extending it with a purified raw oil? Unlike van Eyck's unctuous *liquid varnish*, and because of the suspension that occurs between mastic varnish and leaded oil, the thin, nonresinous, raw oil might well be used in a lesser amount in order to fluidize the compound. Theoretically, such an extension would allow the *lead paste* to retain much of its siccative 'tack' and 'grasp,' thereby benefiting the paint. In addition, with respect to the preparation of the white lead paint, if the pigment were ground and compacted with raw oil, instead of the *liquid varnish* and tempered into paint form with the more oleaginous *lead paste* would it not be made more ductile than the white lead paint of Antonello's palette? This would enable the white paint to be rendered with greater facility and opacity, free perhaps from the need of brush additives of the transparent oleo-resinous pictorial vehicle.

In trials based on the above reasoning, it was determined that to one part of Antonello's *lead paste* medium, but half part of raw oil was required to adequately extend the heavy compound to act, in keeping with the practice of Antonello da Messina, as both the *optical prime* and pictorial vehicle. However, because of the weak raw oil extension of the *lead paste*, the compound failed to 'set' to a necessary fixed structure, posing problems of uncontrolled flow. This centered the focus on the lead-paste medium itself, and how it could be adjusted so as to ingest the desired amount of raw oil, while at the same time creating a buoyant, fixed pomade-like structure.

## The Lead-Wax Medium of Leonardo da Vinci

Although I am not in total agreement with Maroger's reasoning for the formula he called "The Second Lead Medium,"[6] I am in agreement with his proposal that beeswax must have been employed in the technique of Leonardo da Vinci.[7]

Opposing Maroger's idea that the purpose for the beeswax was to add ductility to a certain medium structure, it is herein suggested, instead, that beeswax was employed by Leonardo to firm the otherwise viscous lead *paste* medium. In such a fixed state, the medium might be made to ingest the earlier suggested one-half part of raw oil, and once the immixing process had ceased, would reconstruct itself, via the "setting" or solidifying effect of the beeswax to the point of controlled flow. Following this reasoning, I concluded that no greater amount of wax would have been used than required to "set" the earlier suggested ratio of one-half part raw oil to one part of Antonello's *lead paste* medium.

In reconstruction what will be called Leonardo's *lead-wax* medium, it was finally determined that a ratio of one part beeswax was required to sufficiently firm sixteen parts of the liquids used in the preparation of Antonello's *lead paste* medium. The weight of the oil, litharge, beeswax, and *liquid varnish* were predetermined individually. The oil and litharge were combined and prepared as an *oglio cotto* in accordance with the method of Antonello da Messina. The *liquid varnish* was then added to the *oglio cotto* and stirred until the two were thoroughly blended. The beeswax was then added and stirred until dissolved, after which the rich, dark homogeneous concoction was removed from the fire and while still quite warm, was decanted into a wide-mouthed receptacle and well capped. Rested for several days, a portion of the medium was tested on the stone by whipping with the knife. Although it was of a soft body, it proved interestingly resistant, and upon cessation of the knife's pressure, the softened medium restructured.

## Leonardo's Optical Prime and Pictorial Vehicle

Employing the theory of logical progression, Leonardo's *optical prime* and pictorial vehicle, in keeping with the structures of Antonello da Messina, would be one and the same.

In pursuit of the logic, one part of Leonardo's *lead-wax*, was extended on the stone with an immixture of the earlier determined one-half part of raw oil, both elements measured by volume. Although by the initial agitation of the two elements during their immixture the resulting structure was made quite fluid, the principle of restructuring, experienced in the *lead-wax* medium itself, also applied to the resultant vehicular structure: "setting" the mixture to the point of controlled flow. Thus, we are brought to the first concern, namely the application of Leonardo's *optical prime*, and consideration of the ground on which that structure was applied.

## Consideration of Grounds and the Application of the Optical Prime

Leonardo's directives concerning grounds composed of oil and pigment are, I suggest, theoretical in nature.[8] Paintings of Leonardo and his followers indicated the grounds of their panels were gesso. In some instances the gesso was tinted a sand color by the addition of dry pigment, probably yellow ochre or naples yellow. Evidence of such a ground is obvious in Leonardo's earlier mentioned *Adoration*.

Whether or not the gesso was tinted, Leonardo would have applied over it an isolating coat of meager, soft-jellied glue size. Over that, when dry and in keeping with the traditions of earlier schools, was executed an ink underdrawing. Unlike many of the underdrawings of earlier schools, those of Leonardo and his followers were generally of a bold construction, indicating the more solid and responsive paints to be used upon it.

It was over the above mentioned preparation and ink drawing that the *optical prime* was then applied. However, the *optical prime* structure earlier described, composed as it was of one part *lead-wax* medium and one-half part raw oil, though of proper construction to act as a pictorial vehicle, was too thick to be thinly spread. Fortunately, the means for resolving this structural difficulty had at last come into pictorial use. For the first time in the history of pictorial technique and, to my knowledge, for the first time in technical literature, distilled turpentine was mentioned by Leonardo.[9] While it is true that the process of distillation was known from the 12th Century and, from ancient times, even that an oily exudation could be collected from hot, crude turpentine,[10] I am convinced that the advantages gained from such knowledge was not fully realized until late in the 15th Century, and perhaps through the efforts of Leonardo himself. It was, no doubt, in reference to washing oils and distilling turpentine, and probably oil of spike, that Vasari referred to when he noted—taking his excessive license with technical procedures—that upon receiving a commission from Pope Leo, Leonardo immediately began to distill oils and herbs for the varnish.[11]

If I am wrong in suggesting that Leonardo was the first to perfect the distillation of turpentine, then I at least am correct to state that Leonardo was the first to mention distilled turpentine in the capacity of a pictorial element. Its use within the practice will be here considered, being of the most logical reasoning.

Oil or essence of turpentine is both a thinner for fixed oils and a solvent for resin -both uses, as will later be shown, being known to Leonardo. Thus Leonardo's rationale for its use would have been to simply add oil of turpentine with the brush to the *optical prime* structure, in order to facilitate the thin spreading of that otherwise resistive structure. Since oil of turpentine is evaporable, leaving but little trace, the remaining optical structure would be essentially unchanged from its initial material make-up.

Such a prime is easily spread and brushed thinly and smoothly. Also, it dries within six to eight hours, producing a low-level coating in both body and vitreous shine, both qualities acting to the tactile and visual advantage of the paints to be worked over it. A prime structure that, I might note, was designed more in the interest of liaison advantage than optical reward.

## The Palette Preparation of Leonardo da Vinci and the Introduction of an Auxiliary Diluent

As earlier noted, Leonardo's pictorial vehicle was of the same construction as his *optical prime* structure—one part *lead-wax* medium to one-half part raw oil, both elements measured by volume and immixed with the knife.

Regarding the preparation of Leonardo's palette, raw oil replaced van Eyck's *liquid varnish* as the grinding vehicle for all the colors including white lead. Using the palette knife, each pigment was in turn tightly compacted with raw oil and tempered to ductility with no less than an equal part of Leonardo's pictorial vehicle. Along with the prepared colors rested on the palette was placed a globule of the pictorial vehicle itself to be used as the source for transparency when needed during the course of the painting.

In addition to the above palette preparation was introduced for the first time in the history of the new oil techniques an auxiliary diluent, used to execute line-drawing, laying-in of the basic forms, and details. The directive for this diluent, which shall be referred to as painting-oil, was recorded by Leonardo as follows: "…to make good oil for painting…one part of oil, one of the first turpentine, and one part of the second."[12]

In analysis, the oil referred to was a purified raw oil in its thinnest state, either linseed or walnut, though in all probability the latter was meant. Leonardo's numerical terms for turpentine refer to distillation, the spirit or oil of turpentine from the "first" distillation being somewhat more resinous than that of the "second."

Exactly when Leonardo developed his *painting oil* is impossible to determine. Undoubtedly it was employed in his *Adoration of the Kings* (1481), evidenced in the "bite" of the free flowing umber line drawing into the optical-prime, and also in the "laid-in" washes of color. There are certain indications that it may even have been used by Leonardo in conjunction with the palette preparation of Antonello da Messina. The evidence of that use can be seen in the far from perfect, but nevertheless interesting, paint employed in the *Benois Madonna*, Leningrad, Hermitage.

Because of the turpentine's rapid evaporation, Leonardo would have regarded his *painting oil* as no more than an auxiliary diluent—a fluid aid to be used in conjunction with his strong, oleoresinous pictorial vehicle.

## *Trial by Employment and the Picture Varnish of Leonardo da Vinci*

When employing the aforementioned pictorial elements and technique, in addition to their successful tactile response, one realizes, as is evidenced in numerous Florentine paintings throughout various museums, which unlike the schools of Jan van Eyck and Antonello da Messina equity of shine could not be assured through either Leonardo's paint structure or pictorial process.

This was due primarily to the use of raw oil, which in addition to borrowing siccativity, was also forced to borrow luster from the basic *lead-wax* medium. The problem was further complicated by the process used by certain Florentine and Milanese painters to achieve the effect known by the Italians as *lo sfumato*. In order to achieve those filmy or smoky qualities and optical grays, so characteristic of Leonardo's style, they often worked over a dry, tone-modulated burnt umber underpainting, with varying degrees of semi-transparent flesh tones. The resultant optical grays, when dry, were then enhanced with half-pastes and glazes and contrasted with solid structures of light. By this method, subtle transitional nuances lent naturalism and atmosphere to the object painted. Unfortunately in such a technique, the principle of applying too closely related paint structures was considerably abused, and the painting dried with unacceptable inequities—which brings us to consider the nature of Leonard's picture varnish.

Recorded in one of Leonardo's theoretical preparations for panel is the following directive: "...you must coat it over with mastic and turpentine twice distilled...."[13] Though nowhere in his writings does Leonardo direct such a varnish be used upon the surface of a painting, it would be unthinkable to believe it was not so employed.

Unlike the oleoresinous pictorial vehicle, which functioned as the protector of the paints, Leonardo's picture varnish was simply cosmetic. Since a surface varnish becomes grimy or "smoked by time," Leonardo's varnish was no doubt designed for easy removal. His surface varnish was fluid enough to spread easily, yet contained sufficient resin to dry with a low-level shine, nurturing—without overwhelming—the paint film.

Leonardo did not record the proportions for his spirit of turpentine and mastic resin varnish, nor the method by which they were combined. These decisions, however, were the least problematic of all others in this present work, since the type and preparation of varnish that it is herein proposed Leonardo developed has remained in use throughout these many years.

The proportions Leonardo most likely preferred for his surface varnish consisted of one part mastic resin to three parts oil or spirit of turpentine, measured by weight. Since turpentine is an evaporable element the ingredients were put in a glass container, well capped, and placed in a bath of boiling water until the pulverized resin was dissolved. The varnish was then strained into a clean glass bottle, well capped, and rested until the insoluble particles had settled, leaving the varnish clear as crystal.

No picture varnish is simpler to prepare, nor more effective in use. Although embellishing its powers, it was, in all probability, the varnish that Dürer referred to in his letter to Jacob Heller in 1509, having learned of it during his second trip to Italy in 1506.[14]

## In Summation

Commenting on Leonardo's role in Italian painting, Sir Charles Eastlake observes: "He is to be regarded as the founder, strictly speaking, of the Italian process of oil painting."[15]

I differ with Eastlake's observation and propose Antonello da Messina as founder of the Italian process of oil painting. Nevertheless, Leonardo was a major contributor to that process and developed an Italian style so expressive in spirit that it obscured Antonello's true role in the history of Italian painting. To cite all of Leonardo's aesthetic and pictorial achievements would require a volume of itself. For our purpose, they would be better read in the paintings of that Florentine master and in the paintings of the artists he influenced.

Notwithstanding the many improvements made by Leonardo to the technique of oil painting, greater freedoms were yet to come—not from those most closely associated with Leonardo's aesthetic and technical contributions, but from a youthful painter residing in a clime and cultural milieu different from that of Florence and Milan.

# *Fourth Key*
## *Giorgione da Castelfranco (1475—1510)*
## *The Light of Venice*

Sometime in January in the year 1500, Leonardo da Vinci journeyed from Milan, his residence since 1482, to Venice. After stopping briefly in Mantua, he arrived in Venice in late February or early March of that year. Venice at that time was experiencing a period of change and growth in culture and in commerce. Her artists and craftsmen were no less ambitious, eager, and industrious than her merchants. It was a society free of stifling academic tradition, a society where individuality was applauded and esteemed, as were beauty and intellect. Her painters were both searchers and disseminators of knowledge.

It is inconceivable that a painter bearing the credentials of Leonardo da Vinci would have visited Venice without communicating with the leading artists and their apprentices. We may be certain there were painterly contacts and demonstrations of Leonardo's new technique. The Venetian painters, who at that time were employing the medium and technique of Antonello da Messina, may have questioned both the wisdom of Leonardo's use of oil in its raw and thinnest state and the employment of thin bodied turpentine as a spreading vehicle for the optical *prime*. They may also have questioned the theory of his painting oil and the principles involved in his revolutionary surface varnish. Leonardo's answers undoubtedly allayed their fears and were persuasive enough to encourage the use of his *lead-wax* medium. Evidence of such use is limited however, and requires careful study of Venetian paintings executed between 1500 and 1504. By 1505, evidence of Leonardo's method had waned, having been replaced by a buoyant style of softness, light, and atmosphere as typically Venetian in taste as the more considered method of Leonardo was typically Florentine.

## The Contribution of Giorgione da Castelfranco

In his Lives, Vasari once again offers an entree to our subject when he writes:

> Giorgione had seen certain works from the hand of Leonardo, which were painted with extraordinary softness, and thrown into powerful relief, as is said, by extreme darkness of the shadows, a manner which pleased him so much, that he ever after continued to imitate it....[1]

Had Vasari used the word emulate rather than imitate, the above reference would be far more acceptable.

Not only did the eager young Giorgione view Leonardo's work, he may well have witnessed its execution during a demonstration by Leonardo in the atelier of his master, Giovanni Bellini (c. 1428/30—1516). Through such a demonstration and inevitable trials, Giorgione would have become fully aware of the pros and cons of Leonardo's technique. Once evaluated, and believing Leonardo's technique could be advantageously enlarged upon, he would have sought the necessary changes.

That Giorgione succeeded in his search is obvious in the paintings, and in the descriptive words of Vasari, where he speaks of the "dry, hard, laboured manner" employed by Giovanni Bellini and the young Titian, adding:

About the year 1507, Giorgione da Castelfranco, not being satisfied with that mode of proceeding, began to give to his works an unwanted softness and relief, painting them in a very beautiful manner, yet he by no means neglected to draw from life, or to copy nature with his colours as closely as he could and in doing the latter he shaded with colder or warmer tints as the living object might demand, but without first making a drawing since he held that, to paint with colours only, without any drawing on paper, was the best mode of proceeding and most perfectly in accord with the true principles of design.[2]

Obviously, the manner described in the above quotation does not reflect the technical methods employed by Leonardo da Vinci.

In the role of a "pathfinder," and with what I hope will not appear an arrogant stride, I shall attempt to retrace the steps leading to Giorgione's more rewarding pictorial technique.

## A Founding Principle

For the convenience of reconstruction, let us assume that Leonardo had explained the reasoning for the proportions of his *lead-wax* medium and advised that although a more tractable pictorial vehicle could be realized by using a double portion of wax, and when extending this more suspended medium, an additional portion of raw oil, the resultant pictorial vehicle would be so diminished in siccativity and brilliance that the technique would be unacceptable.

Pondering Leonardo's explanation, Giorgione may have theorized as follows: if indeed a double wax proportioned *lead paste* medium could be extended with additional oil, when forming the pictorial vehicle, to a softer and more rewarding tractability, but these advantages are sacrificed because of the lack-luster raw oil, the fault must rest not with the double portion of wax, but with the raw oil.

Giorgione reasoned, what if oil could be kept in its essential state of fluidity and at the same time made brilliant and independently siccative? If so, such an oil need no longer borrow those properties from the medium and could be used as an extending agent in a significantly rewarding amount. Might not those qualities be obtained through a weakened *oglio cotto*?

Giorgione knew that in a strong *oglio cotto* the large amount of lead suspends in solution and he may have reasoned that the pigment content of a less leaded *oglio cotto* could, by some means, be made to deposit, leaving the oil reasonably thin in body, free of pigmentation, yet siccative and optically charged.

Although the above speculation is made in hindsight, the basis for its reasoning is confirmed by written evidence. As is often the case, evidence does not stem from the source and time of the discovery, but from dissemination of knowledge to painters from a distant land and a later time.

## Maroger and the Black Oil of Giorgione

"Black oil" is a term coined by Jacques Maroger[3] when referring to what the 16th and 17th Century masters called "drying oil," "cooked oil," or "boiled oil." Maroger's term is descriptively simplistic, and had the masters so described their drying oils, needless speculation concerning the color of such oils could have been prevented. Maroger has often been criticized for this term and for his belief that lead-compounded oils, employed by the masters, were optically dark. Indeed, his beliefs continue to be criticized, including his declaration that lead was an essential ingredient in the preparation of the masters' drying oils.

When properly prepared, leaded oils are superior in every way to oils in their raw state. To deny they were used by the masters is to ignore extant written evidence and betrays gross ignorance of the craft of painting. It should be noted when such "leaded" preparations are opposed, it is usually by quoting 19th or 20th Century sources.

Maroger's error was not in the principle involved in black oil, but in his misunderstanding the method of preparation Added to this error was his belief that it was the sole siccative ingredient involved in Giorgione's Venetian Technique.

In truth, the evidence Maroger cited with respect to Georgione's black drying oil stems, not from an Italian 16th Century source, but from a 17th Century source, namely a directive contained in the manuscript of Dr. Theodore de Mayerne as related by a certain M. Sallé. Maroger, presumptively, but I believe correctly, associated this directive with both Giorgione and Rubens. That evidence of Giorgione's black drying oil may indeed have survived through a 17th Century source is not surprising, for all master techniques are linked and in this instance the directive for the preparation communicated through a 17th Century Northern source survived, possibly without change, from the technique of the 16th Century Venetians.

Undoubtedly the preparation of Giorgione's black drying oil was his most difficult technical decision. We are indeed fortunate that a recording for its preparation was communicated to de Mayerne, wanting though it is of certain explanatory details, and that Maroger identified that 17th Century recording with its 16th Century inventor, Giorgione da Castelfranco. The directive reads as follows:

> It is made equally with walnut or linseed oil, but that made with the walnut is better. Take a half a pint of the oil (by weight of Paris) which weighs about half a pound, put this into a new, glazed, earthenware pot and add to it half an ounce of litharge of gold very finely pulverized. Stir it a little with a wooden spatula and allow it to boil over a slow fire, under a chimney or flue, or out of doors in a courtyard. for a period of two hours; this oil will boil away to some degree, but not very much.[4]

## New Thoughts on an Old Theme

Armed with the above quoted communication and discontented with the black oil devised by Maroger,[5] trials were begun in order to add greater meaning to de Mayerne's wanting directive. Holding with the use of walnut oil and litharge, as well as the ratio proportions, believing that these designated amounts had a relationship with procedure, all was then focused on what that mode of procedure might have been.

As a result of numerous trials culminating in what I believe to be unqualified success, it was concluded that de Mayerne had not been informed, or failed to record, what must have been two of the most stringent rules to be followed in preparing the litharge enforced black oil.

Regarding the first rule: when working with the eight ounces of raw walnut oil and one-half ounce of litharge, the volume of the weighted oil, when placed in a cooking vessel, should range in depth not appreciably more nor less than one-half inch. These proposed shallow depths of oil might explain why a painter such as, let us say, Rubens—for I am convinced of the relationship of this directive with that master—chose to prepare but a half pint of oil when it was said of Anthony van Dyck (1599—1641), whose techniques will be considered in depth in the Fifth Key, that in his preparation of a white lead enforced drying oil, he employed "a pint of nut oil"—twice the amount employed by Rubens!

Undoubtedly Rubens, whom we know was a highly productive painter, surely would have employed, given an equal length of time, as much if not more drying oil than did van Dyck. The only alternative is that Rubens would have had to prepare black oil at least twice a month!

Going on the afore proposed theory regarding the depth of oil, it should be noted that a weighted eight ounces of either walnut or linseed oil would require a cooking vessel with an inside diameter of seven to eight inches. Correspondingly, if one were to cook sixteen ounces of oil in a half-inch depth the circumference of the cooking vessel would be so extremely large that its use would be implausible.

While it is true that "chance" (which Pasteur observed "favors only the prepared mind") led me to an unshakeable belief that there were indeed rules of depth employed by the 16th and 17th Century painters when preparing their black drying oils, I am forced to admit that nowhere in extant evidence pertaining to the masters' practices are rules of depth unequivocally stated. The reason would rest, as so often is the case, with the masters' atelier system of oral and visual teaching wherein the written word was deemed unnecessary.

The earlier mentioned second stringent rule, which for one reason or another was not addressed by de Mayerne, deals specifically with procedure and timing. I have come to realize that within the two-hour cooking period mentioned by de Mayerne there must have been two distinct assignment periods. The first was the incorporation of the litharge into the body of the oil, and the second, the period wherein the incorporated litharge was made to lead-saturate the body of the host-oil. That de Mayerne failed to record these two assignments may well have been a misunderstanding on the doctor's part, rather than a deletion on the part of the communicator of the directive.

It is possible that in knowing of de Mayerne's awareness of certain procedures as related to him by various painters, the communicator too casually alluded to the incorporation of the litharge, just prior to his more in-depth remarks regarding what should be considered the lead-saturation period. Thus the good doctor may have believed that the incorporation of the litharge into the oil was achieved by the advice to "stir a little"—a process which was employed solely for the purpose of distributing the litharge more evenly over the bottom of the pot.

It is important to realize that in the directive the term "slow fire" is associated with the collective two-hour cooking period and indicated not a low fire, but a steady even heat, such as produced by a determined level of glowing charcoal. But then, what of the period prior to what must be thought of as a saturation timing, that necessary first step in which the lead is incorporated with the oil? Of considerable importance is the fact there is no mention in the directive of stirring the oil during the cooking process. Thus it was concluded that the incorporation of the litharge was achieved solely by the force of the heat. Persuaded by empirical resolve, it was determined that no specific time may have been set for the incorporation period. In that case, it is not surprising that the time required for the incorporation of the litharge was not specified, but merely linked in with the two hours mention in de Mayerne's recorded directive.

Uncharacteristic of the general scheme of this research, we will bring into focus the use of a thermometer. We know, of course, that the masters of the 16th and 17th Centuries had no access to such an instrument which if our proposals are correct regarding the method of preparing their drying oils makes the resolve of those oils all the more admirable. In truth, repeated trials and proper assessment eventually led the master to the successful resolve of their black drying oils. Observation was their thermometer, visually determining by signs, a necessary result within a given time frame, not unlike the process employed by this researcher.

It has been my practice throughout this long term search for the truths regarding the masters' drying oils to always check visual signs of action and reactions occurring with the oil, and to note at what degree or degree range these signs occurred. Early research led to the determination that to achieve any reasonable success with the preparation of earlier experimental litharge enforced oils, it was necessary to reach degree range of between 200° C to 210° C, after which time the oil was rested for the remainder of the designated two hours. In time it was further concluded that the incorporation process must be as rapid as possible, and that the greater the degree of heat, the more rapid was the process of incorporation. It was further determined that those oils which had turned black and smooth within approximately fifteen minutes, give or take a minute or two from when the oil was first set over the heat, were superior to those oils requiring a greater amount of time. Moreover, the temperature of those superior oils ranged from the acceptable low of 230° C, hopefully not to exceed 240° C.

It should be noted that if we are correct in stating that in the lead-incorporation period it is necessary that the litharge be quickly dissolved and set into the body of the oil, and that this is achieved solely by the force of a high heat. Logic dictates that a shallow depth of oil would heat more quickly and that the lead would saturate more thoroughly. This would lend to the oil the maximum power of siccativity.

Respecting the problem of designated time frames, it was at the end of the incorporation period when the oil was black and smooth exhibiting no signs of the litharge working in the oil that the heat must be reduced by available means, thus beginning the lead-saturation time frame during which the oil was rested over the "slow fire" for the remainder of the designated two hours. At the end of this time, the oil was deemed finished and was removed from the heat source.

The above described black oil is of sufficient body so that the lead content is suspended and unacceptably slow to deposit. Were one to accept, as complete, Maroger's translation of the earlier recorded entry from de Mayerne's manuscript, that on which we have based our resolve for the preparation of Giorgione's black drying oil, one might presume that the communicant of that directive made no mention of the clarification of that drying oil—a function that must be deemed absolutely necessary.

## A Matter of Clarification

Following the earlier quoted directive which Maroger recorded and, we are convinced, properly identified as the "black oil of Giorgione" he noted:

> This formula produces an oil that contains 6% of litharge.
> De Mayerne details other receipts in which the percentage
> is higher. In certain of them he recommends that after
> the oil is sufficiently cooked and has been cooled off, a
> small quantity of essence of spike might be added to it.
> The purpose of this is undoubtedly to cause the lead, in
> suspension in the oil, to settle to the bottom of the bottle.[6]

In analysis of Maroger's statement, it is the term, used in regards to the addition of "essence of spike," where he stated "might be added" which brings us to question: Why did not Maroger translate and quote the last sentence of that directive?

A sentence which calls for the *thorough settling*, *pouring off* and *decanting of that embodied drying oil.*

It is obvious, with respect to the necessary settlement of the unwanted lubricating spent-litharge, prior to the pouring-off of the finished drying oil, that there must have been an understanding of a certain time frame involved with the *settling process.* A time after which, sight unseen, the oil may be decanted without allowing the entrance of the spent-litharge. It is certain that if this strong drying oil were properly litharge-saturated over the required 2 hours cooking time, and then let settle, the spent-litharge would take so long to settle-out of the accelerated drying oil, that it would lose much of its siccative value having, as it does, but one month of peak, siccative life.

The above having been noted, our technical reasoning turns to the suggested use of "essence of spike." Not an undetermined amount to be used only in the case of over-cooked and excessively thickened black drying oils nor by whim of the painter, but instead a given amount of that hydrocarbon (or the counterpart, essence of turpentine) to be used for the clarification of all litharge-saturated oils. An observation which again I must question my master's technical reasoning. Why did not Maroger record de Mayerne's *in-margin* directive? The formula was situated directly opposite the directive under discussion, a placement which clearly indicates a relationship between the two formulas.

Cutting to the issue at hand, the marginal directive calls for "oil of linseed 2 lbs," "litharge of gold 4 oz." and "for penetration [dilution] oil of spike 2 oz."

Unlike the primary directive, that which Maroger dubbed "the black oil of Giorgione", it is my belief that the marginal note, despite the recommended large amount of metallic dryer to be used in its preparation, was a less tensive and siccatively aggressive oil. It was most likely an oil which was measured in considerable depth, perhaps as great as 2 inches, cooked without concern for the rapid-heat incorporation period in a steady, moderately high heat, ranging from 190° C. to 210° C. plus. This was a method wherein the litharge is not quickly thrust into the body of the oil as was the case with the black oil of Giorgione. Such an oil would require substantially more litharge in order to assure ordinary siccativity, without regard for possessing or encouraging siccative-grasp; subsequently, a less embodied oil requiring far less hydrocarbon in order to facilitate the depositing of the lead. An industrial type oil to be used, with respect to pictorial technique, for the preparation of the pliable, knife ground white lead paste employed by the 16th Century Venetians for their scraped-on grounds of canvas. And with respect to the 17th Century Flemish, the preparation of a weakened structure of Flemish medium as well as the pliable white lead paste, the combined elements which formed their ground-primes of canvas.

Thus, without further proposal or speculation, we may assume that the cooked drying oil was of a thick consistency and must be diluted in order to allow the suspended "spent" litharge to deposit, settling out from the body of the oil. A given process not to be dismissed as arbitrary, the proportion of hydrocarbon undoubtedly determined by the reasoned strength and structure of any and all "litharge- saturated" black drying oils.

As to the "black oil of Giorgione," while we should note that oil of spike was often employed by the 16th Century Italian painters, spirit or essence of turpentine was equally acceptable and generally preferred by the painters of Flanders and Holland. In interest of the problem at hand, either of the two hydrocarbons would necessarily displace the fixed-oil body of Giorgione's black drying oil. In light of that fact it was determined that no greater amount of the diluting agent would be used than deemed necessary to facilitate the depositing of the spent-litharge. In time, employing small batches of experimental oils in the ratio of 1:16 parts litharge to oil, it was determined that in accord with the 16 parts of oil, one eighth part of either of the above mentioned hydrocarbons, by weight, was sufficient to weaken or dilute the body of the black drying oil and allow the spent-litharge to settle within 24 to 48 hours: double the ratio proportion as proposed by de Mayerne in the recorded in-margin directive. The process employed in our experimental black oil, was simply to add the hydrocarbon to the finished black oil when sufficiently cool; stir the oil and hydrocarbon together and decant the diluted oil into a bottle, which was then well capped.

After resting the bottle of black oil for the necessary time, as noted above, the appearance of the well delineated deposit will vary in tone from a lighter to darker tan, depending primarily on the degree of heat sustained during the saturation period. When tilting the settled oil to the side of the bottle in which it was decanted and examining it before a lamp, it proved to be of a clear, brilliant amber color and of a pleasant embodiment.

When test spread on a glazed white tile, the oil dried within eight hours to a lustrous, cohesive film. The amber color or tone noted when first spread, dissipated to no more than a slight hue—a phenomenon, as earlier noted, associated with leaded oils.

It should be realized that this lead-saturated black oil, although simply devised, is highly sophisticated in physical structure and reasoned principle. An oil such as this is in no way to be equated with heat or sun thickened polymerized oils.

The black oil, herein proposed, acted in conjunction with the Venetian medium (next to be considered) as a fluid-magnet, so-to-speak, coaxing oxygen into the paint film, thereby, "setting" the paint, via the action of lead-resin suspension. This allowed for a freer and more immediately responsive execution and tonal range than had been experienced in any of the earlier oil painting techniques.

## Giorgione's Venetian Medium and Pictorial Vehicle

Unfortunately, there is no source evidence describing the medium with which Giorgione's black oil would have been used. Nevertheless, in the belief that my reasoning for Antonello da Messina's *lead paste* medium and Leonardo da Vinci's revisions of that medium are correct, I am confident that the make-up of Giorgione's Venetian medium was the least difficult of his technical problems.

Just as Leonardo revised Antonello's medium by adding one part beeswax to sixteen parts of the liquid content in Antonello's *lead paste* medium, Giorgione revised Leonardo's *lead-wax* medium by adding an additional portion of wax in a ratio (by weight) of two parts wax to sixteen parts of the liquids used in Antonello's basic *lead paste* medium.

In concocting such a medium, a portion of Antonello's *lead paste* medium was duly prepared to which was then added (measured by weight) an eighth part beeswax (the litharge content of the *lead paste* medium not to be taken into account in this ratio weight.) After the wax was completely melted, the mixture was allowed to cool but slightly and decanted into a wide-mouthed container. When completely cooled, the resulting paste which we have earlier referred to as *Venetian Medium* appeared much like Leonardo's *lead-wax* medium. However, by calculated design, this waxier medium was necessarily more suspended.

Regarding the preparation of Giorgione's pictorial vehicle, logic prevailed. A measured portion of Giorgione's *Venetian Medium* was placed on the stone and extended by immixing with the knife an equal measure of Giorgione's black oil. In kind with the pictorial vehicle of Leonardo da Vinci, the structure became quite fluid, but allowed to rest a short while, it restructured to a controlled soft puddle-pomade, because of both the beeswax content and the action of lead-resin suspension.

## New Visions—Giorgione's Color Preparation and the White Lead Paste

No less sophisticated than the reasoning for Giorgione's black drying oil was his reasoning for the preparation of colors. I am convinced Giorgione held that the only acceptable oil was that which was controlled by the black drying oil enhanced Venetian medium, the earlier described soft and oleaginous pictorial vehicle. In light of that realization, the proposal is put forth that the preparation of Giorgione's colors was unique in the history of pictorial technique, and, with the exception of white lead, oil was not employed as the grinding vehicle.

The reasoning behind this decision was spurred through experimentation and investigation involving the practices of 17th Century Flemish painters. As Maroger had proposed that the evidence of Giorgione's 16th Century black drying oil was preserved in a 17th Century recording contained in the manuscript of Dr. Theodore de Mayerne, so it is herein proposed that, contained in that same manuscript, evidence was preserved regarding Giorgione's method for grinding colors.

The communication came from Rubens who was well acquainted with Venetian methods as indeed were all Flemish painters who utilized those which lent advantage to their own techniques. One such method was that employed for the grinding or, more correctly, compacting of colors. The practice is so unique that the recording of the method has virtually been ignored by modern researchers. Moreover, in the one case when it was cited by Eastlake, I believe his reasoning with respect to the application of the directive to be completely wrong.

De Mayerne's directive is recorded in Italian, as it was no doubt dictated by Rubens, and reads as follows:

> Il Cavaliere Pietro Paulo Rubens. Il signor Cavaliere Rubens a detto che bisogna che tutti i colori siano presto macinati operando con aqua di raggia che migliore a non tanta fiera come l'oglio di spica.[7]

In translation it should read:

> Sir Peter Paul Rubens said that all colors should be quickly ground, employing for this purpose spirit of turpentine, which is better than spike oil, and not as strong.

The wording is elemental and with reference to procedure. When one is cognizant of the manner in which the masters tempered their color globules to ductility, its meaning is obvious.

Turpentine evaporates and is of low binding power. Therefore, since all pigments should be ground into tightly compacted globules using as little grinding element as possible the process must be executed quickly, otherwise the colors would cake and crumble prior to their being tempered to ductility with the black oil extended Venetian pictorial vehicle.

The advantages to the procedure are obvious. Oil, even when thoroughly lead saturated, is a fat and would thereby fat saturate any pigment ground with it. In addition, since all colors absorb oil at a different rate, its use as a grinding element would offset the predetermined oleous balance of the given pictorial vehicle. Also, turpentine is essentially a non-fat element and when pigments are tightly compacted with it and duly tempered with the traditional no less than equal part of the extended pictorial vehicle, the resulting paint structure—once the turpentine has evaporated—consists of naught but pigment and pictorial vehicle preserving much of the intrinsic color force. The result, a ductile but significantly less oil-saturated paint where the total input of oil to the colors is realized solely through the controlling pictorial vehicle.

However, due to the need for greater density than any other pigment, white lead, as earlier noted, was the exception to Giorgione's innovative practice of grinding colors with turpentine. Necessarily, oil was the grinding vehicle for white lead, and Giorgione's black oil could not function in that capacity primarily because of its accelerated drying power and also because of the initial graying effect the black oil would exert over the white.

No doubt in Giorgione's earliest experiments, white lead was simply knife ground in raw oil in the same manner as that employed by Leonardo da Vinci. However, evidence of the Venetian paint structure clearly indicated that Leonardo's method was quickly abandoned in favor of a far more rewarding practice. This practice was so commonly employed by painters throughout the many years since the institution that no one had thought to pinpoint its origin nor designate the inventor. I refer to the preparation of a concentrated white lead paste of determined proportions, ground in oil, and stored for use.

Giorgione simply reasoned that the more pigment employed when preparing the white lead, the denser and less fat would be the initial structure. This density, while necessarily offering malleability, would withstand the tempering with his soft and buoyant pictorial vehicle. At the same time it would offer greater body than any previous palette preparation of white lead paint.

Regarding proportions, Giorgione would have concluded that by weight, one part of raw oil could be made to ingest twelve parts of the finest pulverized white lead pigment. As to the method by which those ingredients were combined, the total amount of white lead and oil were placed together on the grinding stone and blended with the palette knife until the oil was thoroughly dispersed throughout the body of the pigment. Following the blending, the muller was used to press and grind together the seemingly dry mixture. In time, aided by the pressure and strength of the worker's arms and upper torso, the ingredients showed signs of compacting, becoming a flattened stiff mass. Gradually, through continued grinding, the mass began to soften and the grinding was pursued until the mixture could be softened no further. The resultant malleable white lead paste was scraped from the stone and formed into a globule that was then placed in a receptacle filled with water.

One might question why was not the white lead paste simply stored in a bladder akin to the tubed white lead paste found in today's art store trade? The answer is two-fold. First, such a paste , proportioned in a twelve to one ratio, is uncommonly thick and could not be squeezed from the bladder. Second, due to the physical properties inherent in the masters' water washed raw oils, the heavily leaded structure, even when deprived of air, formed dry flecks throughout its body thus adversely altering its consistency and shortening the useful life of the white lead paste to a month or so.

In summary, Giorgione's palette was prepared as follows: to insure the most perfect structure of the palette white, Giorgione would have employed measure by volume, tempering to ductility one part of the white lead paste with an equal part of his pictorial vehicle. The logic of this reasoning being that the greatest opacity for the white paint could only be achieved through the initial palette preparation, whereas greater transparency could be had by brush additives of the pictorial vehicle during the course of the painting.

Regarding the colors, each in turn were tightly compacted into globules with spirit of turpentine, and gauging with the eye rather than exact measure, they too were tempered to ductility with approximately an equal part of the pictorial vehicle.

In addition to the paints, a portion of the pictorial vehicle was also placed on the palette to aid during the course of the painting in the spreading and when needed to make the paints transparent. It is my belief that Giorgione's pictorial vehicle was designed to act as a total vehicle, requiring no such auxiliary as the *painting oil* such as devised by da Vinci which was not controlled by his strong basic Venetian medium. Even in the preparation of the white lead, although oil was necessarily retained as the grinding element, it was so lowered in amount that the free oil content of the white lead paste exerted negligible adverse effect on the paint structure.

## A Replacement Diluent

While, in reiteration, I am convinced that Giorgione designed his pictorial vehicle as a total vehicle, I am equally convinced that an alternative to Leonardo's *"painting oil"* was introduced, relatively early into the 16th Century Venetian technique. Respecting the nomination of the innovator or inventor of what is best thought of as an auxiliary diluent, I suggest one of three painters: either Giorgione himself; his master Giovanni Bellini; or the young Titian (c. 1487—1576).

Once again we turn to a communication between Peter Paul Rubens and Dr. Theodore de Mayerne. In that the directive primarily reflects the technical habits of Rubens, it will be dealt with, in depth, in the Fifth Key of this work.

The concern at this time is with reference to the properties of the diluent and to the mode of its preparation. De Mayerne writes of an element called "clear essential oil of Venice turpentine" noting that it is "distilled in a water-bath."[8]

Venice turpentine, named after the area of its prominent use, is a viscous, sticky balsam, gathered by tapping the heart of the European larch. The preparation of this extremely thick balsam is merely to cut it with turpentine, the "essential oil" portion referred to in de Mayerne's recording. Since this diluent was to be used with preparations that were accelerated in drying power, such as the pictorial vehicle of the 16th Century Venetians, the Venice turpentine must be so thinned with spirit of turpentine that the diluent itself should appear more in the character of the thinner than that of the balsam. Otherwise, if used in a thick state the leaded, oleaginous structures would "lock-up" the slow drying balsam and, over time, cause extreme lesions in the paint film.

The primary use of this diluent was for the "laying-in" of the bold, inventive strokes of a burnt umber or Venetian red macchia. This had the advantage that the thin bodied paint would easily "flow" and quickly "set" the dark paints, thus allowing for a wet-into-wet application of the lighter, white lead based paints into the dark washes without mixing and muddying the tones. In addition, the diluent allows for the execution of details such as may be viewed in certain works of Giovanni Bellini and, generally in the smaller works, of Paolo Veronese (1528—1588).

## Theory and Resolve of Giorgione's Optical Prime

Although canvas is generally equated with the 16th Century Venetians, in Giorgione's early research and oeuvre tradition dictated the use of optically primed gesso panels. Whereas the preparation of gesso grounded panels required no revision of structure, the same was not true of the necessary optical *prime* coat.

Giorgione, being fully cognizant of the material revisions he had made to the pictorial technique of oil painting, most likely would have reasoned from the outset that since the pictorial vehicle and paint structures were considerably more oily than the *Venetian Medium* itself, the prime structure on which they would be worked might well consist of naught but the *Venetian Medium* itself. Using the principle of working fat over lean, this then should realize a better siccative liaison grasp between the prime and the palette structures which would in turn allow for a more painterly response in accord with the handling of the paints via each individual master.

Holding this reasoned speculation to be the case, Giorgione would logically have retained the spirit of turpentine, believing that the heavy and resistive body of his Venetian medium could be made buoyant by knife immixtures of turpentine and could then be easily taken with the brush and spread with additional turpentine. Such a diluted preparation could be easily spread in a low-level coating, and once the turpentine had evaporated, the film of medium would be left materially unchanged.

In practicing the above reasoning, it was found that the coating dried within six hours leaving a low-level prime free of vitreous shine. The amber tone noticed when the prime was first spread dissipated to a nearly imperceptible tone. These qualities encouraged the earlier noted speculation regarding liaison value and the handling of the soft and tractable paints.

## The Venetian Technique and Panel

In trial copies, working on such a prime as described above, both the anticipated advantages and limitations of the earlier proposed palette preparation were realized. Of considerable importance and in keeping with Vasari's praise of Venetian technique, a prearranged underdrawing was no longer needed and the more immediate chromatic range from the coloring was greatly enhanced over earlier proposed systems of painting.

However, as can be readily witnessed in certain unfinished 16th Century Venetian works on panel, there were limits as to how far a painter might go in the first sitting. Although a design could be freely conceived and directly rendered in paint, the 16th Century Venetian technique was, nevertheless, one of a studied nature and a totally successful *alla prima* method of painting was not possible.

It is important to remember that paintings that are reasoned through a studied process do not necessarily require a labored manner of application. When a painter understands the limits of his palette and pictorial means, the rationale of his labor is directed so as to offer the greatest possible rewards. If superimposition of an embodied paint, wet-into-wet, cannot be conveniently practiced in a first sitting, but similar effects may be easily achieved in a second sitting then, sensibly, a painter would not choose to labor for the effect but would instead plan for its achievement through technical procedures. Thus in Venetian painting and particularly those executed on panel, both the light and shadow areas were kept relatively thin in body and simple in construction. Then they were fused and softened with the brush in the first sitting so as to unite the paint film into the most receptive and unobtrusive *imprimatura* structure possible.

According to the taste of the painter, further embellishment of tonal values and nuances could be executed in yet another sitting, adding mystery to that which might otherwise appear overly didactic. The total effect was that the colors were more brilliant and exciting than those of Leonardo da Vinci even though the two pictorial processes were in certain aspects related.

While it is true that once the Venetians began to employ canvas supports and panel was used with less frequency, it is not surprising that Titian, no doubt for reasons of optical advantage, chose to paint on panel his large *Assumption of the Virgin* (1517—1518), Friar's Church, Venice, even though the intricacies involved in the preparation of canvas had been solved for years prior to 1517.

## Oil and Pigment Ground and Optical Prime of Canvas

In his comments on certain works executed by Titian in 1514, Vasari noted, "In the same year Giorgio Vasari was in

Venice, where he passed thirteen months." Perhaps during that visit Vasari became acquainted with the Venetian method of preparing oil-pigment grounds for canvas that he later recorded.

Vasari informs us of the initial reason for employing fabric supports, stating: "In order to be able to convey pictures from one place to another men have invented the convenient method of painting on canvas, which is of little weight, and when rolled up is easy to transport." Continuing, Vasari directs:

> Unless these canvases intended for oil painting are to remain stationary, they are not covered with gesso, which would interfere with their flexibility, seeing that the gesso would crack if they were rolled up. A paste however is made of flour and walnut oil with two or three measures of white lead put into it, and after the canvas has been covered from one side to the other with three or four coats of smooth size this paste is spread on by means of a knife, and all the holes come to be filled up by the hand of the artist. That done, he gives it one or two more coats of soft size and then the composition or priming.[9]

Vasari's reference to the first three or four coats of smooth size could only have been intended for an excessively rough and loosely woven fabric. My observation is strengthened by Vasari's recommendation for a paste composed of flour, oil, and white lead, rather than one composed simply of oil and white lead, the oil ground generally used on Venetian canvases. Flour not only nurtures, it also aids in filling, without obliterating, the weave of extremely rough textured fabric.

Perhaps the most interesting reference in Vasari's directive is in his last sentence, calling for the application of one or two more coats of soft size over the oil-pigment "paste," followed by what he termed "composition or priming"—referring, I propose, to what we have herein termed the *optical prime*, the same preparation earlier offered as an application over the soft jelly sized gesso ground of panel. Had Vasari intended by his terminology simply another coat of the oil-pigment paste, there would have been no need for the additional coats of soft size, since such a heavily pigmented structure would have dried quite well over an undercoating of similar character. Experience has taught me that this is not true when scraping on a coat of tinted *Venetian Medium* over an unsized oil paint ground. In such a case, although the undercoating is completely nonabsorbent, the oleoresinous medium for some unaccountable reason, is slow to dry and remains tacky for an inordinate length of time. However, if but one or two coats of a meagre jellified soft glue is spread over the dry oil paint ground, as recommended by Vasari, the tinted *optical prime* dries quite satisfactorily without tackiness.

Thus Vasari has identified an indispensable technical procedure which points obliquely to the characteristic nature of the 16th Century Venetian medium and reflects the validity of the reconstructed medium proposed in this treatise.

## Gesso Ground and the Optical Prime of Canvas

Gesso grounds on canvas were more commonly employed in 16th Century Venetian painting than many researchers realize. They were simple to apply and when properly rendered posed no threat to longevity.

In early painting, canvas was *marouflaged* to an inflexible support. It was then sized and gesso grounded with the same preparation used for panel. Later, however, when canvas was stretched on frames, the preparation was revised.

A clue to that revised preparation is found in Giovanni Batista Volpato's 17th Century manuscript, *The Mode to be Observed in Painting*. "To use gesso is to tempt fortune," he warns. Commenting of Bassano's paintings, he notes:

> ...Those pictures which have been primed with but little gesso are in good preservation... and you may distinguish them from the others by the texture of the canvas, the threads of which are visible, although being painted they are covered with gesso, priming and colors; while others which have smooth surfaces, from having too much gesso, scale off.[10]

Concerning the quality of the glue-water used in preparing gesso for canvas, Volpato cautions that it may be "neither too strong or too weak" but recommends "weak glue is best, because the strong absolutely spoils the canvas." In the vernacular of painters "strong" glue indicates the strength used in a gesso preparation for panel, whereas "weak" glue indicates the strength of the soft jelly size used to isolate the gesso ground of panel. The same strength as the "smooth size" which in the proceeding directive Vasari noted was used to size the canvas—prior to the spreading of the "flour, walnut oil" and "white lead" ground. The very same size that was also used to isolate that oleagenious ground.

When applying a strong glue-water gesso, which becomes increasingly brittle with age, the preparation grasps too forcibly the surface of the fabric, filling the weave and by its rapid "setting-up" is increased in thickness wherever the brush strokes overlap. However, the weak glue-water gesso can be thinly brush spread, leaving, as Volpato said, "little gesso."

In truth, not only is the glue strength of the gesso to be weak but the pigment count which forms the body of the gesso must also be considerably lowered. Such a preparation sparsely coats the canvas and withstands without cracking the expansion and contraction of the flexible support. In all, a meager structure which when dry, is lightly pumiced and isolated with one or two coats of the same soft jelly used to size the raw canvas.

Returning to Giorgione and the nature of the prime coat for the above described canvas ground, it would have been reasoned, for both liaison and optical values, in line with the *optical prime* of panel. The preparation was naught but the *Venetian Medium*, tinted by thoroughly immixing with the knife a bit of dry burnt umber pigment. The tinted mass of *Venetian Medium* is then simply scraped thinly and evenly with a knife or spatula, over the glue isolated gesso grounded canvas; nurturing and mellowing the arid ground.

## Consideration of Style

Among the many descriptions extolling 16th Century Venetian technique, Maroger's is one of the most painterly, and I could do no better than quote his words. Of the "step forward" he wrote:

> Thanks to the velatura, made possible by the new medium, it was no longer necessary for the single figures in a picture to stand isolated in their surroundings; they could become an integral part of their landscape, melting into it, as they were, or also standing out, according to the intention of the artist. Henceforth, figures and landscapes combined intimately to make a picture, in contrast to the style of Van Eyck's and Antonello's periods when the landscape seemed to be joined onto the figures. The picture could now take on an effect of unification. By his line, by the undulation of light and shadow, by the play of colored arabesques, which struck against or supported one another, the artist could guide the eye of the spectator to the center of interest of his work.[11]

Never had Maroger's words meant so much to me until I employed the sophisticated medium and technique described in this Fourth Key. The freshness, harmony, and vivacity of coloring were achieved without effort, and although the process was one of a studied nature, the pictorial invention and drawing were created with delightful abandon.

With respect to the 16th Century Venetian medium and technical procedures, I have no doubt of the correctness of my proposals. If asked whether there was a Venetian "secret," the reply would be, none was intended. The Venetians simply understood and employed the superior medium and pictorial process developed by Giorgione which have been since lost. Giorgione's technique of oil painting was an evolvement, no less obliged to the contributions of Jan van Eyck and Antonello da Messina, than was the furtherance of those contributions by Leonardo da Vinci. When Vasari refers to the great works of

Venetian painters as having been executed "in oil," to believe an oil-simple vehicle was intended would be extremely naive.

## A Venetian Tragedy

Over these many years since the 16th Century, Venetian paintings have undergone numerous and sometimes unnecessary cleanings. It is true there was that awful period when museums allowed master paintings to be coated with a dreadful, dark, fixed-oil varnish, in the false belief that the resulting diminished light and muted colors were harmonious with the desire of the masters. On the contrary, from the time of Jan van Eyck onward, dark values sought by the masters were not obtained by superficial dark varnishes. Toning of color was always done during the course of the painting. Dark tones were painted dark and light tones were mellowed by the optically charged pictorial vehicle with which they were tempered. When ordinary surface varnishes did come into use, they were for the most part of the lightest color, and turpentine was their fluid base.

Unfortunately, the later removal of the dark varnishes damaged many 16th Century Venetian paintings. Their deplorable state has become so much the norm that one painter might exclaim to another—"Have you seen the Bassano in the Norton Simon collection? Oh, you must—its glazes are still intact—but hurry, before the tragedy of over-cleaning occurs!" While at the same time, the modern art theorists and critics, who hold the quality of cement to be superior to crystal, write glowingly of the "marvelously unsuspected quality uncovered by the museums' restorers."

In truth, the solvent-filled pads and swabs in the heavy hands of some restorers tear through the thin glazes and *velaturas* to the very *ébauche* of the masters' first inventive brush strokes. Witness the atrocities perpetrated on Venetian paintings by the so-called restorers in museums, great or small. The flayed remains of master paintings, indeed, of all schools may be counted in alarming numbers.

Alas, the carnage continues but this painter's outcry has been made, and with that outcry, leaves this segment of our research to travel back to Flanders, and to a system of pictorial technique that has never been equaled in either sophistication of structure or style of rendering.

# Fifth Key
## Jan Bruegel the Elder (1568—1625)
## Flemish Lumiére

Flemish medium, the subject of the Fifth Key, is a generic term used to describe the basic, but variable, structure of medium employed by Flemish and Dutch painters in the late 16th Century and throughout the 17th Century. Maroger, who credited its invention to Peter Paul Rubens, wrote: "The change he brought about in the medium of the later Italians converted it into the most facile and versatile vehicle that any painter has ever had at his disposal."[1] Maroger also credited Rubens with the invention of the transparent, striated "colored tone" employed on white gesso grounded panels, a device often noted in 17th Century Flemish painting.[2]

According to Maroger's theory, which he frequently repeated to his students, Rubens effected his changes in the Italian medium during his stay in Italy from 1600 until late 1608. Shortly after his return to Antwerp, Rubens disseminated those changes to his fellow Flemish artists who in turn spread knowledge of the new technique to the painters of Holland.

History does not substantiate Maroger's theory. It is herein proposed that Jan Bruegel the Elder was the inventor of the

Flemish technique. Jan has left evidence that the brilliant, facile and versatile vehicle Maroger credited to Rubens was in use as early as 1591, nine years before Rubens embarked upon his Italian journey. This date is inscribed on a small painting executed by Jan Bruegel on copper and entitled *In Front of the Village Inn*, now in Hanover, Landesmuseum.[3]

Evidence of the "colored tone" or, as it will herein be referred to, striated *optical prime*, occurs before the end of the 16th Century in Bruegel's *Harbor with Christ Preaching*, Munich, Alte Pinakothek, signed and dated 1598, and his *Iris Bouquet*, Kunsthistorisches Museum, Vienna, dated 1599, assuming that this date, found on a coin in the painting, is also the *date* of the painting's execution. There is a catalogue of paintings executed by Jan and others who employed his methods—dated or datable—both before the departure of Rubens for Italy in 1600 and his return to Antwerp.

Convinced that the elder Jan Bruegel was the inventor of the new Flemish medium and technique, I offer the following hypothesis.

Even before Jan's departure from Flanders to Naples in 1589, he would have been acquainted with many of the structures and devices of Italian techniques, and would have sought to make them more responsive to his Flemish taste. That he succeeded in his quest by 1591, prior to his departure from Naples to Rome, is realized in his earlier cited *In Front of the Village Inn*.

In Rome, between 1593 and 1595, Jan enjoyed a friendship and technical exchange with the Flemish painter, Paul Bril (1554—1626). During that period, Jan would have explained to Bril the details of his invention. Thus, following Jan's departure from Rome to Milan in 1596, and shortly thereafter from Italy, Paul Bril became the Rome based disseminator of the new technique, relating Jan's discoveries to the members of his "Netherlandish circle." One of the painters who gathered around Bril and profited from his knowledge was the German painter, Adam Elsheimer (1578—1610). Adam, whose studio in Rome was meeting place for northern scholars and painters, became an important disseminator of Bruegel's invention. Two of the most outstanding recipients were the Dutch painter Pieter Lastman (1583—1633) and the rapidly ascending Flemish painter, Peter Paul Rubens. Whereas Lastman may have learned of the new Flemish technique as early as 1604, Rubens seems not to have acquired that knowledge until sometime during his second trip to Rome, between the years of 1606 and October 28, 1608 when he described himself as "Mounting horseback" for his return to Antwerp and to fame matched only by the greatest Italian masters.

Returning to the pattern of dissemination, we find Jan, while traveling through the Netherlands in the summer of 1596, becoming the first northern disseminator of his discoveries, informing his Dutch compatriots of the technique that soon became so well accepted that all others were abandoned. The painting *Moses Striking the Rock*, by Abraham Bloemaert (1564—1651), New York, Metropolitan Museum, painted on a solid toned *ground prime* of canvas was obviously executed in the new Flemish technique. Significantly it is signed and dated 1596, a date that coincides with Jan's first visit to Holland, and no doubt Utrecht, following his departure from Italy.

By September 1596, Jan had settled in Antwerp and shortly thereafter communicated his technique to the artists of that city. One might question why did not Rubens learn of Bruegel's invention during the three intervening years between Breugel's settling in Antwerp and Rubens´departure for Italy? Was it simply that Rubens was too involved with the duties of Otto van Veen's studio, where Rubens worked from 1596 to 1600, even though he had already been appointed membership in the Antwerp Guild in 1598? Certainly in 1599, Rubens would have been working on designs for the pageant entry into Antwerp of the Archducal pair, Albert and Isabella. Also, at that time, Rubens was no doubt preparing for his forthcoming trip to Italy.

Whatever the reason, Ruben's late 16th Century paintings and those emanating from his 17th Century Italian oeuvre—at least for the first six years of his trip—indicated he had not learned of the Flemish medium nor of the luminous striated panel prime nor of the brilliant and marvelously facile pictorial vehicle. This theory is added substance by the fact that in two small studies executed by Rubens prior to 1607, namely *The Entombment*, Curnmer Gallery, Jacksonville, and *The Judgment of Paris*, Vienna Academy, are executed on solid toned, lead-primed copper, employing the 16th Century pictorial vehicle. The same technique as that employed in his small portrait of *A Geographer (?)*, Metropolitan Museum, executed in 1597 prior to his Italian period.

During Rubens' last two years in Italy there is evidence of his employment of the new Flemish technique. Among the earliest examples are his sketch and finished altarpiece, *Saint Gregory the Great and Other Saints Worshipping the Madonna*, executed in 1607.

The finished altarpiece, now in the Grenoble Museum, is a large work on canvas, and was intended for the high altar of the Chiesa Nuova in Rome. The sketch for the altarpiece, now in the collection of Count Antoine Seilern, London, displays both the vitreous pictorial vehicle and the striated panel prime that were to become hallmarks of Rubens' technique. Although in 1607 the Flemish method was relatively new to Rubens, the sketch and altarpiece exhibit a sureness of handling befitting his genius.

In brief, we may be assured, had Rubens possessed the rich and facile Flemish technique during his entire stay in Italy beginning in 1600, the forthcoming grisailles, color sketches, and studies executed after sculptures and paintings would have been staggering in number and with qualities of consummate beauty.

To hypothesize the material nature of the 17th Century Flemish technique would be to pretend that valuable source evidence has not survived, when in fact it has. Unfortunately, only circumstantial evidence in paintings, dates, and coincidental events support my claim for Jan Bruegel the Elder as inventor of that technique. Therefore, let us journey to the more fertile land of facts which, although limited and not as neatly packaged as we might wish, are facts nevertheless.

## The Golden Threads

Extant 17th Century written evidence describing the material make-up and compounding of the 17th Century Flemish medium involves but one painter, Anthony van Dyck (1599—1641) and deals with the medium structure that he employed sometime after 1621 while in Italy and continued to employ throughout the remainder of his career. The technique took him "from splendid youth to admirable maturity." His pictorial technique was so pervasively different from that which he employed prior to his visit to Italy prompted the 19th Century painter and author Eugene Fromentin (1820—1876) to nominate it the "new manner" and even to state: "We should then no longer call van Dyck the son of Rubens, we should add to his name, master unknown: and the mystery of his birth would be worth the historical study."[4]

The truth is that when leaving for Italy in 1621 the young van Dyck carried with him all the intellectual and artistic accoutrements necessary to achieve the pictorial ends to which Fromentin referred. The unknown master was not a master at all, but was instead a set of technical means by which those ends might best be achieved. His was a search for a pictorial technique that would free him from the technique which produced what has been termed his "rough style"—a style born of a medium and pictorial vehicle that, although in time he tamed and commanded it, seldom comfortably fit his hand and artistic mind's-eye vision.

The fact is that sometime in the early years of his Italian sojourn he did succeed in his quest. Also, beginning shortly after his return to the North in 1627 bearing with him the technical fruits of his labor, more young painters of both Flanders and Holland were persuaded toward the use of this soft and facile structuring of medium and pictorial vehicle than toward the structure which fostered that change.

That evidence exists regarding the material make-up of van Dyck's "new manner" may be credited to both the inquiring nature of Dr. Theodore de Mayerne and, to borrow the words of Sir Charles Eastlake, "a collection of memorandum containing successive accounts of the methods of painters who practiced in England from the time of van Dyck to that of Kneller"—a collection, herein to be referred to as the *English Document*.

It was Maroger who assigned the following directive to de Mayerne "Speaking of the technique of Van Dyke...," he wrote:

> Walnut oil, slightly warmed with white lead to increase its drying power, in combination with mastic, dissolved in the proportion of 1:2 in oil of turpentine, was his medium for grinding colors; for grinding the white he used only walnut oil.[5]

If an attempt were made to reconstruct van Dyck's medium and methods from the above directive, the information would prove inadequate. However, when combined with the information contained in the *English Document* the results offer far more substance. Particularly is this true when considered in the revealing light of earlier proposals made in this present work concerning the technique of the 16th Century Venetians—founding-stone for the construction of the 17th Century Flemish pictorial technique. The following segment concerning the *English Document* is quoted from Eastlake verbatim: "To make Vandyck's drying oil—take an oz. and half, or two oz. is better, of white lead, and a pint of nut oil; set the oil upon the fire in a large earthen vessel; put in the lead by degrees, as the oil simmers very slowly over the fire till the whole is dissolved [diffused]." The oil was then clarified by straining and by repose. The writer adds:

> This oil should be used fresh. Vandyck... always had it prepared in his own house, and never kept it by him more than a month; after that time it begins to lose its good qualities; it is believed that Cornelius Jansen, as well as

Vandyck, used this drying oil." The next extract is: "To make Vandyck's mastic varnish—take 1 lb. of gum mastic, carefully picked; powder it and set it in an earthen vessel with 2 lb. of spirit of turpentine. Set this in a sand heat, or any other heat that is less than will make the spirit boil: let it remain (shaking it well continually) till the gum is dissolved. Take it from the fire and let it stand till the contents are cold. The varnish is then to be poured out, and separated from any little foulness it may contain. The best way is to make a quantity of this varnish at a time, and keep it in bottle closely stopped, exposed as much as possible to the heat of the sun. Take 1 lb. of this varnish and half a pint of the drying oil; shake them well together; put them, in a bottle, to simmer on the fire for a quarter of an hour, when the mixture will be complete. But if it should curdle as it cooks, it must be set on the fire again, and simmered until, when cooling, it does not curdle, but appears like a white jelly.

Elsewhere: "He (van Dyck) kept all his colours dry, except white, which was ground with nut oil, and kept under water. His colors were tempered as he used them with the oil and varnish [above described]."[6]

Eastlake cautions that since the original manuscript is lost, and the name of the transcriber unknown, the information contained in the document must rest on it own merits.

Concerning the materials and methods employed by Anthony van Dyke, the *English Document* is more explanatory than the directive recorded by de Mayerne. Nonetheless there are important similarities that cannot be ignored and the information that they contain must be reasoned in the light of pictorial practices. Both documents refer to leaded oils, specifically walnut oil, as the base oil employed. Although the *English Document* gives the exact proportions for van Dyke's accelerated drying oils, and notes that the lead was cooked until dissolved, it does not sufficiently explain the method of cooking.

The same proportions are given in both documents for the spirit of turpentine based mastic varnish used by van Dyck, and states that his drying oil (which the English Document specifies was to be clarified, a point to be considered later) and mastic varnish were combined to form his medium. Of considerable importance, the English Document gives specifics on how that combination was achieved and notes that by that union, a jelly was formed. The method for combining van Dyck's drying oil and mastic varnish is best interpreted as employing the heat source of boiling water, especially considering the low flash-point of spirit of turpentine, and the danger of fire were any other kind of heat used.

Exactly how the jelly was employed, very little is told. De Mayerne states that the colors were ground with the "medium," whereas the *English Document* uses the term "tempered," both sources leave the actual procedure disturbingly vague.

Both documents agree that van Dyck used walnut oil, not only for the preparation of his drying oil but also to grind his white. The *English Document* adds that the resulting preparation of white lead paste was kept under water. Regrettably, no mention is made in either document, (nor, I might add, in any source evidence emanating from the master period) concerning the ratio proportions of white lead pigment to oil, the method of grinding, and the characteristics of the resultant white lead paste. The preceding proposal for such a preparation, contained in the Fourth Key, offers, we believe, the missing information.

The *English Document* will be the primary guide in reconstructing van Dyck's Flemish medium. Correct analysis of that less than perfect source, supplemented with reasoning and practical experience, will answer many of the technical problems concerning Flemish methods, heretofore unresolved.


## The Black Oil of Anthony van Dyck

With respect to the development of a white lead-saturated black drying oil, the thought had been entertained that it was of 16th Century origin. This would have been a seminal oil, preceding the development of Giorgione's litharge-saturated black drying oil. However, in experimentation involving this oil, and the realization of how it was to function within the 17th

Century Flemish technique, I was persuaded that this siccatively strong, yet structurally soft black oil was actually developed by van Dyck himself, an element that was designed specifically to go hand-in-hand with an equally soft mastic varnish such as described by both de Mayerne and the *English Document*. It is understood that the masters did not go naïvely into their studied resolves of technical devices. Their techniques were total systems, dependent on a particular design of medium, pictorial vehicles, auxiliary diluents as well as the related grounds and primes of panel and canvas.

It was the function of the black oil, within the 17th Century Flemish techniques, to set and suspend the mastic varnish and thereby form the medium. In addition, it was the black oil in league with the medium that formed the pictorial vehicles, the element used to compose the paint compounds, and eventually, call oxygen into the paint film at a sufficiently rapid rate so as to allow by the tack and pull of the mastic varnish component, superimposition of the paints' "wet-into-wet" which is the means necessary in order to achieve a true *alla prima* rendering of the paints.

It was in reference to the white lead-saturated black drying oil that van Dyck noted to de Mayerne: "Oil is the principal thing which painters should be choice in, endeavoring to have it good, colourless, fluid, for otherwise, if it be too thick it alters all the finest colours, especially the blues and whatever is made with them, as the greens."[7] This observation, especially when considering the remark "if it be too thick" and noting the ill-effect such an oil would exert over the colors could not have referred to guild approved, fluid, pale-golden toned raw linseed or walnut oils, readily available to the painters of 17th Century Flanders. And with respect to sun and fire thickened oils, save for rare and limited use as a varnish component, they had become obsolete as vehicles for painting, following the improvements made to 15th Century oil painting technique by Jan van Eyck.

It is important to note that when van Dyck proposed the qualities that the painter should endeavor to achieve in the preparation of his drying oil, the resultant structure was equated by comparison to the heavy, dark amber-toned black drying oil developed by Giorgione and employed by Rubens. The very structure of oil that led van Dyck to seek means and methods more suitable to his artistic vision and pictorial demands. This brings to mind the oft referred to observation: "While Rubens used heavy oils, his pupil van Dyck was said by his contemporaries to use light oils."[8]

Holding with the belief that van Dyck's observation referred to a white lead—saturated black drying oil it must be pointed out that such an oil would be thickened and consequently darkened only when cooked at temperatures well exceeding 210° C and then over a sustained period of time. That van Dyck deemed it necessary to caution against the thickening of such an oil suggests that such an unwanted effect was not that uncommon. Just as did van Dyck's use of the word "endeavoring" suggest that when cooking an oil the necessary degree-range sought by a painter and an excessively high degree-range which the painter endeavored to avoid were not all that distant, one from the other, and that the length of time necessary for the complete lead-saturation of the oil might be reasoned to have been exceedingly long.

The above rationale would dismiss any consideration as de Mayerne had suggested in the earlier quoted observation, that the ingredients of walnut oil and white lead need only be "slightly warmed." Such an oil would be but minimally increased in ordinary siccativity, having no power when combined with van Dyck's mastic varnish to properly structure the resultant medium nor would it be effective in any of the pictorial chores to follow thereafter.

The above observations concerning van Dyck's white lead-saturated black drying oil having been made, consideration will be given to the logical resolve and process employed in the preparation of that oil: the 2 to 16 ratio of white lead to oil noted in the *English Document* as the "better" proportion deemed of primary importance. Although the means employed by the 17th Century painters for the cooking of this oil would be interesting, the concern of this present work is with the ends achieved by those means, namely a drying oil which is thoroughly lead-saturated, light in color, fluid in body, and after straining—as recommended in the *English Document*—would clarify within a reasonable time of "repose."

In defense of the simple logic about to be proposed, it should be noted that in the brotherhood of painters, the painters of past times were not unlike ourselves. They did not ignore the inventions of their predecessors; they defined their pictorial and painterly needs and then, rationalizing in accord with known materials and methods, sought ways to relate them to their own pictorial desires.

From the outset, let it be noted that when preparing the various structures of the lead-saturated black drying oils, linseed oil and walnut oil are interchangeable. However, the same cannot be said of the metallic drying agents, litharge and white lead. They are different chemicals and offer to the oil distinct and differing qualities and values, both tactile and optical. It was in that knowledge that van Dyck was persuaded toward the use of white lead. How much van Dyck may have known with respect to the qualities and effect on the colors that drying agent would offer to a cooked oil is difficult to say. What we may be sure of is that the youthful van Dyck even prior to entering Rubens' atelier employed the same technical methods as did Rubens, taught to him by his master Hendrik van Balen (1575—1632). Therefore he well understood the preparation of the dark and thick litharge-saturated black drying oil which was as one with the black oil employed by virtually all the Flemish and Dutch painters of that time. Thus, van Dyck, knowing the preparation of one oil, might well theorize the preparation of another, one wherein white lead would function in place of litharge as the drying agent.

Unlike Giorgione's method for the preparation of his black drying oil, where litharge was added to the cold oil and more evenly distributed over the inside bottom of the pot by brief stirring prior to being placed over the heat source, the *English Document* advised that in the preparation of van Dyck's drying oil that the vessel of oil be placed over the heat source first. And as the heating oil began to show signs of slowly working, ill-described in the document as a "simmer," the white lead was then "added by degrees," and in doing so was no doubt evenly distributed over the surface of the oil in order to prevent a pile-up of the pigment. Procedurally there are important reasons for the different methods of combining the two drying agents with the oil for had the white lead been added as was the litharge to the cold oil, distributed by brief stirring, and then set over the heat, the hydrates and carbon dioxide present in the white lead would, as the oil heated, force plaques of the chemical to the surface of the oil. This would fail to allow the individual particles of the lead pigment to work through the body of the oil, thus reducing the degree of the drying agents siccative charge and saponifying effect.

It was a slow "undulating" or "churning" motion of the oil, rather than a "simmer" which helped to separate the descending pigment particles allowing for a more effective lead-charge as the particles repeatedly descended and ascended in a threading action through the body of the oil expelling, as the lead was being dissolved into the hot oil, the above mentioned hydrates and carbon dioxide forming an ever changing and rising layer of spume and bubbles. This was, in fact, the beginning of the "incorporation period."

While we have noted the differences between cooking with litharge or white lead, there were also shared principles regarding the two types of drying oils. First, and of utmost importance, in line with our reasoning for the black oil of Giorgione, never during the cooking of the white lead-saturated black drying oil should the ingredients be stirred—an action that, as earlier noted in this work, actually prevents lead-saturation. This reasoning is mutely attested to by the fact that neither de Mayerne or the *English Document* when dealing with the technical methods employed by van Dyck for the preparation of his drying oil never mention stirring during the cooking.

Secondly, since the *English Document* proposed that both the white lead and oil proportions designated for the preparation of van Dyck's drying oil were as much as double the amount of those employed in what we have herein offered for the preparation of Giorgione's black drying oil, logic dictates that both the depth of van Dyck's oil, and the length of the total cooking time, comprised as it is of an "incorporation period" and a "saturation period" would also be increased. Through empirical resolve, it was concluded that van Dyck would have called for an oil, ranging in depth, from ¾ to 1 inch. And, instead of Giorgione's approximate 15 minutes "incorporation period" and 1 ¾ hours "saturation period" for a total of two hours, van Dyck would have employed a total 4 hour cooking time consisting of a 45 minute to 1 hour "incorporation period" with the remaining time representing the "saturation period."

It was at the end of the four-hour cooking time that the oil was removed from the heat, and then it had to be clarified. At this point van Dyck's technical method took leave from the process employed for the fostering, litharge-saturated black drying oil, wherein, you will recall, spirit of turpentine was involved. Fortunately the *English Document*, although lacking in specifics, does provide us with the necessary steps for the clarification of van Dyck's black drying oil.

Immediately following the brief and inadequate directive for the cooking of the oil, the document simply informs us that the "oil was clarified by straining and by repose." One might reasonably assume from this statement that the oil, when sufficiently cooled, was decanted by straining through a cloth or sieve into a vial or bottle and then well-capped to await the appropriate time of "repose," allowing for the depositing of any remaining spent-lead. This however, was not the case. It is a fact that when the black oil is strained shortly after having been duly prepared the dissolved and transparent particles of white lead penetrate even a closely woven fabric. Based on that fact, it became the habit of this researcher to decant the experimental preparations of the white lead-saturated black drying oil prior to the straining process in order to visually monitor the oil for any change that might occur over an extended resting period. In doing so, it was realized, tilt-testing the oil before a light, that the first perceived thin bodied, clear, and richly amber-toned black oil after resting several hours became sluggish in body and lackluster in tonal quality thus betraying from top to bottom of black oil the presence of a suspended bulk of resolidified, tan-toned lead, undoubtedly the reason for the *English Document*'s recommended straining process.

After five or six hours of resting, when it was deemed that the gathering of the lead was complete, the black oil was redecanted by straining through a closely woven linen cloth into another glass bottle that was then well-capped and allowed to "repose." Within 24 hours or so, when examining the bottle of oil in front of a light, there was clearly evidenced a sharply delineated, compact tan deposit. In tilt-testing the oil, it was found to be fluid, thoroughly clarified, and richly—but not darkly—amber-toned. A realization of an end, so evasive and long sought, leaving only to be tested empirically—used that is in the preparation of van Dyck's medium, prime and grounds, palette preparations, pictorial vehicles, and under the brush. In other words, means and methods that only painters are capable of assessing value.

Worth noting, before proceeding to the actual employment of this oil, is that the *English Document* states that van Dyck's "drying oil should be used fresh," for after a month "it begins to lose its good qualities"—remarks which lend credentials to the proposals we herein have put forth. In employing this black oil, I have, myself, encountered the same result. Although after one month this drying oil retains ordinary siccativity it fails to sufficiently induce oxygen rapidly enough into the pictorial vehicle and color preparations so as to allow for the superimposition of the paints wet-into-wet. Such a dissipated oil is unfit for the preparation of the Flemish medium and indeed any pictorial chore other than to act as a simple siccative oil used for the preparation of the ground and ground-prime of canvas.

## Flemish Medium: Parent Structure of the 17th

## Century Flemish and Dutch Pictorial Techniques

While we will deal with the preparation of Anthony van Dyck's Flemish medium, procedurally, all Flemish and Dutch medium structures were prepared in the same fashion. The difference between them was in the various strengths and types of black drying oil, and the resin strength of the mastic varnish.

Although both de Mayerne and the *English Document* agree on the ingredients and proportions of van Dyck's spirit of turpentine based mastic varnish, it is the latter named reference that is relatively explicit respecting the fabrication of that varnish.

Regarding the preparation of van Dyck's Flemish medium, once again it is the *English Document* that provides the necessary information. Listing ingredients, the document calls for a pound of mastic varnish, and one-half pint of drying oil. While the wording implies that the varnish was weighed and the black oil was measured by volume, since both ingredients share a common weight, the simplest rationale is to employ, by volume, two parts of mastic varnish and one part of the black oil. The ingredients were then poured into a heat-tempered glass jar, and stirred with a palette knife until combined. In keeping with the principle of lead-resin suspension, the mastic varnish and black oil, after a short while, formed a jelly which, due to aeration, was noticeably cloudy. The jar was then tightly capped and set on a trivet, previously placed in a pot of boiling water.

The jar was then rested in the pot of boiling water for an appropriate length of time, occasionally swirling the ingredients to insure their combination. When removing the jar from the water and examining the content in front of a light, the contents no longer appeared cloudy, but revealed in tilt-testing to be a clear, lustrous, amber-toned liquid. However, had a portion of the content remained jellified ("curdled") as it was referred to in the *English Document* the jar would have been returned to the boiling water until the content was completely liquefied because the purpose of the procedure was to create a non-aerated, homogeneous structure. The liquid was then decanted into a wide-mouth receptacle and well capped. When tested after cooling, the content had restructured, via the principle of lead-resin suspension to a soft, optically dark jelly.

One might question the obvious discrepancy between the dark jelly I have described and the "white jelly" referred to in the *English Document*. The explanation being that the author of Eastlake's "modern manuscript," that which we refer to as the *English Document*, was not a painter and confused the color of Van Dyck' s medium with known remarks made by "Henry Tilson (1654—1695)," a pupil of Peter Lely, concerning the painting medium of a certain "Sebastiano Bombelli (1635—1724)."

Mansfield Kirby Talley, in his most engaging volume, through oversight of an important caveat regarding the color of the leaded painting medium employed by Bombelli, a medium which we believe was in kind to the medium devised by Anthony van Dyck, notes, "What is clear is that Bombelli is the one who used an oil varnish painting medium that looked like a white jelly." A misidentification which lead Talley to further propose that, Bombelli's painting medium "must have been a sort of megilp."[9] The basis for Talley's mistake related to Henry Tilson's description of what he termed Bombelli's "oil" noting, in complete contridiction of that descriptive word, that it "looked like a white jelly" adding (Talley's missing caveat), "when you keep it long." While elsewhere, along that same line of description, Tilson observed (using the words of Talley), "He kept it in a pot next to him and it looked like a white jelly" significantly adding, "after some time."[10]

By those two time frame references we are told, in effect, that Bombelli's "oil" or more correctly, jellified medium, was not white from the outset—leaving us to reasonably speculate that it was, instead, a toned preparation. In kind, we propose, to that which we have described in our Fifth Key text as the "optically dark jelly" devised by Anthony van Dyck. Remember, although Bombelli was Venetian, Van Dyck developed his medium and new mannered "airy style" while in Italy and left numerous examples of enviable portraiture throughout that land. Just as he would no doubt have left evidence of the medium and method in which they were executed. Little wonder that his style and technical means would have been adopted by certain portrait painters of Italy. After all, it was a technical system which offered them much the same *sfumatic* effect as was achieved by the greatest 16th Century Venetians, only with greater speed and far less difficulty. A technical system which by the time of Bombelli would no longer have been associated with its roots and the elegant inventor from the North.

In reiteration, it is a fact that when cooking oils with lead, be it white lead or litharge, they are turned—in relation to degree of heat and length of cooking time, to variant shades of amber. It is also a fact that when such oils are prepared in a lowered heat range from 185°C to 200°C and combined with a soft mastic varnish such as that herein proposed for Van Dyck, the resultant amber toned jelly will, in time, lighten in tone even to the point of becoming white. I have experienced this process time and time again. A technical system largely based on the information cited in the *English Document*, Eastlakes's "modern manuscript without a name." An imperfect but basic document which we have no doubt was linked to the technique of Anthony van Dyck. A design for the preparation of van Dyck's soft Flemish medium structure, although leaving much to be resolved concerning the mode of fabrication and manner of employment. That rich, optically dark, amber toned jelly which through correct usage, allows for an amazing airiness told both by its tactile response and optical rewards.

For those who have difficulty with the idea of an optically dark preparation, while it is true that mastic varnish can be set in suspended solution with an oil by merely stirring white lead, litharge, or even lead acetate into the mixture, it is also true that jellification is the primary reward. Such meager preparations were the basis for certain 19th Century megilps and never should those naively simple and wanting mediums be compared with the highly sophisticated preparations employed by the masters which, I believe, are reasonably reconstructed in this present volume.

The masters demanded that their drying oils be totally lead-saturated because only by that process were the oils rendered brilliant and abundantly siccative while at the same time kept reasonably thin in body. Unlike the 16th Century Venetian medium, with its oil-saturated, active lead content which siccatively charged the *oglio cotto*, the black oils employed by the Flemish painters represented the primary source of siccaativity. The unique advantage was that the mastic resin present in the varnish structure, by way of its combination with the spirit of turpentine carrier, is set into suspended solution free of oil saturation. This enabled the resin to act as a thoroughly lean element, unlike the mastic resin present in van Eyck's *liquid varnish* and thereby the 16th Century Venetian medium. This was their primary drawback to employment of a true *alla prima* technique.

And so, by the foregoing analysis and proposal for the medium employed by Anthony van Dyck, is laid the groundwork necessary for resolving variations of other Flemish and Dutch mediums based on that structural theme. While logical progress would, perhaps, be to continue explaining the means and methods employed by van Dyck, I deem it best to first reason and identify the structure of Flemish medium from which van Dyck took his material leave. The strength and structure of medium that we propose was developed by the Elder Jan Bruegel and employed by Jan's devoted friend and collaborator, Peter Paul Rubens.

## *Peter Paul Rubens: Indications of Strength*

If there existed no other indicators to suggest the material make-up of Rubens' medium, other than those perceived through visual assessment of his paintings, it must be concluded that Rubens' medium perceived through the pictorial vehicle which formed his paint film was of a strong and vitreous nature, and from the obvious wet-into-wet, *alla prima* application of his paints was greatly accelerated in both ordinary siccativity and "siccative grasp." A multifaceted structure, able to be rendered in many free styles, full in translucent and opaque opalescence, and body, paints that could be thinned by dilution to a near watercolor consistency, qualities which could be rendered side-by-side, lending contrast, variety, and vitality, all within the same painted plane.

It was a durable structure, low in oil saturation, one that retained luster and brilliance despite the ravages of time and with notable exceptions the attacks by heavy-handed picture-cleaners. It was a vehicle capable of producing rich enameling effects which, in light of the fact that "enamels are pigmented varnishes"[11] points directly to a strong, resinous make-up.

That resin was a dominant element in Rubens' medium, and therefore his pictorial vehicle, is confirmed when observing the embodied impasto of the white lead paint structure so prevalently displayed in Rubens' paintings—an effect directly related to lead-resin suspension and not, as Maroger suggested, through the use of beeswax.[12]

In addition to visual assessment of Rubens' paintings, there are certain written source evidences which also support the belief that Rubens' medium and pictorial vehicle were of significant resin strength. Theodore de Mayerne, in commenting on the character of Rubens' pictorial vehicle (using the word "medium") wrote: "His medium was so heavy that he had to wet his brush in essence of turpentine, although it was not to paint with the latter."[13] From this observation it may be reasoned that since the turpentine was not used to paint with, it must have been used to clean brushes that had become clogged by Rubens' thick, oleoresinous pictorial vehicle and the paint structures that it formed. The clogging or buildup of the pictorial elements was the result of a combined spirit of turpentine based mastic varnish, suspended by a lead-saturated black drying oil, a consequence owed more to a large percentage of resin than to the lead-saturated oil.

Such a theory is lent credibility through the known facts concerning the proportion and preparation of the oleoresinous medium employed by Anthony van Dyck which, as earlier noted with respect to technique, was essentially the same as that employed by Rubens. The primary difference, herein proposed, is to be accredited to a significantly greater resin strength, coupled with a tenacious drying oil—the earlier discussed black oil of Giorgione.

The above reasoning is supported by yet another bit of source evidence. A directive (selected parts of which have been discussed in the Fourth Key) stemming directly from Rubens, concerns a preparation and pictorial practice which, I propose, reflects on the strong and resin-resistive nature of his basic medium and pictorial vehicle structures. Recorded by Dr. de Mayerne the complete directive is as follows:

> To make your colours spread easily and consequently unite well, and even retain their freshness—as in the case of blues and indeed all colours—dip your brush lightly, from time to time while you paint, in clear essential oil of Venice turpentine, distilled in a water-bath; then with the same brush, mix your colours on the palette.[14]

In useful repetition, Venice turpentine is a thick, viscous balsam which can be successfully employed as a diluent—and this is to be stressed—only when thinned with spirit or oil of turpentine (the "essential oil" portion of what Rubens termed "clear essential oil of Venice turpentine"). So thinned, the diluent appears more in the character of the "thinner" than the balsam.

When the essential oil of Venice turpentine was used as a fluid diluent for soft color compounds, as witnessed in certain free-flowing sketches by van Dyck, the diluent often broke the paint compounds, depriving the colors of their vitality and causing the white paint to appear gray. Obviously the same was not true with respect to the palette preparation of Rubens. In the above quotation we are obliquely advised by Rubens' own words that his paints were of a resistive body and somewhat suspended, for unless his "clear essential oil of Venice turpentine" was employed "from time to time," they would not "spread easily" nor "unite well." Thus it might be concluded that Rubens' pictorial vehicle and paint structures were of such strength that they were not only advantaged by the use of the thin bodied Venice turpentine, but judging from the evidence of his paint film, acted in turn as the protector of even the most diluted paint (save for certain works which have been most rudely over-cleaned). As with the first bit of written evidence earlier cited, the above evidence also points to Rubens' medium, the base element used to form his pictorial vehicle, being of a strong and embodied structure. A strength and structure that when viewed in the evidential principle of lead-resin suspension, points directly to a greater mastic varnish strength than has reliably been associated with the technique of Anthony van Dyck.

Most enlightening is a modern indicator that further suggests a significant concentration of mastic resin was employed in the medium and palette preparations of Peter Paul Rubens. This was realized during a visit to Munich in 1964 when studying Rubens' small *Last Judgment* in the Alte Pinakothek shortly after the painting had been attacked with acid by a madman, it was noted that while the acid had depleted areas of its shine, visible only in an angled view, there was no significant damage to the paint film itself. Mastic varnish, it should be realized, is a "stop-out" varnish used in etching to prevent—where unwanted—acid penetration of the metal plate. Thus, the indication was that Rubens' paint film, in this case an epidermal velatura layer of paint, must have contained a significant amount of that "painters' resin," limiting the deleterious effect of the acid.

Unfortunately, while the painting did withstand the attack, it could not withstand the harsh cleaning it subsequently underwent by the time of a later visit to Munich in 1966, a cleaning which left the nacreous quality of that work significantly diminished.

Thus are a few of the evidences that helped to lay the groundwork for developing Rubens' strength of Flemish Medium, requiring proof by trial: the majority of negative results to be put aside in favor of those more positive.

## Mastic Varnish and the Medium of Peter Paul Rubens

Advantaged by the knowledge of the proper preparation of Giorgione's tensive 1:16 ratio litharge-saturated black drying oil, the oil, which Maroger proposed, was in kind to that employed by Rubens. As well as the many resolves concerning the proportion and fabrication of Van Dyck's strength of Flemish medium, a series of experiments were begun in order to determine the mastic varnish strength most able to lend the various qualities and characteristics evidenced in the works of Peter Paul Rubens. Each experimental varnish was proportioned, by weight, for both the mastic resin and the spirit of turpentine, prepared in a similar manner, as was the earlier discussed mastic varnish of Anthony van Dyck. In addition, each trial varnish required extended time periods of use before their worth could be properly assessed.

The strength of mastic varnish that we deemed most able to lend rewards associated with the technique of Rubens is proportioned by weight in a ratio of one part mastic resin to a corresponding equal part spirit of turpentine. When duly prepared, such a varnish is of sufficiently heavy body, that in order to encourage the deposit of insoluble debris, the recommendation found in the *English Document* to keep the varnish in the heat and light of the sun, proves especially useful.

In the preparation of Rubens' basic Flemish Medium, both the proportions and method of cooking as earlier proposed for the preparation of Anthony van Dyck's Flemish Medium strength prevails. Thus, by volume measure, two parts of Rubens' strong mastic varnish is poured into a heat-resistant jar, to which is added a one part corresponding measure of Rubens' litharge-saturated black drying oil. The ingredients are then stirred with the palette knife, resulting in a strong gel. The jar is then to be well capped and placed into a pot of boiling water where it is allowed to rest until the gel structure is completely liquefied. The resulting homogeneous, non-aerated liquid is then decanted into a wide-mouthed jar, then to be well capped and kept for use.

It should be noted that in any and all envisioned strengths and structures of the Flemish Medium, the siccativity is always granted by the type and strength of the black drying oil, be it prepared with white lead or litharge, whereas the body structure is always determined by the mastic varnish strength. This having been said, as well as the proposed resolve of the Flemish Medium strengths employed by Peter Paul Rubens and Anthony van Dyck, the two most artistically persuasive Flemish artists of the 17th Century, we will now consider the first chore assigned to those mediums, namely, the nature of the primes employed on both panel and canvas.

## The Grounds and Striated Optical Primes of Panel

Van Dyck leaves no doubt regarding the importance of panel and canvas preparations when he remarked to De Mayerne: "The ground and priming for pictures is of great consequence."[15]

There is no mystery surrounding the grounding of panel. In the North, hardwood panels such as oak and walnut were grounded in the traditional manner, i.e. gesso, isolated with a soft jellified glue size.

As to the priming of those grounds, traditional theory prevailed. A continuous, transparent oleoresinous coating was required which, when dry, would act as an optical milieu and liaison attractor for the more oleoginous palette preparations of pictorial vehicle and paints to be worked over it. The relatively lean make-up of the Flemish Medium, acting in accord to its materially reasoned, architectonic design dictated its use. In the case of a striated *optical prime*, a device readily evidenced in the 17th Century Flemish painting, a portion of the Flemish Medium was tinted with a bit of dry pigment, generally brown or black, and broadly brush spread over the glue isolated gesso ground.

Due to the resistive body of the Flemish Medium, particularly a medium as strongly resinous and suspended as that employed by Rubens, spirit of turpentine was immixed with the knife into the tinted medium, sufficient enough to produce a soft and buoyant pomade. This pomade was then quickly spread with a large bristle bush, over the glue isolated gesso ground. Aided when necessary with brush additives of spirit of turpentine, in order to insure fluidity and desired thinness of the priming element. Turpentine thins the body of the Flemish Medium without disturbing its integral make-up leaving, once the turpentine evaporated, the same unencumbered oil to resin ratio.

The purpose for the tinted striations that, depending on the pigment used, ranged from blond or pale gray to shades of darker brown or black, was threefold. To subdue the glaring whiteness of the gesso ground; to add variety to the translucent paint film to be worked over it; and to display with greater force those areas where opacities prevail so that, as Maroger wrote "…the whites can detach themselves from the darker ground becoming visible immediately [as] they are laid on."[16]

The striated primes employed by different masters reveals the character of their medium. The *optical prime* so prevalently displayed in Rubens' unfinished *Lion Hunt*, London, National Gallery, is extremely tensive. The smooth character of its somewhat suspended body suggests that a great deal of spirit of turpentine was used to insure fluidity. Judging from the resistive character of the striated bush strokes, this had to be replenished during the application of the prime. Also most informative is the character of the striated prime structure found in several small panel sketches of modellos housed in the Brussels Museum of Fine Arts. Both the *Boy Riding a Dolphin* and *Neptune and Amphatrite* reveal that the striated *optical prime*, composed as it was of dry pigment and Flemish Medium, was spread with but a small amount of spirit of turpentine. The striations are quite prominent, forming hills and valleys of Rubens' thick suspended medium, on which, as is easily perceived through the existing paint film, a maverick crayon line ruled by Rubens at some earlier time adheres to the *hills* while skipping over the *valleys*. A raised form which could hardly be identified as a hygroscopic glue coat.

Other Rubens' panels, such as those employed for the sketches executed in league with his *Marie de Medici Cycle*, now in the Alte Pinakothek, Munich, reveal the use of much spirit of turpentine, rendering the striations of a watery quality. In all cases, however, whether unctuous or watery, the prime is quite capable of supporting and suspending over the underlying reflective white gesso ground, the paints worked upon them. What we do insist, contrary to the opinions of certain Rubens scholars, is that Rubens' striated *optical primes* were never prepared by a hand other than that of the master himself. It is in the laying on of the *optical prime*, wherein is felt an abstract pleasure, no less personal to the master than are the paints to be rendered over them.

There is however, one example of Rubens having employed a striated *optical prime* not of his own making, but then, neither was the Flemish Medium used in the application of that prime, nor were the pictorial vehicle and paint structures employed in the execution of the work rendered over it. The painting is Rubens' portrait of his second wife, *Helena Fourment*, Brussels Museum of Fine Art. This uncharacteristically soft, gossamer like paint film may well have been rendered at the request of the young Van Dyck, prevailing on Rubens to employ the panel and paint preparations that constituted the younger painter's "airy style," which he had developed during his Italian sojourn. Executed most likely, during a planned visit by Rubens and his stylish young wife to Van Dyck's Antwerp studio, there are signs in the rendering of the paint which Rubens would have considered as less appealing than that of the more enameled paint structures to which he was accustomed. The reason, perhaps, that we find no other evidence in Rubens' pictorial *oeuvre* of that soft and "airy style."

As earlier noted in this work, the Elder Jan Bruegel was the Flemish initiator of the tinted striated *optical prime*; however, he was not the inventor. To this writer's knowledge, the first example of a striated panel prime used in oil painting is found in

Titian's *Christ Crowned with Thorns*, c. 1542, now in the Louvre. In the foreground of that painting, the lowest step leading to the stage where the tragedy occurs remains free of paint. In that area, the broad, striated *optical prime* coat composed of a black pigment tinted and turpentine spread *Venetian Medium*, is readily perceived. Unlike Flemish 17th Century painting, the grayish striations are obliterated in the painted areas, the purpose being to depress the glaring whiteness of the gesso ground, rather than to add optical advantage to the paint film.

Yet another early evidence of the striated *optical prime* is found in the Elder Pieter Bruegel's *Ships in a Storm*, Vienna, Kunsthistorisches Museum, often proposed as his last painting. Striations can be seen through the translucent paint film of the umber surrounded, light toned center area of the painting. The striations, composed of a dry pigment tinted preparation of Antonella da Messina's *lead-paste* medium based, oleogeniously upgraded pictorial vehicle, lent to the paints worked over it, when dry, rewards in kind to those found in the paintings of Pieter's son Jan, and those painters who followed his lead.

As to where the elder Pieter Bruegel may have learned of the application of the striated *optical prime*, we cannot ignore a reference regarding such a practice as recorded by Carel van Mander. In his *Schilderboeck*, Van Mander notes in the life of Jan de Hollander: "He frequently made use of a method by which he covered the ground color of his canvas or panel with a light wash, so that this ground color contributed to the final effect of the painting." Then, significantly, he adds: "Breughel took over this method from him."[17]

Due to the lack of sufficient evidence to uphold the accuracy of the above reference, let us term it "a literary curiosity," worthy of pondering in leisure time. This is a luxury that old age and failing health now deny me.

Turning to what is indeed a reasonable theory regarding source knowledge which may have led to the general use of the tinted, striated *optical prime*, it may well be that the Elder Pieter Bruegel learned of the Titianesque device when in Italy from 1552 to 1554, having viewed Titian's *Christ Crowned with*

*Thorns* which was housed in the Church of Santa Maria della Grazie in Milan.

Thus we have two possible sources by which Jan may have learned of the tinted, striated *optical prime*: from handed down knowledge of his father's technique, perhaps even having viewed what may have been his illustrious father's last painting, *Ships in a Storm*; or having viewed, as did his father, Titian's *Christ Crowned with Thorns* during his visit to Milan in 1596.

With respect to the 17th Century Flemish pictorial technique, in general, it is safe to say that tinted, striated *optical prime* of panel was preferred by those painters who employed highly resinous and siccativity strong preparations of Flemish Medium, as opposed to the soft and lowered resin strength of medium, such as employed by Anthony van Dyck.

## The Preparation of Canvas—Preferred Support of Anthony van Dyck

Seventeenth Century Flemish and Dutch painters seldom employed extremely rough textured canvas, preferring, instead, canvas of moderate to smooth weave. As was the custom when preparing canvas, the stretched material was sized with one or two coats of soft jellified glue, in order to break the absorption of the fabric and protect the fabric from direct contact with the oil compounded ground coat.

As with the ground coat employed by the later 16th Century Venetians, Flemish grounds were composed of a solid russet toned, tan, or gray tinted white lead and siccative black drying oil (with or without inerts), knife prepared to a pliable paste consistency, and scraped over the glue sized canvas. However, unlike the earlier described Venetian ground coat, the Flemish oil compounded ground coat, when dry, required no subsequent isolating coat of jellified glue, prior to the application of the final "composition or priming." This brings us to consider the necessary difference between the Flemish *optical prime* of panel and what we will call the ground-prime of canvas.

Whereas a transparent *optical prime* coat of the lean Flemish Medium, which it should be noted becomes brittle with age, could be used on the inflexible support of panel; such a lean coat could not be employed on the flexible support of canvas without splitting and cracking. Therefore, it is necessary to render the final ground-prime coat sufficiently fat and elastic so as to allow for the movement natural to fabric. At the same time it must be kept lean enough to act in liaison attraction for the more oleaginous pictorial vehicle and related paint preparations to be worked over it.

Elasticity for the ground-prime is achieved by simply immixing with a palette knife or spatula equal amounts of the above described ground preparation and pure Flemish Medium. This prepared ground-prime is then simply scraped over a lightly sanded, dry ground coat. It is the material make-up of this ground-prime that nurtures and refines the arid and abrasive textured underlying ground coat while offering, when dry, both optical and tactile advantage and rewards to the materially related pictorial vehicle and tempered paints to be rendered over it.

As to the reason for scraping, rather than painting on the ground-prime, it is to prevent the over-loading and thereby cosmetic smoothing and disguising of the weave of canvas. It should be noted that if a smooth field is desired, the painter must begin by employing a canvas of smooth texture.

Such a ground-prime as above described allows, via the oil content, for the expansion and contraction of the canvas without cracking. The toleration of movement is especially effective when employing a medium such as herein proposed for van Dyck. This is an important point, since it was the degree of cracquelere seen in the canvases of van Dyck, as compared with those of Rubens, that aided in determining the difference between the medium structures employed by the two painters. The greater the resin strength of a medium, the amount of the greater cracquelere will eventually develop in the ground-prime. A medium containing a lesser strength of mastic resin will, in the main, exhibit fewer signs barring, of course, works which have been ravaged in time.

## Order of Concern: Rubens and the Alla Prima Sketches and Studies

Being left to our own wit and reason, it must be noted that nowhere in surviving source or near-source evidence is there a designation for such a preparation as the pictorial vehicle. In fact, the *English Document* after having described what must be considered Anthony van Dyck's medium, implies that it was as one, both a medium and a vehicle used in the rendering of the paints stating: "his colours were tempered as he used them with the oil and varnish above described." All that one need to do to dispel that implication is to consider the imbalanced ratio of two parts mastic varnish to one part drying oil used in the formation of the medium in order to realize that the greater portion of varnish by its extreme leanness and fluid base of evaporable spirit of turpentine would unacceptably impede both the spreading and manipulation of the paints. A structural leanness which, while offering a most desirable *optical prime* coat, would hardly answer the need for a reasonably tractable pictorial vehicle or "color carrier."

Unlike 16th Century Venetian painting, where the technique was based on the principle of controlled fat offering but one relatively fat-saturated pictorial vehicle and related paint structures, 17th Century Flemish pictorial technique was based on controlled lean, offering no less than three forms of pictorial vehicles and their related paint structures. Each varied in degrees of structural body, siccativity, and tactile force by way of black drying oil extended temperings. As is true of all pictorial vehicles, they serve to bind the pigments into paint form and are the carrier of the colors. Acting at the same time as the extender of the paints, allowing for tractability and ease of spreading. Compositionally, all pictorial vehicles as well as their related paint preparations must be no less fat and preferably fatter in construction than the priming material over which they are worked.

It is by way of the lead-saturated black drying oil, the very source of fat, which when duly prepared and proportioned in the forming of a pictorial vehicle structure, lends a siccative effect over the lean mastic varnish content of the vehicle and the vehicle bound paints, encouraging the rapid intake of oxygen, setting and tacking the paint film, thereby creating the siccative grasp necessary for the superimposition of the paints wet-into-wet. This serves the hand and pictorial needs of the individual painter, allowing for his various identifying pictorial style and personal calligraphic rendering, be it *alla prima* or a sequence of wet-over-dry layerings.

It is the concern for siccative grasp that, in time, we came to reason with respect to working on the lean *optical prime* of panel that the most powerful structure of pictorial vehicle—the first and leanest of the three earlier mentioned structures, is that which is kept in relatively close material proximity to the Flemish Medium itself. The very same medium which, when tinted with a bit of dark pigment and brush spread with spirit of turpentine over the glue isolated gesso ground of panel, served, when dry, as the *optical prime*. This striated, lean oleoresinous field which acted to physically attract the pictorial vehicle and its related paint structures lends through the striations, particularly noticeable in the works of Peter Paul Rubens, variation and visual vitality to the enamel-like paint films.

Regarding the fabrication of this pictorial vehicle, it is as simplistic in preparation as are the many rewards sophisticated. Employing a determined 1 part, volume measure, of the Flemish Medium, placed on the grinding stone, thoroughly immix with the palette knife 1/3 part, in corresponding volume measure, of the appropriate black drying oil. The resulting mixture, although fluid when first prepared, soon structures to a fixed soft gel. The direct result (as might be anticipated) is of the oft-repeated principle of lead-resin suspension. The more resinous the mastic varnish, as well as the heavier bodied and darker toned the lead-saturated black drying oil produces a cohesively denser and darker vehicle than would be realized in the use of softer and lighter toned pictorial elements.

## *Setting-up of Palette: Preparation of the Paint*

It is by the mention of a pictorial vehicle that we are obliged to deal with the preparation of the paints. Except for the difference of the grinding vehicle or element, used in the compacting of the color pigments, all procedures are the same whether employing the leanest structure of pictorial vehicle or those of greater fat, *i.e.* oil content, yet to be discussed. Respecting the make-up of the paints, we shall begin by considering the preparation of white. A determined measure of the earlier described white lead paste is placed on the stone, into which is thoroughly immixed with the palette knife, an equal volume measure of the appropriate, above described, pictorial vehicle. Although the resulting mixture appears somewhat grayed, due to the amber tone of the tempering pictorial vehicle, the discoloration, after resting on the palette soon dissipates leaving gleaming, enamel-like, white lead paint. The degree of the body of the compound being in direct accord with the resin strength of the pictorial vehicle used in the tempering, i.e. the body of Rubens' white lead paint being heavier and more suspended than that of van Dyck. Both preparations, however, were sufficiently yielding so as to be taken from the palette with the brush sans diluent.

Concerning the preparation of the colors, there is no mystery about the element employed for the grinding and compacting of the pigments into globules. Through earlier noted directives related to Theodore de Mayerne by both Rubens and van Dyck, it is known that Rubens, in reflection of what has herein been proposed to be of 16th Century Venetian origin, employed spirit of turpentine, whereas van Dyck, in what we believe must be considered as a wholly Flemish method, employed his soft, lean Flemish Medium. As to the formation of the paint, each tightly compacted color globule, in turn was tempered to ductility (by judgment of eye) with an approximate equal measure of the respective, duly prepared pictorial vehicle. The colored paints were then rested on the palette along with the white.

In addition, and in keeping with the tradition of all previous schools of painting, a portion of the pictorial vehicle was also placed on the palette to act as an embodied transparent paint. This would be added to the real paints with the brush when needed during the course of the painting.

Undoubtedly, the relationship between the *optical prime* of panel and *ground prime* of canvas, as well as the paint structures, were materially close. In fact, with respect to the mastic varnish strength employed by Rubens, were we to break down the oil to varnish ration of those elements, they would prove to be of equal lean to fat construction. Most interesting is the fact that if we were to consider the amount of purified raw oil employed in the preparation of the tightly compacted white lead paste, coupled with the evaporation of the spirit of turpentine inherent in the palette preparations, the ratio amount of fat to lean would bring this vehicle and related paint structures to the ratio of fat to lean (*i.e.*, oil to resin) proportions of what we believe comprised the improved liquid-varnish devised by Jan van Eyck.

## *The Diluent "Essential Oil of Venice Turpentine"*

In support of the earlier proposal regarding the preparation of the pictorial vehicle related paint structures, wherein that designated vehicle was the sole oleaginous source, (save for a controlled amount of raw oil present in the white lead paint), there exists a bit of evidence, oblique though it may be, which lends credence to our reasoning.

The 18th Century French painter, J.B. Descamps who recorded the famed "maxims" which are attributed to Peter Paul Rubens wrote:

> In the pictures of Rubens the obscurer masses have scarcely any substance of colour: this was one of the grounds for criticism by his enemies, who objected that his pictures were not painted with sufficient solidity, that they were little more than a tinted varnish, calculated to last no longer than the painter.[18]

While it is true, as Descamps then stated with regard to the longevity of Rubens' work—we now find that this criticism has no just foundation. The same is not true with respect to Rubens' enemies noting that his pictorial technique involved the use of "varnish."

We must consider that Rubens' enemies lived at the time of the painter and would, no doubt, have known of the preparations used in the mixing and rendering of his paints. For indeed, the pictorial vehicle that helped to form Rubens' paints and was used during the course of the painting was essentially a varnish. This brings us to a discussion of Rubens' pictorial technique and a consideration of the "essential oil of Venice turpentine," yet another indisputable varnish form.

While we are convinced of that diluents general employment by the 17th Century Flemish and Dutch painters, we admit that it is difficult to point to a variety of paint films, particularly in the more finished paintings, and state unequivocally: There is the concrete evidence of that diluent's use.

When examining Rubens' recommendation (found in the earlier quoting of Rubens' directive), "dip your brush lightly, from time to time while you paint, in clear essential oil of Venice turpentine… then, with the same brush, mix your colours on the palette…," we may better understand why it is difficult to visually identify the use of that diluent. Quite simply, Rubens made no mention of that element being added directly into the white paint. This is understandable. After all, it is that paint structure which lends both opacity and impasto, qualities that could be jeopardized were the diluent brush added directly into that compound. Thus we might conclude that the diluent generally found its way into the white paint and the tones that it helped to form, by insinuation of the colors via their recommended "from time to time" brush immixture of that diluent. It is, therefore, not surprising that easy identification of the diluent's presence in the more opaque tones would be difficult.

This identification is further complicated by the fact that when degrees of translucency were desired for the opaque tones or even the pure white paint, the chore was best served through the use of the master painters most unique structure: the pictorial vehicle. This element lends a fixed and embodied transparency while at the same time adds protection to the paints and tones in which it is mixed, extending that protection to even the thinnest of structures, wherein the diluent might play a significant role. It was this diluent which Rubens deemed so important to his technique that he himself described the mode of employment.

Seldom in Rubens' vast *oeuvre* is the use of the essential oil of Venice turpentine so clearly evident than in his sketches, particularly those executed on toned, striated *optical prime* of panel. These works comprise a living microcosm of the painter, conveying to us, so distant from his time, the intellect and artistic essence of that Flemish master. Be it a bozzeto, color sketch or study, the work was executed *alla prima* and, save for sketch-like modellos, never do we find corrective repaint. More than any other painter, Rubens through the vitality of his sketches, illustrates the importance of pictorial devices and materials, the means by which he attained what has been termed his "technical fluency." The excitement of these works rest with the fact that they are never merely painted but are instead written in the most intelligent and legible pictorial calligraphy possible— wedding the mind and hand by way of technical methods.

He viewed all subjects be they human kind or beast, still life or landscape, not in the puny photographic process that has entrapped many of the "realist" painters of our time, but in the painterly science of draughtsmanship and the analytical, critical observation of nature. Although Rubens lends to all that he painted an undeniable sense of nature, it is never nature alone but nature adorned and embellished, through punctuating accents and forceful articulation. Flesh was his forte and anatomy was his structural guide. All of which was translated into paint, employing the most perfect pictorial elements and technical system of painting ever devised. He turned what would otherwise be a pictorial chore into an act of painterly love.

Due to the fact that Rubens' siccativity strong and highly resinous pictorial vehicle and color preparations were not specifically designed for sketching, the "essential oil of Venice turpentine" must be considered as an indispensable aid. This diluent acted for Rubens as the "painters ink" par excellent, allowing for a speed of execution consummate with the immediacy of his rapidly developing thoughts. It is important to realize that with respect to the two ingredients which form the diluent, it is the superior amount of oil or spirit of turpentine that acts as the actual diluent, used to thin and run the paints and this is of paramount importance—it is the dual function of the lesser ingredient amount of Venice turpentine to set and control in both line and wash, the free flowing oil of turpentine, lending luster to that otherwise lusterless and luster-depleting hydrocarbon. Collectively allowing for the colors to "spread easily and consequently unite well and ever retain their freshness," a freshness that, it should be noted, was lent by the inherent richness of the pictorial vehicle tempered colors that formed the paint structure.

It is not surprising that the use of the "essential oil of Venice turpentine," as directed by Rubens himself, has been virtually ignored or, despite the indisputable extant evidence, changed from the directed mode of employment. The failure rests with the fact that, until now, both the medium and palette preparations employed by Rubens had not been correctly identified, rendering Rubens' directive ineffective. It was precisely because of the resin strength and suspension of Rubens' palette preparations that this diluent was employed. It may well be that it was Rubens' extensive use of this additional varnish form, coupled with the varnish-laden Flemish Medium and pictorial vehicle that, as earlier noted, prompted Rubens' critics to question the stability of his technique—a fear that would be well founded had the Venice turpentine been used in a thick state.

It is important to understand that the "essential oil of Venice turpentine" is not a painting medium. That is the province of the pictorial vehicle and the paints that it helps to form. It is but a diluent, an aid that by its properly reasoned use allowed the powerful palette structures employed by Rubens to yield to his pictorial will. It served as a means by which to adjust the paints to fit particular pictorial chores.

At the risk of infuriating the literati with respect not only to Rubens' sketches but to his entire pictorial corpus, commencing with the year 1607, we should stress the fact that the luminous and immediately responsive technique employed by Rubens was owed more to the nature of the pictorial materials and devices which comprised his technique than to his genius. I would even say that despite his masterful draughtsmanship and invention, had Rubens not possessed the facile Flemish technique, the rewarding qualities that artists and laymen alike recognize as "typically Rubens" would not have been so well pronounced. That many great masterpieces executed in the 16th Century Venetian technique would have been forthcoming from the hand of Rubens is assured by his genius. However, they would have been less chromatically intense, transparently vibrant, and richly enameled in quality. Their manner of rapid execution would have been adumbrated and their number severely curtailed.

It would even be safe to say that the toned, striated *optical prime* of glue isolated gesso panel would not have acted as Rubens preferred preparation and support. Instead, he would have continued to use, as evidenced in many of Rubens' paintings executed prior to 1607, the dark gray or red bolus ground-primed canvases in kind to those employed by the later 16th Century Venetians, coupled with the necessary layered building of the paints that their technique demanded. Little wonder that Rubens so favored the Elder Jan Bruegel, even allowing himself to be referred to by the older painter as "my secretary."

## On Painting "Finished in Every Detail"

It was Rubens himself who in a letter written to Peter de Vischere on April 27, 1619 concerning a commissioned painting noted: "I hope that the work will be finished in every detail within two months," adding, "but one must consider that paintings need to dry two or three times before they can be brought to conclusion."[19]

In view of the above remarks and the fact that Rubens was an undisputed master of *alla prima* technique, we propose that the wording of his letter to DeVischere alludes to a pictorial system: a series of defined stages, requiring three or four wet-over-dry sittings. This proposal is diametrically opposed to that espoused by Maroger.

In his *Secret Formulas*, Maroger took exception with the belief that, as he stated, "beneath the painting of Rubens and Van Dyck there must be a very skillful underpainting, and that each session of their painting was planned in a very exact order." Instead, seemingly unaware of Rubens' letter to DeVischere and perhaps believing that such a process is too limiting, Maroger offered what he proposed to be a refutation of such a procedure, quoting a "dictum… attributed to van Dyck" wherein it is stated: "Endeavor as far as possible to complete your work *alla prima* because there is always plenty left to do afterwards."[20]

With respect to our belief, we find no difficulty in accepting and combining the words of Rubens and the above advice purportedly given by van Dyck. In fact, the very wording of both of the above quoted advice informs us that additional work was yet to come. We must consider that the reasoning behind the architectonic design of the basic Flemish Medium structure lends to the principle of subsequent fluid adjustments, a means of variation by which the artist can control differing oleaginous tempering of pictorial vehicles and their related paint preparations. In acceptance of the above rationale and speaking as a painter, we are convinced that the majority of 17th Century Flemish masters when executing works to be "finished in every detail" would have employed a pictorial system: a set of stages; a layered but not labored process, and an adjustable means by which to attain the most perfect pictorial ends. This was a studied process which, fortunately, has escaped the fate of obscurity, adding yet another ever strengthening thread in the weave of our research fabric.

Contained in Dr. Thomas Marshall's (1621—1685) *Commonplace-Book* is a "four page manuscript in archaic Dutch dating from the 1640s." In this document the author of what has been entitled *The Observations of Anthony van Dyck* offers a certain amount of information concerning "artistic theory" and, more relevant to this present treatise, a four stage pictorial system involving what we propose to be three structures of pictorial vehicles and their related paint forms, recorded as follows:

1. *Sketch*
It is important to sketch in the forms, so perfectly, that afterwards there will be no reason to make a change.

2. *Dead-colouring*
He must, following the rules, choose lean colours (tempered colours), so that the first layer, when it will be dry enough, have a light tone; he has to see to it, of course, that those colours used in the dead-colouring are basically the same as those with which he is going to do the final painting, that is, that dead-colouring of nudes will always be done with carnation colours, and clothed figures will have a dead-colouring in a darker paint, without trying to accomplish in this rough work a degree of finish which will closely anticipate the final colour; it must be noted that this dead-colouring should be lighter in some places and darker (browner) in others as is seen fit by the artist in view of his final conception.

3. *Modeling*
The painter should realize that, when the dead-colouring is dry, that when he gives final form to his figures he will use darker colours; which means that, he will pay special attention to a correct rendering of those parts of his body, such as muscles, when he does his final modeling in accordance with the pre-modeling he did in the dead-colouring. But here the painter should see to it that he will not attempt to accentuate the round forms with highlights, which means that the round forms should not be brought forward by highlights but only through the use of darker (browner) colours.

4. After the round forms have dried the painter should put in the darkest shadows, whereby the colours of the clothing should be glazed in some places with lakes, ultramarine, and other colours in accordance with the work. This is the way the work was carried out by Titian, Giorgione, Pordonone, Palma Vecchio, and many others who left us such extremely fine works.

5. *Drawing*
Proper drawing means to get the hand used to it that it will function so assuredly that the proportions in the drawing will be so correct that they will be in accordance with that which the eye perceives, that it will not be possible to confuse one element for another. Dead-colouring is called *la maniera lavata* which is a washing process; because the space within the contours seems to have been touched up with a wash only, The second manner is called *maniera sbozzata*, or the modelling or forming process; because it is supposed to give the entire work its final form. The third one is called *la maniera finita*, which is the finishing or completing process; because this one gives the work its final touch.[21]

In clarifying certain of the information contained in the above directives, it should be understood that the "sketch" (which it is noted was not assigned a 'maniera') and the "dead-colouring" share the same material form of pictorial vehicle and paint preparation and may be rendered together wet-into-wet. However much depending on size and difficulty factor, the painter may find it preferable to render the brown guide "sketch" over which, when dry, may then be rendered the "dead-colouring." In either case completed two stages form what is in effect the primary paint film. Ergo, all of the above being considered, the reason for our earlier mentioned discrepancy concerning a three or four stage pictorial system, based on Rubens' mention of a necessary "two or three times" drying stage "before they can be brought to conclusion."

In following the lead offered in the above quoted "dead-colouring" stage, the advice "to choose lean colours" reflects the practice of tempering, that is, immixing a given amount of one or another of the earlier mentioned three pictorial vehicles into the tightly compacted white lead paste and color globules, rendering them into paint form. The leanest of those vehicles involving a ratio of 1 part volume measure of the Flemish Medium to be immixed or extended with a corresponding volume measure of 1/3 part of the black drying oil, the same preparation earlier given for the pictorial vehicle used in *alla prima* sketches and studies. This will be referred to as the *primary pictorial vehicle*, the mode of rendering being the principle difference between the two pictorial structures.

Of considerable importance, the author of the four pictorial stages leaves no doubt that the "dead-colouring" involves a full palette rendering, stipulating that the "colours" be of a light tone but basically the same as those to be used in the "final painting," be they "carnation colours" such as used in the "dead colouring of nudes" and, of course, all flesh, or the "darker paint" employed when painting "clothed figures."

Regarding the fully achieved rendering of the "dead-colouring" underpainting, the author of the "observations" refers to it as a "rough work," a term meant to describe an in-progress, planned pictorial understatement, with the degree of finish calculated in accord with needs and demands of the initiator, guided in the mind's eye-view. The "final form" was dependent on yet another pictorial stage and material adjustment of the Flemish Medium. A second vehicle structuring, to be used in a wet-over-dry rendering of paint which, in relation to its designed function, we will term the *epidermal vehicle*.

It is the numbered "3, modeling" stage found in the earlier quoted 4 stage pictorial system, wherein the epidermal vehicle and its related paint forms will be employed. As earlier noted in this Fifth Key section, it is by way of the oleous adjustment of the Flemish Medium, which forms the various pictorial vehicles and their related paint structures. Thus regarding this second pictorial structure, this epidermal vehicle, save for the amount of black drying oil adjustment of the Flemish Medium, all else procedurally remains the same as that used for the preparation of the primary pictorial vehicle. Whereas that initial vehicle requires a ratio proportion of I part volume measure of the Flemish Medium immixed with a 1/3 part, corresponding volume measure of black dry oil, the epidermal vehicle, is proportioned with 1 part Flemish Medium immixed with 2/3 part black drying oil. The difference between the two vehicles is somewhat softer gel structure of the epidermal vehicle. A sufficiently oleaginous structure so as to allay agglutination of the epidermal paint structures that except for use of the epidermal vehicle, are identical to those paint preparations employing the primary pictorial vehicle, especially important in regards to the pigment density of the white lead paint. Pigments advantaged in dispersement by way of the greater oil content of the epidermal vehicle are able to be rendered in degrees of translucency, so as to utilize the light force of the underlying "dead-colouring."

This highly tractable vehicle has the advantage of insuring an ease of spreading the related paints and, therefore, is less dependent on the diluent "essential oil of Venice turpentine" and is a material source used in the creation of optical effects, which defy easy detection. It is in section rendering that when dry retains a depth of shine equal to that of the "dead-colouring" over which the "modeling" or epidermal paints are worked. Moreover, that resolved the "form," called for in the untitled, number 4 stage of the *Observations* involving the darkening of "shadows" and glazing of "clothing."

In following a pattern of logical progression, the glaze vehicle and color preparations employed by the 17th Century painters of Flanders and Holland must necessarily be of a fatter construction than the primary and epidermal vehicles and paint preparations. Such glaze elements must be highly tractable, drawn out from a fixed-from-flow body, able to be rendered quickly and broadly, fairly gliding over the understructure. A glaze vehicle likened to a lucid matrix was envisioned by the inventor of the 17th Century Flemish technique by way of the principle of lead-resin suspension: the desired pictorial ends were constantly held in mind.

In consideration of the aforementioned requirements set for the glaze vehicle the following preparation is offered: using volume measure, immix with the palette knife on the stone one part Flemish Medium and an equal part black drying oil, until thoroughly blended. The resultant mixture although quite fluid when first prepared will soon structure into a highly tractable soft gel.

Respecting employment of the glaze vehicle and palette preparations, it is important to note, borrowing from a succinctly stated observation made by my friend and fellow painter, Gerald Doyle, "that glazes are not intended to act as a tonal value system." Quite simply, a painting must be able to stand on its own right as a tonally achieved work, and only then, when dry, might the work visually profit from the application of unifying, tone-enhancing glazes which at times may be rendered so thin that they are told more by way of their optical quality rather than pigmentation.

Thus, despite their valued effect, glazes are to be considered as cosmetic veiling, a velatura layering that may be rendered over a dry understructure in a continuous or in section paint film, unifying graduated tonal forms into a pictorial whole.

The above being concluded, we are brought to the end of the 4 stage pictorial system, leaving only the interpretation of a second number 4 entry entitled, "Drawing."

By the use of the word "drawing" and the demands for accuracy placed on the hand that wields the brush—"that it would not be possible to confuse one element from another"— is meant to reflect not only on the brown guide "sketch" but on the full palette wet-over-dry rendering of both the "dead-colouring" and the "modeling" or "final form." In other words drawing with the paint, a constant process well summed up by Sir Peter Lely (1618—1680) who was credited as having said "that painting was nothing else but draft"[22] a simple explanation of a challenging truth.

Concluding the *Observations* van Dyck romantically nominates in Italian the three-stage root process which nurtured the 17th Century Flemish pictorial system. Paying homage to the

16th century painters of Venice who inspired and spurred van Dyck to seek material means by which to express himself in a wholly personal manner—collectively his "new manner" and, as one, his "master unknown."

All of the information contained in this Fifth Key having been said, though far from exhausting our thoughts and theories concerning 17th Century Flemish pictorial techniques, we shall turn our attention to the painters north of the Province of Brabant, those whose excellence of craft inspired the title, "The Golden Age of Dutch Painting."

# The Dutch Addendum

## Variations on a Theme

What political and religious forces could not do to unite the once undivided people of Holland and Flanders, the love of painting shared by them equally acted to unify in a brotherhood of pictorial techniques the painters of both lands. As it is to speak of the pictorial mediums and vehicles employed by Peter Paul Rubens, so it is to speak of the same pictorial elements employed by Pieter Lastman, Frans Hals (1580—1666), and Rembrandt van Rijn (1606—1669). Also, when recalling the pictorial system developed and employed by Anthony van Dyck, so it is to recall the same pictorial techniques employed by Bartholomeus van Helst (c. 1613—1670), Melchior Hondecoeter (1636—1695), and Jacob Ruisdael (c. 1628—1682).

The greatest change between the painters of Flanders and their Dutch brethren, other than personal pictorial calligraphies, is found in their cultural *milieu* and aesthetic insight. But then, to involve ourselves in such matters, save for the calligraphies, would unwisely increase the pages of this treatise.... Our concern is with the craft of painting and things technical, aesthetics being best left to those who ponder such intangibles, and in doing so aid painters like me in the literary transfer of their scholarly knowledge.

Believing our observation concerning the invention and dissemination of the 17<sup>th</sup> Century Flemish pictorial technique is correct, it was the mannerist painters of Catholic Utrecht, namely Abraham Bloemaert and Joachim Utewael (1566— 1638) who in 1596, via Jan Brueghel himself, were the first northern painters to be informed of the new pictorial technique. Pieter Lastman following his return from Italy back to his native Amsterdam in 1607 furthered this technical dissemination.

Whether it is just or not, many believe that Lastman's greatest claim to fame rests with the fact that for a brief six months sometime in 1625 he taught and influenced the youthful Rembrandt van Rijn. Not only were there painterly skills taught to the young painter, but in all probability Lastman would have shared with him important insights regarding the three-year tenure with his own master, the Rome based painter Adam Elsheimer. The master who by his excellence of pictorial invention and knowledge of the then new Flemish technique, provided the metal from which Lastman forged what has been called "a better and profound manner." It was Adam, you will recall, who introduced the Flemish pictorial system to Peter Paul Rubens and following Adam's death in 1610, brought forth a note of sentiment not commonly displayed by that sophisticated Fleming.[1]

Be that as it may, the fact is that Adam's pictorial invention exerted great influence over Rembrandt, as it did over many of the painters who knew Adam or knew of his inventions primarily through engravings. While the mere mention of Adam's name never fails to stir our interest, for we also have fallen under his spell, it is best that we return to the subject at hand, recommending that our readers delve as deeply as possible into the art and influence of the cerebral German.

While we agree with Maroger in his noting that "Rembrandt… employed the same medium and technique as Rubens," we disagree with his proposal that Rembrandt employed "the maximum quantity of wax in his impastos."[2] It is true for Rembrandt as we had earlier proposed for Rubens, that with respect to the white lead based impastos, it was the presence of mastic varnish within the pictorial vehicle which, combined with the densely pigmented white lead paste, triggered the oft referred to lead-resin suspension. Thus was formed the pliant body of the white lead paint be it that employed in the make-up of the primary, epidermal, or glaze vehicle.

In further discussion of Rembrandt's pictorial techniques, it was Bredius who best summarized Rembrandt's late style when noting "toward the end of Rembrandt's life smooth, finished style was what the public most admired, whereas Rembrandt's own technique was becoming broader and broader, and more spontaneously inspired."[3]

It was that rendering of the paints that André Félibien wrote "his style which is so far removed from that of others has removed us from him."[4] This style, Maroger noted, "towards the end of his life, his more important paintings were very much worked over."[5]

It was due to such layering that, save for a small number of more traditionally executed works on the *optical prime* of panel, Rembrandt employed the oleaginous ground-prime of canvas. It is a style recognized by areas of layered thickness, not rightly to be termed impasto, that is, the laying down of a thick *alla prima* loading of paint. These layers are identified by the effect of agglutination, a piling-up of paint when rendered in various wet over dry layerings, more common to a pictorial system involving evaporable hydrocarbon such as spirit of turpentine. This tell-tale effect informs us that the various paint layers were of like material construction—a rendering that stands in complete opposition to the pictorial system and reasoned use of oleaginous differing pictorial vehicles as offered in the *Observations of Anthony van Dyck*.

In brief, while most Dutch painters sought to avoid agglutination Rembrandt seems to have embraced it. Perhaps this bold and experimental maverick painter, "this old lion," worked in defiance of the routine common to all other of his fellow painters. His was a highly personal technique no doubt based on his hearsay knowledge of Titian's late style. A system devised by Rembrandt to serve both the vision of his inner-eye as well as his reasoning of tactile response. A mode of rendering designed as above noted for use on the oleaginous ground-prime of canvas, a field devised for repaint

It might be said that Rembrandt's intrigue with the matiére of paint slanted toward the sensual, a need to dominate and mold paint into a form identified with himself and no other than himself.

As for certain technical specifications to be found in the preparation of the pictorial vehicle and related paint forms, we suggest a 1/3 part volume measure of the black drying oil to a 1 part corresponding volume measure of medium, a preparation to be used throughout the building process, regardless of the number of wet over dry sittings. Where we do believe a change of pictorial vehicle and related paint forms is to be employed is the very last process of glazing. The preparation being typical of that employed in the traditional manner namely equal volume measure parts of the black drying oil to medium. That we hold Rembrandt's late style of rendering to be a corruption of the earlier described Flemish technique is true. However, it must be said that while Rembrandt may have been *lesser the polished technician*, his pictorial inventions proved him to be *greater the artist*.

## Pictures, Pride, and Pronck

Although we have made mention, albeit brief, of certain outstanding Dutch painters and their general relationship to the two most persuasive structures of Flemish pictorial techniques, we would be remiss if we failed to mention those painters whose simple genre oriented works attracted in their own time, as in ours, viewers who were as the painters themselves less complicated and intellectually aloof.

We are speaking, without intending to denigrate, of those who are intrigued by pictorial neatness and minute details, who seek subjects and styles to which they can better relate and are more comfortable with paintings of small size. Those who in spite of their love for painting may tire of large Christian and pagan mythologies: crucifixions, murderous martyrdoms, rape, and other mayhem.

Those are the more gentle souls who enjoy most the stuff of everyday life: a child standing in a doorway, her blond hair illuminated by rays of sunlight; skaters on a frozen pond; horse drawn cart on a country road; portrait of a prized animal; a goldfinch perched on the rung of a feed box; a moonlit night; and seascapes. Also there were the up and coming doctors, lawyers, and entrepreneurs, who would add a touch of class to their lives and surroundings by commissioning paintings depicting their newly acquired treasures, boasting of their gold and silver mounted pearly nautilus shells; ornate chargers; gleaming wine urns; and glistening Venetian glassware. Those tour de force works we know as *pronck*.

There were also those who found richness and distinction in their mode of dress, a satin gown or fur trimmed velvet jacket for the lady; and for the gentleman, the latest white puffed shirt to go with his well tailored black breeches, coat, and cape, finished off by a black ribboned, broad-brimmed hat and matching ribbon adorned shoes. There were also rich displays of flowers, fruit, and family feasts; young girls slyly and coquettishly eating oysters from the half shell; writing love letters; and playing musical instruments.

There were also those who were amused by the antics of frolicking peasants: as well as the more serious and sobering *vanitas*: an extinguished flame, a time piece, and skull, warning that all things, they themselves (even as you and I) and the aged rocks will in time become dust.

These varied subjects and more were the provenance of those painters whose works, due to size and not their artistic merit, have been referred to as the "Little Masters." These painters included such as Jan Steen, Carel Fabritius, Pieter de Hooch, Gerard ter Borch, and the most celebrated of these masters, Jan Vermeer of Delft.

## Resurrected Phoenix

Undoubtedly the spell cast by the paintings of this artist—this Vermeer about whom we know so little, "succeeded in creating" as Frithjof van Thienen noted in his *Jan Vermeer of Delft*,[6] "a strange, dreamy, lyrical atmosphere—comparable only to that achieved by the Venetian, Giorgione," sharing through their paintings a magical and mystical "aura of nuances of light" and refined technique, created tonal transitions which "seem more breathed onto the canvas than painted," who reigned supreme amongst his peers and whose name should be linked with those of Frans Hals and Rembrandt forming, thereby, the *Ruling Triumverate — The Coryphaei of the Golden Age of Dutch Painting.*

Being a technically oriented painter, I tend not to believe, as has often been proposed, that Vermeer's pictorial technique was "laborious" and that he required "a protracted time period such as months" to bring to completion what were often very small works. Such laborious methods (if one equates number of sittings with labor) would better describe those employed by the painters of 15th Century Flanders, when the first successful method of oil painting was instituted by Jan van Eyck.

The most likely scenario was that Vermeer, as were all other 17th Century Dutch painters, was indebted to his Flemish brethren who developed and helped to disseminate to their northern brethren pictorial techniques that to this day have not been equaled. It was, we propose, the soft and highly tractable Flemish medium and pictorial methods employed by Anthony van Dyck that offered to Vermeer the basic devices on which to construct a medium and the necessary pictorial devices that would best serve his own artistic needs.

Sir Charles Holmes in concern for the surface structure of Vermeer's paintings noted that "smoothness, for once, is not feebleness, but is an essential factor in securing the exact adjustment of each tone, to its neighbour." He then speculated on the physical structure of Vermeer's paints and the fact that the pictorial components were often leveled or as he stated "fused without any trace of brushwork remaining" and that "by this fusion Vermeer prevents any casual gradation of his light." Then, after expressing amazement that successive application of paints when rendered over the dry underpaint "left no trace of its superimposition," incorrectly suggests that the surface quality of Vermeer's paint film was the result of "some process of smoothing or polishing the surface while the work was approaching completion."[7]

Collectively, the earlier noted qualities of "softness" and "subtle tonal nuances" generally associated with Vermeer's paint structure, wherein he employed what has been referred to as a "*pointille* (dotted) technique", credited as the means by which he achieved the "effect of moving light" while undoubtedly related to the pictorial practices and materials employed by the earlier mentioned "little master" Gabriel Metsu, Gerard ter Borch, and Pieter de Hooch. This displayed a significant structural independence that could have been achieved only by a physical revision of the basic pictorial elements.

Quite simply, the aerial qualities and smooth and luminous freshness of Vermeer's paint film could not have been achieved through a process of blending. All too often blending, when viewed through judgment of the discerning eye tortures and sullies the quality of the paints. This is especially true when the paints are themselves of a soft and rather evenly distributed pigmentation.

It is such a structure of paint that Holmes referred to when remarking of Vermeer: "His tones meet whether sharply or gently with the exact definition of nature, and with a surface so even that the effect remains quite unaltered however the lighting of the picture may be changed." These are qualities more often associated with paint structures wherein the pictorial vehicle used in the bonding of the pigments is itself of an extremely soft construction, fixing the paint compounds close to the point of flow. This was so close that the brush stirring the paints, including the white lead which occurs in their mixing of the various tints, tones, and hues, renders them sufficiently soft so as to appear when they are laid onto the pictorial field of panel or canvas as blended, when in fact no such process is necessary.

It was such a pictorial method, combined with the enviable inner vision, heart, and hand of Vermeer, that created what Holmes referred to as "this magical process," all the magic, we would suggest, is to be found in the man himself, freed in his mode of expression by the materials and pictorial method which he employed. However, speaking as I do strictly as a painter, regrettably sans genius, it might be said that had Vermeer not been born in the time that he was, his storied fame as a painter might have been quite different from what we know it to have become.

And so, we are brought to the discussion of materials and processes which, we suggest, would preclude any thought of Vermeer's having devoted "months" at a "laborious chore of painting." That there were long intervals between the paintings that constitute Vermeer's mature *oeuvre* we would agree. The reason, however, being that Vermeer, as Wilenski conjectured when comparing the meager output of paintings by that most wonderful master Adam Elsheimer to that of his admirer Peter Paul Rubens, was "more a man of thought rather than action, a man driven more to ponder on the nature of art than to turn out pictures."[8]

Based on the rationale that Vermeer's basic *medium* structure was designed to be softer than that employed by van Dyck, which in Vermeer's *unknown* early *oeuvre* he certainly would have employed, we propose a mastic varnish strength composed, by weight, of one part gum mastic tears to 3 parts spirit of turpentine. Respecting the preparation of Vermeer's black drying oil we propose the softer ratio strength to consist of, by weight, of 1 ½ parts white lead to 16 parts linseed oil. Since I am not a chemist and have no means to determine which of the fixed oils Vermeer employed, it would however be true that walnut or poppy oil would lend greater content by way of fat, the ability to further soften the color compounds and thereby add the limpid quality to the various "dotted" lights, so characteristic of Vermeer's paintings.

The above preparations having been stated, all other preparations and procedures were the same as those herein proposed for Anthony van Dyck. This would also be true regarding the preparation of Vermeer's preferred pictorial field, and support namely the solid toned *ground-prime* of canvas, with but one exception. We are referring to *Young Girl with Flute*, Washington, National Gallery, the only known panel painting by Vermeer. Through a cursory examination of this painting we have concluded that the paints were worked over a transparent, nonstriated, light enhancing and tactilely rewarding, dry *optical-prime coat* composed of Vermeer's ultra-soft and highly tractable medium, spread either with or without brush additive of spirit of turpentine over a glue isolated gesso ground. We were encouraged in this belief by the fact that in a laboratory study conducted by the Doerner Institute, Munich, investigating the 'Pigments And Grounds Used by Jan Vermeer' (Report and Studies in the History of Art, 1968, Washington, D.C.) while the analysis of this particular painting revealed a ground consisting of "chalk (yellow ocher)" no mention was made of what we propose must have an oleoresinous coat resting atop the glue isolated ocher toned gesso ground and *under* the first layer of *real paint*. The reason for this oversight in the Munich study was due to the fact that the *optical prime* coat is transparent and since it is made of the same materials as are found in the paint themselves it is not properly identified with the pictorial field but with the initial layer of *real* paint. While the same circumstance would not be true with what we have termed the *ground-prime* employed canvas, the fault in that case is that the paint chemists, failed in their analysis of master paintings to identify resin and specifically mastic resin. Such a failure will, in turn, limit their knowledge not only of paint preparations, but also, the relationship of those preparations to the various primes over which they are worked.

Returning to the specific discussion of Vermeer's pictorial technique, it is our belief that despite the portrayal offered by Vermeer in his *Allegory of Painting (The Studio)*, Vienna, Kunsthistorisches where the painter is shown working from a live model with palette in hand, that it was done so for effect. We offer instead, that he employed a fully rendered, tonally modulated drawing on paper of both the primary subject and lay-out of the all over design. A work that would be transferred by tracing or scaled-up on to the prepared pictorial field as a reference drawing to be consulted throughout the painting process. After which the drawing was simply discarded. This is a varied process (save for cave painters) virtually as old as art itself.

In concluding this discussion of Vermeer and, indeed, the investigative Keys themselves, we shall cite an observation by Frith van Thienen from his earlier cited brief but poignant text: "There were great artists before Vermeer and great artists thereafter, but in his own sphere he was supreme."

# Random Thoughts

## Theories Revisited

Of the principles, practices, and devices herein proposed, concerning the various successful systems of oil painting, all were rooted in the pictorial techniques practiced by the *founding duo*, Jan van Eyck and Antonello da Messina. Working in 'times and climes' distant from one another, it was through the efforts of these two masters that the oil-simple technique described by Theophilus was changed to a *fixed-structure* oleoresin technique wherein the paints were increased in plasticity, brilliance, and siccative powers. Ever developing unique, varnish superior technical systems, calling for equally as unique, nonabsorbent, transparent *optical-primes* of panel and solid-tone *ground primes* of canvas.

Pictorial systems are in need of improved investigative means by which to identify resin. An identification we propose would reveal mastic resin—the so-called "painters' resin" used throughout all systems of master painting from the 15th through the 17th Centuries. This was the resin that helped to form the body of their mediums, *pictorial vehicles*, color compounds and even the primes over which the paints were used. This resin was also to be found in certain of the masters' cosmetic varnishes, most importantly litharge enhanced, sun-thickened drying oil varnish. A preparation described to de Mayerne by no less a painter than Peter Paul Rubens and will be discussed in the Directives of this treatise.

No less important than resin is the need to identify yellow beeswax, an element that would prove Maroger *correct* in his proposal that beeswax (that 'complicated fat') was employed by Leonardo da Vinci seemingly associating its use with a failed technique. Such identification would, on the other hand, prove Maroger *incorrect* in his proposal that Rubens and Rembrandt immixed beeswax with their white lead paint in order to achieve impastos. This structure which, in degrees of elevated form, we have credited to the mastic resin strength of the turpentine based mastic varnishes. A structural element automatically inherent in the *pictorial vehicle* tempered, raw oil compounded white lead paint, able to be taken from the palette with the brush free from the need of additional softening.

As for our present research, while we were greatly aided by Maroger's resolves, both positive and negative, we often found it prudent to revaluate the message found in source and near-source information which he employed and, significantly, was first to identify and associate with a particular master. Unlike Maroger who, unknowingly, all too quickly sought to change the dictates found in such early documents, in order to fit his current line of reasoning, we have stubbornly held to what we believed to be valid, though at times somewhat convoluted messages. These frayed bits and pieces of technical evidence have survived over a period of some three hundred years. In fact, by the reasoning of your author, I would fix the time as early as Pliny and his reference to the "Atramentum of Apelles" (400 B.C.).

Let it be understood that mediums, vehicles, and methods are the essential bases by which painters may more easily achieve *style*. That abstract individual "mode of expression" which Cust observed "the man of great strength may do much without style, but would do more with it."[1] It is in fact the means by which such masters as Titian, Tintoretto, Rubens, Van Dyck, Frans Hals, and Rembrandt were allowed unfettered freedom to express their core emotions—the meat on which art historians and aestheticians feed. We note that with respect to all schools of Italian master painting, while both the transparent *optical-prime* and glazes of pure lac colors would reveal, by means of microchemical analysis, substantial lead content, it would not be in the form of opaque white lead pigment or yellowish litharge. Thus, by the lead presence, providing evidence that the lead content had been incorporated and the transparent, particularized molecules equitably distributed, forming the thick body of the optically darkened *oglio cotto*. The only means by which those processes might occur is through cooking the oil and lead over a relatively high heat.

Believing we are well within the realm of possibility regarding the logical progression of one pictorial structure leading to another we have no doubt that it was Antonello's *oglio cotto* which spawned Giorgione's lead-saturated, black drying oil. A pigment-free black oil where respecting the 17th Century Flemish pictorial techniques, the mastic resin was carried into and combined with the fluid black drying oil by way of the essential oil of turpentine based varnish. The result of the process was the fully awakening of the consciousness regarding the principle of lead/resin suspension. The bases on which the Elder Jan Bruegel reasoned the lean, colloidal, architectonic structure of his Flemish medium. A structure which would act, by adjustment, as the priming element for both panel and canvas as well as the defined parent structure of the oleaginously extended *pictorial vehicles* and their related paint preparations.

Unlike the Italian techniques which, through the *oglio cotto*, contained and functioned by way of an active-lead content, the 17th Century Northern techniques—though no less dependent on siccative powers—relied solely on the lead-saturated strength of the black drying oil. Since such oils must be freed of their *spent-lead* content, prior to use, it might be said that the Flemish techniques worked by way of *lead-effect*. Unfortunately, the absence of pigmentation within the black drying oil defied, by available means, an absolute lead-identification.

In light of these considerations, much credit is to be given the Elder Jan Bruegel in his reasoning of the effect that Giorgione's fluid, litharge-saturated black drying oil would exert over the mastic resin content of an evaporable, turpentine based varnish. This was a rapid intake of sufficient oxygen so as to *tack*, *set*, and *control* the oleoresinous, vehicle-laden paints, thereby lending the power of siccative-grasp, a reward essential to a true *alla-prima* technique.

However, since spirit of turpentine is an evaporable element, it also, as with the case of the above discussed *lead-effect* of black drying oil, defies identification by its inclusion in both the optical-prime and the full bodied paint film, even areas of line and *wash* which betray the use of the diluent *essential oil of Venice turpentine*, a mode of rendering so prevalently displayed in Rubens' *bozettos*, full color sketches, and studies.

It is lamentable that in pursuit of knowledge regarding the materials and technical methods employed by the painters of the 15th, 16th, and 17th Centuries, not being chemist or scientist, we must rely solely on the evidence of tactile and optical rewards, achieved through the rule of empirical resolve. These rewards, while valuable and absolutely necessary, have posed certain questions by way of their success that we are not qualified to answer.

One might query, are the duly lead-saturated black drying oils dependent solely on their litharge or white lead saturation or are there other principles involved? For instance, does the melting and boiling points of the saturated free fatty acids, namely stearic and palmitic, the problematic non-drying acids present in fixed-oils, have something to do regarding their control with a duly prepared black drying oil? Might there actually be a change in the hydrocarbon chains of these saturated fatty acids, by way of an adjustment of restructuring of the bonds from single double bonds to conjugated double bonds?

Since we know that black drying oils have a peak life of one month, may it be assumed that the undesirable fatty acids have not been eliminated but merely neutralized and, thereby, able to restruct? Also, and of no small significance, how would all of these factors influence the glycerides so necessary in oils that are to be used in painting? With that question, and on a base of reckoning more fitted to my knowledge, why is it nowhere stated in technical formulas or from the query of painters, that linseed oil (and possibly all fixed-oils) is unfit for use when newly pressed, due to a *watery* quality, so unlike the necessary viscosity associated with oil?

No less disturbing, concerning the quality of cold pressed oil, is the fact that virtually all commercial producers use some form of purifying and cosmetically lightening the color of the oil. These processes make the oil useless with respect to the reconstructed offerings contained in this treatise. Water-washing, as you will recall, is the only acceptable method of purification.

Returning to our main consideration, the fact is that the words and thoughts above discussed concerning the scientific reasons about the masters' black drying oils, would not have been included in their technical lexicon. Theirs was the 'painters science,' handed down set of pictorial principles, practices, reasonings, and rules. This was a 'hands-on' science, where observation of the various unique preparations made the written word, much to our chagrin, unnecessary.

Theirs was an atelier training of the highest order, as were their materials of the highest grade. A requisite quality that, no doubt, would have been insisted upon by the powerful guilds and the primary consumers of their works—the Princes of both Church and state.

What the painters did understand was the function of lead-saturated black drying oils which when used in combination with a turpentine based mastic varnish, form the molecular suspension of their basic Flemish medium structures. The principle of lead/resin suspension source for the chain of devices ranging from the optical-prime and *groundprime*, to the various oleaginously extended primary, epidermal, and glaze vehicle. Sufficiently extended tractable paint structures, allowed for the use of small palettes, as may be witnessed in numerous paintings wherein the painter is shown with palette in hand.

Rewardingly siccative structures in their rendering were best served, when necessary, by the addition of freshly prepared paints, a condition preferable to employing large amounts of ever thickening paints, housed on an unwieldy large palette.

In summing-up the ultimate purpose of this research, it is in line with the reasoning of Louis Pasteur whom after having studied the works of the Old Masters, noted that it was done so (using the wording of Madeleine Hours), "…in the belief that to conserve paintings well it was necessary to understand as much as possible about them."[2]

In my personal quest to understand the techniques of the masters, it might be said that I have had a long, and enduring romance with 'paint.' As to the honesty of this treatise, that I can unabashedly proclaim. Whether all that has herein been revealed is completely correct, that I can only hope. While it is true that I am not a scientist or chemist, one must remember that neither were the masters who envisioned, devised, and perfected these pictorial elements and technical systems.

That I have taken leave from many of the proposals made by my master, Jacques Maroger, is true. However it was done so in line with my legacy, which without my awareness began many years before his death. Forging a technical bond led Maroger, whom, we might add, was not a sentimental man, to proclaim, "Frank, my boy, you are my son." In light of those words, my regret is that my once allies—time and good health—have abandoned me, leaving certain problems yet to be settled. I hope these problems will be claimed by others who share our concerns and beliefs, if for no reason other than "to wake the dead."

The above having been said, we shall close by quoting a segment from a here-to-fore unpublished letter written by Raoul Dufy (1877—1953) to Maroger, translated from the French expressly for me by Maroger himself. After offering pleasantries, Dufy then writes of "plunging... into the anxieties of research" and "the mysterious role that color plays in painting," concluding:

The principal thing is to know the problem; the solution is the affair of painting, and the mystery can be solved when the brush is in the hand. At the risk of seeming paradoxical, I will say that the important thing is not to solve the mystery, because when one knows, all is finished, and life is without an aim when everything is known. Fortunately I run no such risk, and I hope always to be able to run after butterflies without catching them.

*Finis*

# Book Two

# The Materials

The information contained in the following compendium is offered, not from the view of a chemist, but of a practicing painter. However, one who is keenly aware of the métier of paint, and of the pictorial elements available to and employed by the painters of the 15th through the 17th centuries. Undoubtedly, due to the modern manufacturing methods, certain of those elements have undergone change. It is, therefore, incumbent on the painter to search out and properly assess the elements necessary for the successful preparation of the various reconstructed mediums and vehicles herein proposed.

## Cold Pressed Linseed and Walnut Oils

Prior to any discussion of cold pressed oils, mention must be made of the tireless efforts of the late H. Gluck (formerly of The Chantry House, Steyning, Sussex, England), who was responsible for convincing the leading art supply firm of England to begin the commercial production of cold pressed linseed oil. It was her effort and dedication to the production of cold pressed oil that sparked what has become a thriving art trade business.

Unfortunately, over the years following the death of H. Gluck, most manufacturers of cold pressed oils have in the interest of cosmetic attractiveness, treated the oils by one of the "three general types of refining processes: mechanical, acid and alkali,"[1] all of which adversely effect the free fatty acid content of oil. Oils which have been so treated do not favorably respond to being cooked with metallic drying agents, specifically lead, be it in the form of white lead or litharge. The only acceptable condition for oils used in painting is crude or natural cold pressed state. And the only refining method acceptable for such oils is "water-washing," a process to be dealt with in the Directive Section of this present volume.

Respecting the difference between linseed oil and walnut oil, they rest primarily with the fatty acid content and iodine number; walnut oil being higher in fatty acid content and lower in iodine number than linseed oil. The greater fat content of walnut oil being helpful to painters who used heavy oils and highly resinous structures of mediums and pictorial vehicles such as employed by Rubens and Rembrandt. It was also helpful to those painters in the structuring of the *white lead paste*, adding a greater tractability to that densely compacted preparation. These points being considered, although we know from De Mayerne and the *English Document* that Van Dyck employed walnut oil. De Mayerne, in recording remarks made by Van Dyck as early as 1632, noted "linseed oil is the best of all the oils; it even surpasses nut oil, which is more fat, and that of poppy seed, which becomes so and easily thickens."[2]

I should note that with reference to poppy oil, since I have no interest in using that oil, were one to do so, it must also be of a crude or natural cold pressed state and water-washed.

## Turpentine

The distillate, variably referred to as "essential oil of turpentine," "oil of turpentine," "spirit of turpentine" or "essence of turpentine" and, in the trade, as "gum spirit of turpentine," is readily available and, generally, of good quality. Painters must avoid, however, preparations termed, "double distilled" or "refined turpentine," or any other such labeling which offers greater sophistication than is necessary or desirable and does in fact render the distillate unfit for the purpose described in this treatise. Namely, to act as the fluid base of mastic varnishes and the preparation of the "essential oil of Venice turpentine."

A painter would do well to test each container of turpentine before use. Simply decant some turpentine into a small glass container, cap well and place in a freezer for several hours. Then remove the container from the freezer, wipe the condensation from the container and examine before a light. Any cloudiness or beads of ice will indicate an undesirable presence of moisture; and when shaken, if efflorescence occurs, there is evidence of an undesirable additive.

## White Lead, 2Pb $CO_3$PB $(OH)_2$

For the purpose of this work, the only acceptable white lead pigment or, as it is often termed "basic lead carbonate," is reagent grade, available through the drug or chemical trade. If white lead is listed by color merchant, the painter should request a written statement regarding the chemical formula, and whether on not the lead has been cut with inert filler.

The old Dutch process for making white lead yielded a pigment which was "more or less crystalline in structure;" whereas the newer processes produce a pigment which is "of more amorphous character."[3] Due to the fact that your writer has prepared Dutch or stack method white lead, it should be noted that there is no difference in the use of the stack method and the newer method white lead when employed in the cooking of the various oleous preparations herein proposed. However, the same is not true when using the two different types of white lead for the preparation of paint. It is the Dutch process white lead that, by the joining of the flat crystallizing sides of each pigment particle, seems to glide from the brush to the panel or canvas, offering tactile and visual advantages superior to paint preparations wherein the modern processed white lead is employed.

What might be hoped for is that sometime in the future there will be art trade manufacturers who are dedicated to the production of materials that might deserve the title "Guild

Quality." These products would demand the respect and use by all concerned artists.

## Massicot (litharge), (PbO)

When there is mention of litharge in documents from the 15th through the 17th Centuries, it was the "unfused monoxide of lead made by the gentle roasting of white lead" that was meant. This was the "litharge of Gold," the very finest quality being produced by employing as the base pigment the same grade of white lead used in grinding the white lead paste and preparation of the paint. A fact which was first realized after having determined, by empirical evidence, that the black oils employed by the masters were not to be stirred during the cooking process. It is the light weight body of the roasted white lead that allows for the buoyancy necessary in the "threading" of the pigment from the bottom to the top of the oil—propelled by the force of heat during the cooking of black oil. It was Maroger's use of commercial, fused litharge of the trade[4] which prevented him from understanding the proper method for the preparation of litharge black oil, a fact which, in regard for my master, causes me continual regret.

## Mastic Resin

Commencing with the discovery of Jan Van Eyck's improved *liquid varnish*, mastic was the resin exclusively employed in the mediums of the masters. This statement could be substantiated if the scientists and paint chemists, occupied with analysis of the masters' paintings, would care enough to do so. Unfortunately, either because of lack of concern or unwillingness to involve themselves in such a difficult identification they have, thus far, failed that task.

It was not until the 19th Century that mastic resin fell from favor. The reason was quite simple; the proper means for that resins preparation, with respect to mediums and certain other pictorial devices was no longer understood, and the disastrous effects often connected with that lack of knowledge, dissuaded many painters and pictorial theorists from the use and consideration of that otherwise excellent and, with respect to the techniques of the masters, indispensable element.

Unfortunately, those who have written handbooks of painters "terms and materials," generally paraphrase Sir Arthur Church's assessment of mastic resin—"a poor and weak resin which become in the course of time yellow and brittle, and is liable to be injuriously affected when a picture in which it has been used freely is cleaned." This statement clearly betrays, not the fault of mastic resin, but Sir Arthur's lack of understanding the manner in which that "painter's resin" was employed within the master's technique.

It is recommended that when selecting mastic resin, also referred to as gum mastic, tears, grain, or crystals, is that the lighter in color the resin the lighter in tone will be the varnish made with it, whether prepared with a base of fixed or essential oil. It is also advisable to store the dry resin in containers with little air space, and well-capped, in order to prevent the crystals or tears from excessive hardening due to the evaporation of essential oil and moisture. It is also essential that, prior to the melting of mastic in either a fixed oil or the essential oil or spirit of turpentine, that the tears be pulverized.

## Beeswax

The history of the use of beeswax in art is ancient. It formed the basis for "encaustic" painting, a technique which would have involved wax and, in certain cases, resin. As earlier noted, Maroger was, to my knowledge, the first researcher to propose beeswax to have been used in the medium devised by Leonardo da Vinci, and insisted on its use by the Venetian painters from Giorgione to Tiepolo.

Respecting the quality of the beeswax employed in the forthcoming directives, the best is clean, yellow beeswax, preferably obtained from an apiary, where information may be available concerning the processing of the wax. One must be cautioned to avoid chemically bleached or synthetic beeswax.

## Venice Turpentine

The best grade of the balsam, Venice turpentine, is of a pale golden hue and as thick as cold, heavy honey. Very often, however, the Venice turpentine found in art supply stores is cut with spirit of turpentine and, therefore, is much thinner and lighter in body and hue. While we would recommend the uncut Venice turpentine, either structure is acceptable. The fluid body of the cut Venice turpentine is to be taken into consideration when used in the preparation of "essential oil of Venice turpentine" and various varnishes. What must be avoided is a dark colored product as well as synthetic Venice turpentine.

## Gelatin, Rabbit Skin Glue

The above named adhesives are employed in the preparation of weak and strong glue water sizes and gesso. Sizes are generally employed in the form of a jelly. Weak or soft size is used to break the absorption of porous supports, over which primes are to be applied. Also, the liquid weak glue water size is used for the preparation of the meager, chalk-based gesso employed for the preparation of gesso grounds of canvas.

Strong glue water size is the fluid binder for chalk or gypsum based gesso to be used for this grounding of weak, jellified glue isolated wood panels. By the fact that gelatin bound gesso "sets" and "firms" more rapidly than rabbit skin glue bound gesso, the former is preferred when rendering successive "wet-over-wet" coats of gesso such as used for the grounds of panel.

It might be cautioned that since the gelatin found in the food trade is of less adhesive power than that found in the art supply trade, the former should be avoided when preparing gesso grounds of panel.

## Chalk (whiting) and Gypsum

Chalk whiting (calcium carbonate) was the pigment most commonly employed by the painters of Europe for the preparation of gesso. The finest grade is known as "gilders whiting" and is readily available in the art supply trade.

Regarding the white pigment known as gypsum or terra alba (not plaster of Paris), D.V. Thompson noted: "It may be used in place of whiting, in exactly the same way, and will generally be found better. Gypsum gives a crisper and whiter gesso than whiting, and is regularly used by modern gilders in Italy and France."[5]

# Pre-key Directives

The pre-key Directives deal with preparation known and used by painters prior to the technical methods introduced by Jan van Eyck. Namely, litharge or massicot; gesso panels; and the sizing of canvas,

## *Preparation of Massicot (Litharge) Yellow Monoxide of Lead (PbO)*

Due to the fact that white lead and litharge are toxic, care should be taken to avoid breathing of fumes during the following process:

> Place a quantity of reagent grade white lead in an iron or enamelware receptacle and set it over a moderately high heat. Using a metal or wooden spoon or spatula, gently stir the white lead in order to more equitably distribute and expose the mass of lead particles to the heat. As the white lead begins to react to the effect of the heat, a dust or vapor is formed, consequential to the expelling of the hydrates and carbon dioxide content from the white lead. Shortly thereafter, the white pigment begins to turn a pale yellow, ever increasing in color as the lead continues heating. The cooking and stirring of the lead should continue until the pigment appears relatively golden in color—sans shine. The resultant litharge or massicot, when

sufficiently cooled, should be stored in a moisture proof container, well capped and kept for use.

## Concerning the Gesso Grounds of Panel

Rather than offer what might be viewed as a plagiarized method for preparation of gesso grounds of panel, it is best to recommend the source from which that knowledge came.

It was the late Reginald Marsh, who in the interest of the most perfect panel preparation wisely recommended to me, Daniel V. Thompson's simplified formula for the preparation of gesso grounds of panel.[6] Through my own experience, no better advice could be given a painter, prior to following Thomson's directive, than to read and reread Chapter II of his most excellent and informative work; isolating and reviewing those passages which deal with the subject at hand. What can be guaranteed, is that diligent employment and repeated practice of his method will, in time, be rewarded with absolute perfection.

## An Addendum Directive, Preparation of Weak Glue Water and Soft Jelly Size

Essential to the preparation of gesso grounds employed in oil, technique is a jellified glue isolation coat of what Vasari called "smooth or soft size". The basis for such a size is weak glue water used for the sizing of panel and preparation of gesso. Reasoning the forthcoming preparation of weak glue water on the 1:16 strength gelatin to water proportion of what Thompson calls "standard size solution" (strong glue water):

> In the top section of a double boiler containing 16 oz. of cold water, add ½ oz. by weight, of leaf or granulated gelatin. Allow the ingredients to stand until the gelatin swells and softens. Place the receptacle over the lower section of the double boiler containing boiling water and stir the ingredients until the gelatin is melted. The weak glue water is then removed from over the hot water and set aside. Within twenty-four hours the liquid will become

a smooth jelly, strong enough so as to resist liquefaction when stirred, yet soft enough to be easily spread. In the isolation of the gesso panels, using a wide brush or damp sponge, thinly and evenly spread one or two coats of the soft jelly size.

That we have dealt with the isolation of gesso grounds in this pre-key section, is for the convenience of following in line with the Thompson recommended preparation of gesso panel. As well as the fact that we cannot know when the practice was first instituted.

# Observations and Key Directive

Recalling from the onset that experience is the Ambrosia of painters, we will in the forthcoming Observations and Key Directives refresh the memory of our readers by way of capsulized segments contained in the preceding pages of the First Book. In addition, we will bring into focus certain relevant points that we did not wish to intrude upon the reasoning and story of that text. We will elaborate upon such chores as the water-washing of oil and preparation of black drying oils, as well as the types of grounds and primes employed upon various supports. In-depth explanations recorded in what is in effect A Painter's Handbook.

# *First Key Directives*
## Jan Van Eyck and the 15<sup>th</sup> Century Flemish Pictorial Technique

*Selective Thoughts Concerning the 15<sup>th</sup> Century Eyckian Technique*

Fifteenth century Flemish paintings, save for one unique exception, were always rendered over a glue isolated white gesso ground of panel, primed with an enhanced and structurally suspended, dry, litharge-charged prime coat of *liquid varnish*. A light reflective milieu intended to float the paint, as it were, over the white gesso light source. The smoother and whiter the glue isolated gesso ground and the more determined the ink under-drawing, the more rewarding will be the finished painting.

It is a technique requiring strict discipline, since once the *optical prime* (as we have termed it) is spread and dry, there is little chance for successful change. We fine in Van Eyck's *The Marriage of Giovanni Arnolfini and Giovanna Cename* (London, National Gallery) clear evidence of a repositioning of the Arnolfini's right foot, were all the corrective dark paints were of a similar fat structure, executed in wet-over-dry thin layer upon thin layer, remaining to this day a continuous, crack free paint film. The same however is not true with respect to

Arnolfini's raised right hand. Where the area of dense flesh coloring, which was an opaque, white paint based and, thereby leaner structure than the dry, dark glazed under-painting of Arnolfini's robe, gives evidence of fine, but definite cracks.

The only way Van Eyck could have avoided such a problem would have involved application of many thin, wet-over-dry, fat varnish-pomade charged layers of translucent flesh tones, building-up opaque pigment density. Knowing that each of the thin fat layers of the varnish-pomade charged paint would have required 4, 5, or even 6 days to dry properly, before another coat might be applied, Van Eyck obviously deem the chore unwarranted. A decision which, for our purpose, seeing that pentimenti are a silent teacher, was a relevant value.

It is necessary to understand that with respect to the formation of translucent and transparent paint structures, the chore is placed solely on the *varnish-pomade* pictorial vehicle. A portion of which was always housed on the palette along with the paints. It would also be stressed, that the more thinly and evenly the spreading of the paints, the faster and better would be the drying of the paint film. The reason being, that oxygen, by way of the siccative power of mastic resin—an element present in all Eyckian preparations and pictorial processes, could be coaxed into a lower and even-leveled film more effectively than in denser and heavier structures. Recalling to mind the earlier stated advice of Van Mander: "They laid on their colors beautifully, neatly, and pleasingly and they never heaped them on their panels."

As to the words which best describes the quality of Van Eyck's pictorial element, viscosity and luminosity come quickly to mind. The improved fixed oil based *liquid varnish* and the yolk of egg bound varnish-pomade medium and pictorial vehicles are both highly viscous. It is in fact their characteristic "stickiness" and "oiliness" which lends to their pictorial value. It was D. V. Thompson who in his *Materials and Techniques of Medieval Paintings*, speaking of works to be rendered "on a very small scale" noted, "Generally speaking... the medium must flow very freely even when it is fairly concentrated," further noting: "The one exception is this: that if a medium is very viscid indeed, so that is pulls out in fine threads, like sugar candy, it has another kind of usefulness for very minute works." The words "viscid" and "minute" certainly describes much of Van Eyck's oeuvre, as does "viscid" also describes the *varnish pomade* medium and pictorial vehicle offered in this present treaties as the binding vehicle for Van Eyck's paints and spreading medium for his translucent and transparent color and tonal preparations.

While is it true that the Eyckian pictorial procedure was necessarily of a didactic nature, it was improvised upon by certain masters in accordance with their artistic and aesthetic needs. Hieronymus Bosch (c. 1450—1516) who employed Van Eyck's *varnish-pomade* medium throughout much of his creative oeuvre, executed areas of his painting in a near *alla prima* fashion. In such works as his *Death of a Miser* (c. 1495), the bold, striated line and cross-hatched ink under-drawing in the shadow areas subdues, while not eliminating, the underlying white gesso ground optical primed light source. Deflecting the eye from the shadow area, forcing it to focus on areas where the unencumbered light source dominates through the thin, translucent paint film, creating an illusion of form, further persuading the eye by the addition of form defining highlights.

Also in the *Death of a Miser* we see impatience with the limiting structure of the white lead paint and its need for a thin, laminated rendering. In the arched window shown in the left side of the painting, the light was applied in the structure of the white paint exactly as it was taken with the brush from the palette, sufficiently heavy so that the panes of glass were created by cutting into the wet paint, most likely with the tip of the brush handle. It cannot be said that the white paint employed in that fashion is attractive, however, praise can be given a master whose artistic fervor was so great as to lurch forward by abandoning traditional procedure bending, as it were, the rules of a pictorial system to his own artistic will.

Antonello da Messina was one of the few Italian painters who employed Jan Van Eyck's pictorial technique of oil painting having learned of it, we propose, from Rogier van der Weyden during his trip to Rome in 1450. Among the few examples of his employment of the Eyckian technique are: *Abraham Visited by the Three Angels* and *St. Jerome Penitent* (both paintings in Reggio Calabria, Museo della Magna Grecia) and *Crucifixion* (Sibiu, Romania). All of those works having been executed in a fully achieved pictorial technique; unlike the various works which make up Antonello's experimental oeuvre executed during the period of his search for a leaded, fixed oil based replacement for the yolk of egg emulsifier.

Concluding this summary, with respect to the dissemination of the Eyckian pictorial technique, it is here proposed that the *Lamentation for Christ at His Entombment* (Florence, Uffizi) was executed by Rogier van der Weyden as a demonstration piece rendered before a select group of Florentine painters. Although there is no extant evidence of Rogier having visited Florence during his trip to Italy in 1450, it would be unthinkable to believe that he would not have done so. It was in interest of the dissemination of the Eyckian technique to Italian painters that Rogier selected a motif that was of Italian derivation rather than Flemish, patterning his design after a painting by Fra Angelico (1387–1455), a work which would have been in Florence at the time of Rogier's visit.

## Purification of Linseed Oil

Although walnut oil and poppy oil were known to Jan Van Eyck, it was also known that both oils were fatter and slower to dry then linseed oil. It was for the primary advantage of drying that Van Eyck chose the less fat linseed oil as the fluid base of his improved *liquid varnish*.

A. P. Laurie, referring to linseed oil, stated "the oldest and most satisfactory manner for artist's purposes, regarding its refining, is to expose it to light and air in covered glass vessels."[1] Perhaps it is correct that such a method of refining was the oldest but totally incorrect to proclaim it "most satisfactory."

There is but one method by which oil is made suitable for pictorial purposes—and this is purification by water-washing, No writer on this subject, chemist or artist, denies that the washing of oil was practiced by the masters. Unfortunately, neither do they insist that the practice was essential to the masters' craft nor that it was first instituted by Jan Van Eyck. Eastlake, in his way, may be thought of as an advocate for the "water-washing" purification, and has recorded several directives for performing that necessary task.[2] However, each of the directives fail in one particular respect. When recommending the immixture of the oil and water, none specify that any emulsion is to be achieved. Emulsification is the only condition capable of drawing out the aqueous loving phosphatides and mucilaginous materials, the antioxidants which retard drying. Also consequential to the washing process, is lightening the color of the oil. However, if a good grade of cold pressed oil is used, the golden color of the oil should not be excessively dark to begin with.

It is a fact that painters from the time of Van Eyck until the demise of the great schools of painting never considered linseed or any other of the fixed oils adequate to act as independent painting vehicles. The masters thought of their washed oils as but one of the basic elements that must be combined with other ingredients in order to fabricate their various pictorial preparations. In conclusion, we can offer no better advice with respect to the various proposals made in this present work concerning the water-washing of raw, cold pressed linseed and walnut oil than the earlier quoted observation of Don Alessio— "whenever you find oil mentioned, this purified oil is meant."

## Directive I

The following method for water-washing purification of fixed oils is based on the various processes found in Eastlake's *Materials for a History of Oil Painting.*[3]

Before beginning the process, it is to be noted that the use of common salt and white silica sand are arbitrary. However, salt aids in the creation of the oil and water emulsion, an end result that we propose was essential to a proper purification method. A result all too simply dismissed by the use of such words as "effectually" or "incorporated" or such phrases as "after stirring well"—"well" being the defining word used to proclaim an emulsion.

Regarding the use of silica sand, it acted when settling out of the emulsion to carry with it the unwanted impurities such as mucilage, wax and albuminoid matter. It also acted to denote the degree of purification, of the early stages of washing the sand appears as a discolored, thick and greasy glob which, as the various washings are pursued, the newly added sand proves to be of lighter color and the sand particles become less globulus, freed as they are of binding impurities.

---

MATERIALS
Raw, cold pressed linseed or walnut oil
Spring, purified or distilled water
Common salt
White silica sand (playground sand)

Half fill a glass container with one of the above noted waters and one half that amount with one of the above noted oils. Add a portion of salt and another of silica sand. Cover the opening of the container with one of the suggested sealing materials and cap well. Then, holding the palm of your hand against the top and bottom of the container turn it upside down, several times. Then, turn the container horizontally and shake the contents using a gentle, rolling back and forth motion. After a few minutes of this action, briefly rest the container upright; then again repeat the shaking process.

Gradually the water will be taken into the oil, until at last having repeated the shakings often enough, the ingredients are thoroughly combined, forming a thick emulsion. Always remember that gentle, intermittent shakings of the contents will accomplish the desired ends sooner than vigorous and extended shaking.

Following the emulsification of the ingredients, the container is then rested until the emulsion breaks, leaving the oil uppermost over the water. This may in a shorter or longer time, requiring as much as two or three hours, much depending on the quality of oil. Once the emulsion does break, siphon the sand and water from beneath the oil. Then in a clean container add fresh water, salt and sand and the oil which appears as an opaque, yellowish mass, due to the water still being held in the oil along with the impurities. This is not greatly significant since all the debris will be drawn out of the oil in the necessary subsequent washings.

As for determining when the oil is sufficiently washed, the sand acts as a visual aid. With the impurities withdrawn from the oil, the sand will appear whiter and the grains well separated, moving as the container is tilted, much as sand on a beach.

In the final washing, the oil should be allowed to completely clear; afterwards to be transferred to a clean bottle, the cap set ajar and kept in a warm place (sunshine the best) until the oil is crystal clear. Then it should be capped and best stored where sunlight might shine upon it from time to time, thus further lightening the color of the oil.

During the course of the washing process there is a loss of oil. However, much of that oil may be retrieved by conscious effort. The "reclaimed" oil is simply collected and added to various washings or saved until a sufficient amount is obtained to make a full washing. Reclaimed oil has the advantage of having many of the impurities already removed and thereby produces the finest of washed oils.

Experience, the Ambrosia of painters, will act as the teacher in this purely mechanical process. In fact, any way a painter might devise to carry out the water-washing operation (freezing comes to mind) will do, providing the desired ends are achieved and no injurious elements are used to accelerate the process. On a precautionary note, when placing a container of oil into the freezer in order to freeze the water content and allow for easy pouring off of the oil, it is advisable to place the glass container and its contents in a relatively strong, clear plastic bag, which is then to be fastened at the top. Due to the air locked into the sealed bag, the water freezes slower and reacts less aggressively or harshly upon the glass container, reducing the possibility of cracking.

---

## *The Liquid Varnish of Jan Van Eyck*

*Van Eyck's improved liquid varnish* was the primary constituent for his *optical prime*; grinding element for all color pigments including white lead; preparation of the *varnish pomade* medium and, as one, *pictorial vehicle*; as well as the diluent employed for the execution of various details and accents. The most perfect condition for the varnish is directly related to the purification of the oil to be used as the fluid base and the quality of the mastic resin which embodies that base.

In addition to the technique of the 15th Century Flemish painters, the improved *liquid varnish* was employed in all the Italian pictorial techniques, constituting the resinous varnish portion of Antonello da Messina's *lead paste* medium, the lead wax medium of Leonardo da Vinci, and Georgio da Castelfranco's *Venetian medium*.

It is interesting to note that Albrecht Dürer, who used the technique devised by Antonello da Messina, twice mentions the purchase of varnish during his Netherlandish journey.[4] That it was the *liquid varnish* of Jan Van Eyck; I have no doubt, since Dürer would have used it in the preparation and extension of the Messina *lead paste* medium. Seeing that such a preparation dries with a shine there was no need to varnish paintings executed in that vehicle, ruling out the possibility that the purchased varnish was simple turpentine based mastic picture varnish. Especially would this be true when considering the freshness of the paint films of those works executed during his Netherlandish travels.

There will be those interested persons who, judging from ordinary practices will, no doubt, take exception with our proposal concerning the automatic "shine" of Dürer's paint film. Quoting from a letter dated "24 Aug. 1508" written by Dürer to Jacob Heller, concerning the commission of the famed Alter piece, the artist stated, "the wings have been painted in stone colours on the outside, but they are not yet varnished." It was with concern for varnishing that Madelaine Hours noted in her *Secrets of the Great Masters* (p. 118), "the great painters of the Renaissance recognized the importance of varnish and they completed their work often adding a 'velatura,' mixing certain colours in with the varnish in order to accentuate details and veil the brightness of some tones."

While we concur with the purpose expressed in Madelaine Hours' observation, we must insist that it was not a varnish in the ordinary sense of the word. Instead it was a final unifying and tone enhancing rendering wherein was employed the pictorial vehicle compounded paints; a final layering which in the case of the stone colored outer wings, depicting the *Three Kings, SS. Peter and Paul, S. Thomas Aquinas, and S. Christopher*, would have consisted of black and umber paints rendered transparent by brush additions of the clear pictorial vehicle—a coating far superior to any common picture varnish such as that discussed in the text of our Third Key under the title of *Trial by Employment and the Picture Varnish of Leonardo da Vinci*.

Returning to our primary subject, in the early history of the Eyckian technique before pictorial elements were prepared and sold through apothecaries, apprentices were advantaged by the fact that the studio they had entered would have been well stocked with washed linseed oil as well as *liquid varnish*. During the years of his apprenticeship he would, in all probability, have been rewarded with portions of the washed oil and *liquid varnish* which he himself would have been assigned to prepare throughout his tenure with his master. Hence, when opening his own atelier or studio, he was sufficiently rewarded with supplies that would otherwise have required months of preparation before his own artistic production could begin.

## *Directive II*

---

MATERIALS

    2 parts, by weight, raw linseed or walnut oil
    1 part, by weight, well pulverized mastic resin

Employing a glass or enamelware double boiler, add water to the lower section and set it over the heat source to boil. Combine in the upper section the 2 parts oil and 1 part pulverized mastic resin and set it over the lower section containing boiling water. As the oil heats, stir the ingredients gently until the resin is thoroughly dissolved save, that is for a portion or core of insoluble matter, essentially the rind or outer crust of the mastic tears. Since the heat produced by boiling water would prevent carbonization and thickening of the oil, and assuring longer rather than a possible insufficient shorter cooking time is recommended.

The resulting cloudy varnish is then to be decanted into a jar, well-capped, and placed in an area where the sun might play upon it, even if at but brief intervals, to await the deposit of the fine particles of insoluble, secondary debris. Such depositing may require many weeks or months before the oil clarifies, becoming as bright and clear as crystal. However, the depositing process may be accelerated by decanting the cloudy varnish in a jar of sufficient circumference so as to reduce the depth of the varnish to approximately ½ inch or so; thereby reducing the distance the fine debris will have to travel in depositing.

*Since the above described liquid varnish* was employed in the preparation of the 16th Century *Venetian medium*, given the number of practicing painters and the many and often very large works which they produce, the *liquid varnish* (as earlier noted) would have been commercially manufactured and sold by the apothecaries. The Guild with which they were associated was ideal for tracing the production and perhaps even the material nature of the *liquid varnish but, unfortunately, most likely would not bear the name of the inventor—Jan Van Eyck.*

## *The* Optical Prime

By the institution of the transparent *optical prime*, designed for use on glue isolated gesso grounds of panel, Van Eyck established a principle and practice that was followed throughout all master schools of painting from the 15<sup>th</sup> through the 17<sup>th</sup> Centuries. Not only did the isolating *optical prime* coat, when dry, act in liaison attraction for the related *varnish pomade* enforced paint compounds, but also, via the reflective white gesso grounds, served to illuminate the transparent and semi-transparent paints, surrounded as the pigments were by the reflective and light enhancing matrix, *i.e.* Van Eyck's *varnish pomade*.

## *Directive III*

INGREDIENTS

A portion of liquid varnish
Litharge (made by roasting pure white lead)

Employing the palette knife, immix into the *liquid varnish* a small amount of litharge. Paraphrasing the directive offered by Filarete: according to the amount of litharge employed, the mixture will range from a lighter to a darker tone of yellow. It is not important what color tone it is for once the prime is spread the tone will dissipate, becoming undetectable. What is important is that the litharge-charged pomade is set in suspension and the cohesive prime coat when brushed thinly and evenly over the glue sized, white gesso ground of panel, will dry within 8 hours or so. Thereby the oleous portion of the *liquid varnish was prevented from impregnating and staining the white gesso ground.*

## *Jan Van Eyck's* Varnish Pomade *Medium and Pictorial Vehicle*

While it is true that Van Eyck's reasoning for the *varnish pomade* medium and pictorial vehicle stemmed from a known practice employed in the art of glass painting, as was the essential principle for the varnish structured *optical prime* based on a practice described by Theophilus, Jan's sophistication of those seminal practices should not be minimized. In light of all that came before Van Eyck's contribution to the technique of oil painting, his advancements and refinements were revolutionary—the practice of water-washing of oil acting as the primary step forward toward the development of what properly would be termed oleo-resinous painting.

While the structure of the *varnish pomade* was achieved through the use of egg yolk, never should the quality of 15$^{th}$ Century Flemish painting be attributed to that element. Egg yolk was essential to the Eyckian system to *set* the improved *liquid varnish* in suspension and, thereby, control the flow of that unctuous fluid. As to the function of the *varnish pomade* as a pictorial vehicle, it acted as the binder for the color pigments (including white lead) rendering them into paint form. In addition, it was used to ease the spreading of the paints and acted as the source by which to increase transparency or translucency of the various color or tonal compounds.

Regarding the quality of the *varnish pomade* medium and the paints which it helped to form, once the hydrous portion of the egg yolk evaporated, the paints profited greatly owing to the relatively large amount of mastic resin present in their structural body. This produced a lucid, enamel-like paint film, illuminated by the underlying oleo-resinous *optical prime* coat resting atop the reflective, glue isolated white gesso ground of panel.

## *Preparation of the Yolk of Egg*

Quoting from D. V. Thompson's *The Practice of Tempera Painting* is the following simply stated directive:

> Take a raw fresh hen's egg, and crack it on the side of a bowl. Lift off half of the shell, keeping the yolk in the lower half, and letting the white run into the bowl. Pass the yolk back and forth from one half shell to the other several times without breaking it, so as to get rid of as much of the white as possible; and pinch off between the shells the little white knots which adhere to the yolk.

At this point, since Thompson then continues by noting a practice related to the tempera painting, we will note that the egg yolk is to be decanted into a small jar and well capped. Egg yolk can be kept for several days, in a cool (but not cold) condition. Once the yolk begins to thicken, which generally occurs before putrefaction, it should be discarded and the container well cleaned.

## Directive IV

MATERIALS
Egg yolk
Van Eyck's liquid varnish

Place a given one part measure of egg yolk on the grinding stone and immix with the palette knife a corresponding one part measure of liquid varnish. Then, to the resultant pomade, add one part at a time, yet another two corresponding one part measure of liquid varnish. Each immixture will produce an ever thickening pomade until the final one part liquid varnish which produces a soft, translucent blonde pomade.

## A Matter of Paint and the Reasoning for a Diluent

Respecting the preparation of Van Eyck's paints and setting of the palette, the subject has been adequately discussed in the text of the First Key, under the section heading "The Palette Preparations of Jan Van Eyck."

Regarding the diluent, certainly a must when considering the detail work exhibited in Van Eyck's pictorial oeuvre, there was but one acceptable element available. Essential oil or spirit of turpentine had not entered the field of pictorial technique and the weak and wanting raw oil would have been automatically eliminated from consideration, leaving only Van Eyck's improved *liquid varnish*.

Due to the laminated style of rendering and necessary broad and even spreading of the paints, the *varnish pomade* itself acted as the primary, transparentizing diluent. However, in the execution of details such as seen in Van Eyck's bejeweled, repoussé gold crowns; gold and silver thread embossed robes and hangings; contents of a room reflected in a beveled mirror adorned by ten small rondels depicting the passion of Christ; flower dotted and plant strewn green fields; fruit laden trees; pock-marked and small fossil laden sedimentary rock formations; distant cities with steeple cathedrals, turreted buildings and towered bridges with pinpoint sized travelers and myriad other subjects making fluid dilution indispensable.

It was the calculated use of this fluid dilution that was reckoned in the structural formation of the *varnish pomade* medium and pictorial vehicle. A reasoned body capable of fixing at the point of flow brush additives of the fluid *liquid varnish* into the paint mixtures. A sufficiently restraining suspension via the *varnish pomade*, able to support the fluid varnish—in place, for the necessary time to allow for the "setting" of the liquid and the beginning of the drying process of the paints.

# *Second Key Directives*
## *Antonella da Messina and the 15th Century Italians*

### *Regarding the Contribution of Antonello da Messina*

By the year 1510, virtually all northern painters had rejected the pictorial technique of Jan van Eyck in favor of that developed by Antonello da Messina. Undoubtedly, many painters were persuaded to Messina's technical advancement by the work and word of Jacopo dei Barbari (c. 1440/50—1511/15), who was employing Messina's technical method at the time of his journey to Germany in 1500, and the Netherlands, (c. 1505/09).

Although the basic structure of Antonello's *lead-paste* medium acted as the foundation for advancements made by Leonardo da Vinci and that of Giorgio da Castlefranco, many northern painters continued to employ the original *lead-paste* medium, aided by certain materials and methods offered by the latter named Italian innovator. Most likely a painter such as Elder Pieter Bruegel, would have compacted his color pigments with essence of turpentine, prior to their tempering with *lead-paste* pictorial vehicle; just as he would have employed the tightly compacted raw oil based *white lead paste* and, undoubtedly, the auxiliary diluent "clear essential oil of Venice turpentine."

As can be witnessed in any of the works of that northern master, the freer use of Antonello's pictorial vehicle did not allow for the exclusion of an underdrawing, this embodied and siccative vehicle proved more responsive than did the *varnish pomade* of Jan van Eyck. We do not wish to suggest that evidence of this material change is easily defined between the works of the 15th century Flemish and Italian masters. Although, there is a certain quality that separates the two techniques, the fact of such differences can be proved only by microchemical analysis, and then, only when such a system of analysis can isolate, detect, and identify *specific* natural resins. The identification of a structural body such as the metallic varnish, e.g. *oglio cotto*, unfortunately defying any and all analytical systems; a significant amount of lead being the only possible, albeit oblique, bit of evidence.

## *The* Lead-Paste *Medium of Antonello da Messina*

While Antonello da Messina's *lead-paste* medium is simplistic in the method of preparation, the founding principle is highly sophisticated. The medium is of a dual-varnish construction, one metallic and the other natural resin, both having a fixed-oil base. The calculated design for the litharge compounded *oglio cotto* was intended to act, not only as the drying agent for its raw oil base, but also for the more problematic raw oil base of Van Eyck's *liquid varnish*, as well as the large input of that varnish into the lead-paste medium when forming the pictorial vehicle. In addition and of considerable importance, it was Antonello's introduction of the accelerated drying compound into the pictorial technique of oil painting that allowed painters to choose either linseed oil or the fatter and more fluid walnut oil, the preferred oil of Italian painters.

In brief, the *lead-paste* medium is a complex colloid which lends to the pictorial vehicle that it helps to form both tactile and optical rewards. It was the first preparation of painting medium wherein the principle of lead-resin suspension functioned in creation of its structure. Although this term is of my own invention, there is no doubt in my mind that were we able to travel back in time this term would be readily comprehended by all painters from the pictorial era of Jan van Eyck until the demise of the great schools of master painting. This structural principle might be thought of as a most important technical link, forging the 15th century school of Italian painting with the more sophisticated pictorial techniques to follow.

## *Directive I*

There are in this directive two distinct steps: (1) preparation of the *oglio cotto* and, (2) formation of the *lead-paste medium.*

---

MATERIALS

*2 parts, by weight, washed raw linseed or walnut oil*
*1 part, by weight, litharge (see Pre-Key Directives)*
*2 parts, by weight, Van Eyck's liquid varnish*—set near the heat source for future use when compounding the *lead-paste* medium

## Step 1: Preparation of the *oglio cotto*

Combine into the cooking vessel the raw oil and litharge. Stir the two ingredients and while continuing to gently stir, set the pot over a shielded, moderately high heat source; continuing to stir throughout the cooking period.

After approximately one half hour into the cooking (much depending on the degree of heat) the ever darkening and spongy body of oil and lead will begin to decrease in volume and after approximately one hour into the cooking the foam will disappear. At that time the *oglio cotto* will have turned to a thick, homogenous black solution which, when seen on the inside of the pot during stirring, appears of a lustrous reddish amber color. The *oglio cotto* may then be considered finished. It should be noted, that by the constant stirring of the *oglio cotto* during cooking, the litharge is both evenly dispersed and prevented from lead-saturating the oil. This produces what might be termed a lead-active oil, the exact opposite principle used in the preparation of black drying oils.

Step 2: Formation of the *lead-paste* medium

Keeping the pot over the heat source and continuing to stir, pour into the hot *oglio cotto* the pre-weighted parts of Van Eyck's *liquid varnish*. Stirring may be ceased long enough to scrape the sticky varnish from the sides and bottom of the container from which it was poured. The pot may then be removed from the heat source and when the ingredients are thoroughly combined by further stirring, the resultant *lead-paste* medium while still quite warm, may be decanted into the appropriate sized jar (allowing as little air space as possible) and then well capped.

When thoroughly cooled this *lead-paste* medium appears as a blackish-brown unguent. In actuality, this unguent or medium is a concentrate and is not intended to act independently from further extension of tempering of *liquid varnish*.

---

## Antonello's Pictorial Vehicle and Optical Prime

Antonello's pictorial vehicle and *optical prime* structures are one and the same. They are characteristically an unguent-like gel, akin in structure to Van Eyck's litharge invested *liquid varnish optical prime*.

Through the heat infusion of the litharge dryer and, as one, suspension agent, both the oleous base of Antonello's *oglio cotto* and that of Van Eyck's *liquid varnish* additive, are rewarded in brilliance and enhanced luminosity. The rich amber tone of this unguent structure lending lustrous warmth and tonal depth to both the transparent *optical prime* and the pictorial vehicle prepared paints including the normally, cold toned white lead.

# *Directive II, Preparation of the Pictorial Vehicle*

INGREDIENTS
> 1 part *lead-paste* medium, by volume
> 3 parts Van Eyck's improved *liquid varnish,* by volume

Place the *lead-paste* medium on the grinding stone and immix with the palette knife the full three parts *liquid varnish.* The *lead-paste* medium will soon yield to the input of *liquid varnish* and its thick, tacky body will structure into a puddle fixed-liquid that in a short time will restructure into a soft jelly.

## *The* Optical Prime *of Panel*
In the application of the *optical prime* it is simply smoothly spread with a flat, bristle brush over the finished ink underdrawing executed on a glue isolated white gesso ground. Although this structure appears richly amber colored when first spread the color diminishes to but a pale lustrous hue in but a few hours.

Through the litharge content of the *oglio cotto* portion of this *lead-paste optical prime*, drying is assured in from six to eight hours. However, since each coat of color or paint to follow over this prime is itself changed equally with this powerful drying agent (the *optical prime* and the pictorial vehicle being one in the same structure) it is best to allow at least twenty-four hours before working over the *optical prime.*

## *Another Method: Variation on a Theme*
Incorrectly assigned as an Eyckian practice, Van Mander noted the use of a flesh colored prime. In the section of his *Schilderboeck,* where earlier in this work we had made use of Van Mander's marginal note concerning an "oil-like priming" he notes in the body of the writing after speaking of an underdrawing: "Over this they put, with great forethought,

a thin priming, through, which, however, one could still see everything, and this priming was done in flesh tones."[1]

Regarding the actual method: In application, using the palette prepared paints (soon to be discussed) a flesh tint is mixed with the brush to which was then brush added sufficient amounts of the *optical prime* structure needed to render the flesh tinted prime adequately translucent or transparent. This tinted *optical prime* is then smoothly spread over the ink underdrawing and allowed to dry.

By this practice one would, in effect, combine two applications into one, representing the saving of a bit of time and the decided advantage of working the first full sitting of real paint over a tinted prime—without impairing the brightness of the underlying light source. We might add, however, that unlike Van Mander's implication the practice was employed more as an exception than as a rule.

## Preparation of the Paints and Setting the Palette

The preparation of Antonello's paints was akin to the practice employed by Jan van Eyck. Each in turn the colors including white lead were tightly knife compacted into globules employing Van Eyck's improved *liquid varnish*; then tempered to ductility with an immixture of no less than an equal measure of Antonello's *lead-paste* pictorial vehicle. Each paint preparation, in turn, was placed on the palette. Along with the paints was also placed a portion of the pictorial vehicle to aid in the spreading of the paints and to act as a means by which to render real paints more transparent or translucent, according to need.

Although there are restrictions to Antonello's palette preparations, familiarity with its response lends to a better understanding of the inherent possibilities offered by this improved technique. We might note that it was this palette that functioned for both the disciplined method of its 15th century inventor as well as the free style of the great 16th century Flemish master the Elder Pieter Bruegel.

## The Diluent

In kind with the technique of Jan van Eyck, Antonello da Messina would have employed Jan's improved *liquid varnish* as a fluid diluent. A brush added vehicle advantaged by being fixed from flow by way of the principle of lead-resin suspension, offered through the related construction of Antonello's *lead-paste* medium, a holding power not inherent in the egg yolk bound *varnish pomade* of Jan van Eyck.

It was sometime after 1500, the date of Leonardo's trip to Venice and his introduction of spirit of turpentine, that the "essential oil of Venice turpentine" was introduced into the pictorial systems. This diluent greatly advantaged those Northern painters who chose to employ Antonello's basic technical methods rather then the technique introduced by Leonardo da Vinci or the even more advanced technique employed by the 16th century Venetians. Although a most painterly technique it, nevertheless, failed to excite the eye and taste of such Northern masters as Albrecht Dürer, Lucas Cranach (1472—1553), Albrecht Altdorfer (1480—1538) and Elder Pieter Bruegel (1520—1569), and their love of brilliant, enameled coloring and shiny paint films.

## The Technique of Antonello da Messina and the Northern Painters' Use of Canvas

One of the most interesting techniques developed by Northern painters employing Antonello's *lead-paste* medium and its related palette preparations is evidenced in Gerard David's (1450/60—1523) e.g. *The Deposition*, New York, Frick Museum. Under the paint film of this high quality work, were we able to roll back the various layers, would be found a fully rendered tempera painting executed over a pen or brush and ink underdrawing, transferred from a pre-drawn design. A work that when the paints were dry was then primed with an isolating, *optical prime* of Antonello da Messina's pictorial vehicle. A coating which when thoroughly dry was worked over employing paint preparations keyed in accord with the demands of the opaque lighter tones tempera underpainting as a source of *luce di sotto*.

In accord with the above reasoning, it is our belief that the Elder Pieter Bruegel's *Landscape with the Fall of Icarus*, Brussels Musé Royaux des Beaux-Arts, though often proposed as having been transferred from panel to canvas, instead, originally painted on canvas in the manner above described. Our reasoning for this belief is the presence of a certain static paint layering visible through the thin, translucent, oleaginous paint film, a visual evenness so unlike the active paint field observed in many works by Brueghel executed on an *optical prime* of glue isolated, white gesso ground of panel.

Undeniably, such a technique as above described, would hardly challenge the superior, more painterly technique of the 16th century Venetians and may well have inspired the observation made by Paolo Pino (16th century painter/writer) when stating "Let us leave gouache to the Flemish, we Italians will paint in oil."

# Third Key Directives
## Leonardo da Vinci, Bridge Between Styles

### Leonardo da Vinci in Measured Step

The advantages of Leonardo's palette preparation over those of earlier schools of painting were realized by the lending of a more natural chroma and sfumatic blendability of the paints: rewards directly related to the less transparent, non-varnish extended paint structure. Despite the use of wax and a thin-bodied raw oil, there appears to be no less protection offered to the paint film than that offered through the use of the protective enamel-like palette preparations devised by Antonello da Messina. Also, for the first time in history of oil painting techniques, the white lead paint could be applied with reasonable solidity leaving the decision of the paint structure more to the taste and choice of the painter—rather then the demands of the pictorial elements.

Despite the fluid line employed by Leonardo in his *Adoration* (earlier discussed), it is apparent that among his improvements to the technique of oil painting, playful invention with the brush was not one of them. His works were necessarily well planned and the designs were generally transferred from master cartoons to the panel, indicating that certain restrictive characteristics of Antonello's *lead-paste* medium and related structures still prevailed.

Perhaps the most unwanted consequence with respect to Leonardo's technique was that the white paint or areas where white predominated, often appeared fat-saturated, due to the use of raw oil as a compacting element for the colors and their tempering with the raw oil adjusted pictorial vehicle. It was for that reason Leonardo and his followers sometimes employed sand-colored grounds, believing that the force of this less then perfect structure of white paint would insinuate itself more forcefully on a toned ground than a ground of competitive whiteness as can be witnessed in numerous Florentine and Milanese works.

Prior to the adoption of certain Venetian improvements offered to oil painting technique by Giorgione, Leonardo's palette preparation was not that of a colorist. This may have been the reason that many Florentine and Milanese painters were persuaded away from coloristic pursuits, some seemingly to have convinced themselves that color and form were not compatible.

That in the present writing Leonardo's technical efforts may appear to be criticized more than praised, is because of the hindsight perspective in which his contribution is herein viewed. Understand that our critical analysis involves only the "stepping stone" contribution made by that "divinely endowed" master to the developing refinement of the pictorial technique of oil painting. A step forward, which had it not been made, would have delayed the development of that ever-evolving technique until such a time when another equally valued linkage were made.

The fact is, had Leonardo adequately provided answers to the problems inherent in his step forward in the technique of oil painting, more substantial changes in his method would not have come so rapidly after the dissemination of his technique to the painters of Venice. That those changes did not come from Milanese painters, the first to share Leonardo's technical knowledge, even before his fellow Florentines, may be because their goal seemed to be more toward imitation of the master's style of rendering, rather than toward advancement of technique.

## *The* Lead-wax *Medium*

The basis for Leonardo's *lead-wax* medium was Antonello da Messina's *lead-paste*, Leonardo having merely added to that base structure a given measure of beeswax. Although the principle involved in the structuring of the *lead-wax* medium is relatively simple, it nevertheless represented an important step forward in oil painting technique.

As to the directive for the preparation of Leonardo's medium, the following formula is based on a ratio of 1 part beeswax to 16 parts of the liquids used in preparing Antonello's *lead-paste* medium. With respect to the choice of fixed oil, while linseed oil is acceptable, Leonardo would have preferred walnut oil.

## *Directive I*

INGREDIENTS
> *2 parts, by weight, washed raw linseed or walnut oil*
> *1 part, by weight, litharge (made from the finest reagent grade white lead pigment, prepared as noted in the Pre-Key Directive*
> *2 parts, by weight, Van Eyck's liquid varnish*—set near the heat source for future use when compounding the *lead-paste* medium of Antonello da Messina
> ¼ *part, by weight, yellow beeswax*

Step 1: Combine the raw oil and litharge in an enamelware pot and cook as earlier described for the preparation of Antonello da Messina's *oglio cotto* (see Key Directive).

Step 2: When the *oglio cotto* is duly prepared, add the pre-weighted 2 parts of Van Eyck's *liquid varnish.* Stir the ingredients until they are homogenously blended, forming the *lead-paste* medium of Antonello da Messina.

Step 3: While the pot remains over the heat, add to the basic medium structure ¼ part beeswax. Stir until the wax is melted and the mixture is smooth. The pot is then removed from the heat and, while still quite warm, the *lead-wax* medium is decanted into a wide-mouth receptacle and well capped.

---

## *Leonardo's* Optical Prime *and Pictorial Vehicle* Structure

Leonardo's *optical prime* and pictorial vehicle were as with those of Jan van Eyck and Antonello da Messina, one in the same structure.

## *Directive II*

---

INGREDIENTS
> *1 part, by measure, lead-wax* medium
> ½ part, by measure, raw linseed or walnut oil

Combine the two ingredients by immixing with the palette knife until smooth, thereby, producing both the pictorial vehicle and *optical prime* structures.

---

## *Application of the* Optical Prime

In the spreading of Leonardo's *optical prime*, due to the resistive body of the pictorial vehicle preparation, spirit of turpentine, newly instituted into the technique of oil painting by Leonardo himself, was immixed with the knife into the pictorial vehicle, forming a puddle mass, able to be taken with the brush and quickly and evenly spread over the glue isolated gesso ground of panel.

Such a spreading will yield a coating low in both body level and vitreous shine, preserving the egg-shell like quality of the gesso. A coating which, once dry, aids the tactile response of the paints worked over it, as well as visually and texturally advantaging the sfumatic effect so diligently sought by Leonardo.

Such a prime structure is improved by the thorough evaporation of the turpentine spreading agent and proper drying of the wax content, a purpose requiring from one, or better, two weeks.

The significant advantage for Leonardo, with respect to the mode of rendering and quality of the *optical prime* was the use of spirit of turpentine, assuring for him the thinnest possible liaison structure. It should be noted that generally Leonardo's *optical prime* was applied over a broadly executed ink underdrawing, as can be seen through the paint film of numerous 16th Century Milanese and Florentine paintings. However, since the discipline of Leonardo's technique was less rigid then that of earlier oil paintings techniques and changes could effectively be made during the course of the painting, the guide line drawing might even be traced or drawn directly onto the dry *optical prime*.

Unlike the pictorial vehicle of Antonello da Messina, where the *liquid varnish* tempering of his *lead-paste* medium suspends, via the action that occurs between the combination of lead and mastic resin, Leonardo's vehicle structure never suspends, remaining instead of a soft unguent.

Leonardo's reasoning for his more siccatively responsive pictorial vehicle was based on a simple principle of solidification. In effect, the wax content of his medium was softened by both an oil input and pressure of the knife during the immixing process. It was by cessation of that pressure that the extended wax portion of the immixture re-solidified, holding the oleous input at a point of controlled flow.

## Preparation of Leonardo's Palette and the First True Diluent

In a theoretical step forward but a material step backwards Leonardo, using a well washed, thin bodied raw linseed or walnut oil, knife ground his colors including white lead, into tightly compacted globules. Which were then, each in turn, tempered to ductility with no less than an equal part of Leonardo's pictorial vehicle and when duly prepared were set upon the palette. In accord with tradition, a portion of the pictorial vehicle was also housed on the palette to be used during the course of the painting as a primary means to achieve transparency as well as aid in the spreading of the paints.

Although Leonardo's paints were tractable, it was the heaviness of their construction that called for a thinning diluent, one which would allow a certain freedom of *line* and *wash* and *laying-in* of the colors, particularly in the first sitting.

While the preparation of Leonardo's painting oil is of simplest design, it is important to remember that the ingredients involved, as well as the principle behind the painting oil's employment, were revolutionary for the time. Turpentine was newly introduced into pictorial technique; whereas raw oil, a technical outcast since the time of Jan van Eyck's invention was—though of but brief duration—made acceptable.

In the directive about to be given, it is important to recall that Leonardo recommended 2 parts of the distillate oil or spirit of turpentine, designating "one of the first turpentine" and "one of the second." Obviously, the first distillate turpentine would be more resinous than that of the second. It is in that interest, seeing that the resin present in the first part of turpentine would lend a certain *tack* and *pull* to the feel of the total preparation, that we note the distinct advantage offered through the use of the painting oil with respect to the rendering of *line* and *wash*.

Were one interested in a better understanding of the pictorial element and the technical methods of Leonardo da Vinci through trial application of the elements and methods herein proposed, the following Key Directive is adjusted with respect to the oleo-resinous proportion of the "first turpentine."

## *Directive III*

---

INGREDIENTS
  1 part, water-washed linseed or walnut oil, by volume
  1 ½ parts, spirit of turpentine, by volume
  ½ part, Leonardo's mastic picture varnish, by volume

Simply combine the ingredients in a bottle, cap well, and mix by thorough shaking of the bottle.

It should be stressed that this *painting oil* is not a substitute for the pictorial vehicle. It is merely an auxiliary fluid aid, to be used in the execution of *line* and *wash* during the planning of the initial design and laying-in of the first sitting. A method such as can be witnessed in Leonardo's *St. Jerome*, Rome, Vatican Museum. Since the properties and quality of the *painting oil* do not correspond to those which form the primary pictorial vehicle, the painter soon learns where it should, and should not, be employed. And, seldom would the painting oil be employed, other than for details, past the first sitting.

---

## *Leonardo's Mastic Picture Varnish*

With respect to Leonardo's varnish, there are those who would point to the master's own words, where he recommends as the perfect varnish a "purified nut oil thickened… in the sun." However, to realize that Leonardo was speaking theoretically, all that one need do is to put his recommendation to test. One would then find that although such an oil yellows less rapidly than a purified oil in its thinnest state, it does yellow and to such a degree far greater then any painter would tolerate. A fact to be considered when later discussing the sum thickened oil recommended by Peter Paul Rubens.

I would suggest that when Vasari wrote of Leonardo's "curious experiments to find oil for painting and varnish to preserve the work done," the varnish which he alluded to was a simple spirit of turpentine based mastic varnish, designed more as a cosmetic coating than as a protector of the paints, such protection being the province of the pictorial vehicle and the inherent structure of the paints themselves.

## Directive IV

INGREDIENTS

1 part, by weight, of pulverized gum mastic crystals or tears
3 parts, by weight, spirit of turpentine

Combine the ingredients in a glass jar, gently stir so as not to throw the mastic above the level of turpentine. Well cap the container and place it in a deep water bath, resting on a trivet or some device so as to prevent the jar from direct contact with the bottom of the heating pot.

Bring the water to a boil, never allowing it to evaporate below the level of the ingredients. The jar may be gently swirled from time to time until the soluble portion of the mastic resin is combined with the turpentine. In order to insure incorporation of the resin into the oil, a longer cooking time is preferable to a lesser time.

The varnish may then be removed from the boiling water, the jar wiped dry, and stored, preferably, in an area where the sun's rays might play upon it, even if at but brief intervals. In several weeks to a month or so, the varnish will become as clear as crystal. The varnish may then be re-decanted into smaller containers, well capped and restored to the light or sunny area for future use.

# Fourth Key Directives
## Giorgio da Castelfranco and the 16<sup>th</sup> Century Venetians

*Thoughts on the Venetian Technique*

Were one to search out the identity of a problematic element in the 16th Century *Venetian lead-wax medium* it would, undoubtedly, be fat. The lean mastic resin content of Van Eyck's *liquid varnish* was fat-saturated by way of the fixed-oil base. This is also true of the active litharge content of Antonello da Messina's *oglio cotto*, and beeswax is itself a "complicated fat." Thus, the issue as Giorgione would have assessed it would not have been how to eliminate fat from his new technique but was, instead, how to reduce and control that element, making the preparation in which it served more responsive in values both tactile and optical.

In concern of those values, only painters can truly appreciate the merit behind the painterly principle and tactile reward gained from the preparation of Giorgione's densely compacted, low-fat *white lead paste* and the oleaginous tempering of that preparation with a tractable, oil rich pictorial vehicle. This would also be true of Giorgione's institution of the essential oil or spirit of turpentine as the compacting element for the color pigments, prior to their oleaginous, pictorial vehicle tampering. In addition, none but a painter can experience the difference between the tactile response of the paints when worked over dry, *optical prime* of glue isolated white gesso panel or the umber tinted *optical prime* employed on a glue isolated white lead and oil ground of canvas.

For the first time in the progression of oil painting technique, the 16th Century Venetian technique with its well reasoned palette preparation granted the painters the privilege of inventing with the brush directly over the kindred, pictorial liaison fields, particularly those employed on canvas. This technique, when duly employed, allows the changes in the pictorial invention in wet-over-dry layerings without intrusion of the underlying paint structure.

It was also through the Venetian technique that oil painters became truly aware of the related power of color joined with form. As Boschini noted: "Without this color design would be said to be a body without a soul… color makes us aware of the various hues. Thus color adds the blood to the flesh and can be called a brilliant sun that with its luminous rays lets us see the perfection of each detail."[1]

## *Giorgione's Venetian* Lead-wax *Medium*

While the structural change offered by Giorgio da Castelfranco to the *lead-wax* medium of Leonardo da Vinci may appear to be somewhat nominal, what was not was his envisioning and resolve of the independent siccative and optically charged lead-saturated drying oil to be used in conjunction with that medium.

If the proposals made throughout the Fourth Key of this work are correct and Leonardo da Vinci and Giorgio da Castelfranco in forming their *lead-wax* mediums merely added beeswax to an otherwise unchanged *lead-paste*, then greater credentials are lent to our claims that Antonello da Messina and not Leonardo da Vinci "is to be regarded as the founder, strictly speaking, of the Italian process of oil painting."

## *Directive I*

<small>INGREDIENTS</small>

1 part, by weight, litharge (made from the finest reagent grade white lead pigment, prepared as noted in the Pre-Key directives)

2 parts, by weight, washed raw linseed or walnut oil

2 parts, by weight, Van Eyck's liquid varnish—set near the heat source for future use when compounding the lead-paste medium of Antonello da Messina

½ part, by weight, yellow beeswax

Step 1: Combine the raw oil and litharge in the pot and cook in the manner earlier describe for the preparation of Antonello's *oglio cotto* (see Second Key Directive I).

Step 2: When the *oglio cotto* is duly prepared, add the pre-weighted 2 parts of Van Eyck's *liquid varnish*. Stir the combined ingredients until thoroughly blended, forming the *lead-paste*.

Step 3: While the pot remains over the heat, add to the basic *lead-paste* medium the ½ part beeswax. Stir until the wax is melted and the mixture is smooth. The pot is then to be removed from the heat and while still quite warm the resultant *Venetian lead-wax medium* is decanted into a wide-mouth jar and well capped.

## *The Black Oil of Giorgione*

Black oil, we repeat, is a simple designation given by Maroger for what we propose is a most sophisticated structure of drying oil. It was designed to act as the tempering or extending oil used to soften and make ductile the heavy bodied *Venetian lead-wax medium*. This formed the pictorial vehicle and, in turn, paint structures. This optically darkened oil, a coloring consequential to the process of lead-saturation, when viewed in a thin layer painted on a glazed white tile, proves to be of a bright, rich amber tone, lending both brilliance and accelerated drying power to the oleaginous elements which it helps to form. These qualities need not be sapped from the strength of the Venetian medium as did the raw oil-tempering element employed by Leonardo da Vinci sap strength from his *lead-wax* medium.

Functionally the black oil was designed to induce and control the oxygen intake of the paint film and, by way of its interaction with the mastic resin content of the *liquid varnish* portion of the Venetian medium, it spurred an increase of siccative-grasp, offering—although limited—an *alla prima* response.

In addition, the black oil insured "through" rather than merely "top" drying of the paints preventing "frosting" or "wrinkling" of the paint layer, retaining the luster of the paints and rich glazes that were hallmarks of the 16th Century Venetian technique.

It should be stressed that Giorgione's lead-saturated black drying oil was not intended to act as an *independent* pictorial vehicle. In fact, from the advancements offered by Giorgione, save for the small amount of raw oil used in the preparation of the tightly compacted white lead paste, there were no free oils employed in the technique of the 16th Century Venetian painters.

That this didactically demanding preparation of black oil was so well understood by so many painters in both Italy and the North—prior to the invention of a heat proof thermometer, is a tribute to the atelier system of training. In the preparation of such a drying oil one must understand the nature of charcoal fire—the "slow heat" referred to in various 16th and 17th century documents. Owing to the difficulty of exactness of a charcoal fire, there must have been signs indicating degree ranges of *highs* and *lows*, that is, *over* and *under* cooking. By the fact that undercooking leaves an oil less brilliant and siccatively responsive than over-cooking, you may be assured that the masters would always have erred on the side of strength.

Before offering our directive for the preparation of Giorgione's black drying oil, we deem it best to understand how the masters in using their less sophisticated means might achieve the same end results that we have achieved by the use of an easily changeable heat source and that most important instrument, the heat-proof thermometer.

The Elder Jan Bruegel has provided us with pictorial evidence of the type of stove which would have been employed for the preparation of black drying oils; no doubt in kind to that also employed by Giorgione. It is in one of the large panels from the series, *Allegory of the Five Senses*, Madrid, Prado Museum, dealing with the sense of smell, wherein is depicted a relatively small, cylindrical metal stove. Resting atop the stove, no doubt on a stationary metal plate, is a perfume distiller. Immediately beneath the upper plate is an underlying, movable second metal plate to which is attached a metal handle with a pull-ring. In analysis, both plates would be perforated with a center cluster of holes each, perhaps, an inch or so in diameter. The perforations were calculated so as to be opened or closed either in-part or whole by pulling the handle in a given direction within a determined area of a point-to-point span. Allowed, as deemed necessary, degrees of the built-up heat either to work upon or to deny contact with, the bottom of the cooking vessel which must have fully encompassed the above mentioned clustered perforations.

Toward the bottom of the stove is an open damper-door, one of the means control the degree of heat. Not only was the heat increased by the open damper, but most important, the heat could be quickly raised by the use of a bellows, a designed draught capable of bringing the temperature anywhere from 20, 30, or more degrees above the normally increased highest degree.

In reversing the process, the lowering of the degrees of heat begins immediately upon cessation of the use of the bellows and may be further controlled by the banking of the coals, shutting of the damper door, and the full or partial closing of the perforated lower metal plate situated just below that on which the cooking receptacle rests.

That the preparation of black drying oils was the masters' greatest technical problem, there is no doubt; however, the students and apprentices would have taken heart in the knowledge that all pictorial methods were taught by eye witnessing hands-on-demonstrations and holding with the simple logic, that in crafts repetition tends to familiarize and, thereby, serves to simplify.

## *Directive II*

Understanding that the ratio amounts of 8 oz. oil to ½ oz. litharge recorded in the De Mayerne Ms. (see: Fourth Key text under the heading "Maroger and the Black Oil of Giorgione") represented the maximum amount of drying oil to be prepared at one time, then any reduced amounts of such a preparation are to be based on a 1:16 litharge to raw oil ration proportion; while holding with the rule we have proposed ½ inch depth and the given rule of a 2 hour cooking time and the temperature ranges, herein proposed, for the incorporation and saturation periods.

---

INGREDIENTS

16 parts of linseed or walnut oil, pre-weighted and calculated to measure not appreciably more nor less than ½ inch in depth, when placed in the cooking vessel
1 part, by weight, litharge
2 parts, by weight, spirit of turpentine

Pour the 16 parts oil into the cooking vessel and add the 1 part litharge. Stir the litharge gently and briefly in order to disperse the pigment more evenly over the inside bottom of the pot. Take care not to raise any more than necessary a cloud of litharge. Then place the pot over the shielded, relatively hot fire. It is at this point that the 2 hour cooking time should begin.

Within several minutes of what is the "incorporation stage", the slightly clouded oil will clarify. As the litharge begins to a pin-point threading action, it forms a low-level spume accumulating over the ever darkening surface of the oil. It is essential, for reasons of lead-saturation and, thereby, the maximum degree of siccatively, that the spume and working action earlier noted in the oil completely dissipated within approximately 15 minutes, having reached a degree of no less than 230°C and, preferably not to greatly exceed that degree.

The oil becoming smooth and black and the lead having been fully incorporated, the heat is then to be lowered, to settle at a degree range between a low of 200°, to a high not to exceed 210°C. There to rest undisturbed, save for taking the degree with the thermometer, for the remaining 1 and ¾ hours.

The stage which we have dubbed the *lead-saturation stage*; a period in which there are virtually no signs of working as the lead silently saturated the oil bringing it to the highest degree of siccatively. At the end of the total two hours cooking time, the pot of oil is to be removed from the fire an allowed to diminish in heat below 100°C; readied to be freed of the unwanted, lubricating lead particles.

In the simplest procedure, add the 2 parts spirit of turpentine into the black drying oil, stir well and decant the black oil into the small-mouth bottle and well cap.

An oil such as above described, clarifies within 24 hours to 48 hours (much depending on the highest degree reached in the incorporation stage), the lead content settling into a compact, tan colored deposit. Tilting the oil to the side of the bottle it is realized to be a clear, brilliant amber tone and of a pleasingly thin body—a thinness, however, not to be equated with the weak body of raw oil.

---

## The Pictorial Vehicle

In the design of Giorgione's pictorial vehicle, the intent was to produce a soft but fixed structure that would sufficiently yield under the pressure of the brush so as to be able to render the sfumatic, atmospheric, lyrical qualities generally associated with the 16th Century Venetian painters. It was this extended, highly tractable, pomade-like pictorial vehicle and its related paint structures which it helped to form, that allowed masters such as Titian, Giorgione, Veronese and Tintoretto—all of whom often rendered extremely large works—to employ small palettes.

Although structurally soft, the pictorial vehicle was adequately protective of the *velaturas* and glazes generally employed by Venetian painters. The removal and abrading of their paint films, to be placed directly at the fault of heavy handed and pictorially insensitive paint chemists, certain of whom deserve no better than to be referred to as "picture cleaners."

## Directive III

_____

INGREDIENTS
    Venetian medium
    Giorgione's black drying oil

Place a measured portion of the Venetian medium on the grinding slab and immix with the palette knife an equal measure of Giorgione's black drying oil. Initially the mixture is quite fluid but, owing to the re-solidification of the beeswax present in the mixture, soon restructs to a soft controlled paste. The pictorial vehicle should then be moved to the corner of the stone or grinding slab, to await its use for the vehicle tempering of the paints and setting-up the palette.

_____

## Preparation of the White Lead Paste

In the preparation of the 1-12 ratio raw oil to pigment white lead paste, two principles called for its structure: (1) to reduce to the lowest possible amount the free raw oil used in its compacting. (2) to create a structure of white lead paste of the greatest possible density in order to offset both the effect of transparency as well as the initially dark, amber tone lent by the pictorial vehicle used in the rendering of the white lead paste into a ductile paint form.

Of all the mechanical procedures employed by the 16th Century Venetians and the 17th Century Flemish and Dutch masters none were more physically demanding than the grinding of the white lead paste. It is for this reason that we find in certain works depicting the studio and its various practices an assistant or more likely a hired workman, sleeves rolled-up, bent over the grinding stone with muller in hand, preparing paint. A depiction so unlike the master painter himself, often dressed in rich and stylish garb, brandishing his palette, brushes and maul-stick.

Since all painters, both Italian and Northern, would have employed the same 1:12 ratio, oil to pigment white lead paste, had there not have been a variety of mediums and their oleaginously extended pictorial vehicles all paintings would exhibit, more or less, many of the same characteristic opaque loadings or impastos. Instead, we find a vast difference between the various systems of master painting from the layered method of the 15th Century Flemish and Italian painters to the more immediately responsive technique of Leonardo da Vinci; to the rich coloring and opaque building exhibited in the paintings of Giorgione and the 16th Century Venetians and the rich, enameled quality and alla prime executions of Rubens and Rembrandt; as well as the soft, lyrical "airy style" of Van Dyck leading to the softest structure of paint characteristic of the technique of Jan Vermeer.

As it is herein believed that the white lead paste is at peak quality for a period of three weeks, it is advised that the amount of paste to be prepared, be calculated as to the amount needed for that maximum time of three weeks. I myself made the preparation of the white lead paste a bi-monthly chore.

## Directive IV

INGREDIENTS
    12 parts, by weight, dry white lead pigment
    1 part, by weight washed raw linseed or walnut oil

Combine the total ingredients on the stone and blend together with the knife until an even textured powder is formed. Gather the powder into a pile and with the muller, applying reasonable forceful pressure, grind with short forward and backward, side-to-side action. After a while, the compacted powder is to be scraped from the bottom of the muller and again gathered into a pile and the grinding procedure repeated over and over.

In time, the tightly compacted thin sheet to be found on the bottom of the muller, reveals evidence of the oil content. This thin sheet should also be scraped from the muller and the grinding to be repeated over and over until the mixture begins to yield, giving evidence of a paint form. This form, in time, produces a thick malleable globule, which is then to be placed in a container of water, well capped and kept for use.

In concluding, it should be noted that with respect to the above directive and the presence of free fatty acids that, "in paints that contain basic metallic pigments there will be some degree of reaction between the pigments and the free fatty acids of the oil, which will produce a coating of metal soaps upon the surface of the pigment particles. This coating is an aid to the wetting of the pigment in the grinding process,"[2] an advantage which clearly favors walnut oil over linseed.

---

## Preparation of the Paints

Unlike earlier practices where prior to tempering with the pictorial vehicle the white lead and color pigments were compacted with Van Eyck's *liquid varnish* or, as in the case of Leonardo da Vinci, a raw fixed-oil. Giorgione sought to reduce as much as possible any free oil, that is, any oil not controlled by its inclusion in the pictorial vehicle, be they raw or lead-saturated. The exception is in the preparation of the white lead paste, where the smallest possible amount of free raw oil is used in the compacting of the white lead pigment.

With respect to the soft structured Venetian pictorial vehicle when used in the tempering of the densely compacted white lead paste, it assures not only tractability, but also an enhanced degree of illumination, reducing the demand on rendering the paint in order to reveal the reflective, underlying light source of the transparent *optical prime*, glue isolated white gesso ground of panel, or the tinted *optical prime* rendered over glue isolated, oleaginous white lead ground of canvas.

## *Directive V, White Lead Paint*

INGREDIENTS
   1 part, by measure, Venetian pictorial vehicle
   1 part, by measure, white lead paste

Place the equal measures of Venetian pictorial vehicle and white lead paste on the grinding stone. Thoroughly immix the two ingredients with the palette knife until duly blended. Place the resultant white paint structure on the palette. Initially the paint will be quite soft and tan toned. However, shortly after resting on the palette, the structure will firm, due to lead resin suspension and the restructuring of the beeswax contained in the pictorial vehicle; while the tan tone will dissipate, leaving ductile, gleaming white paint.

## *Concerning Colors*

In accord with the text of our Fourth Key, it was no lesser a master than Peter Paul Rubens, who unmistakably, advised spirit of turpentine as the element to be employed in the grinding of the colors.

Turpentine is no more then an evaporable, compacting vehicle used in forming the globules of color pigment in order to visually gauge the necessary equal amount of pictorial vehicle that would act as the tempering element to be immixed with the color globules in order to render them into paint form. The advantage of the evaporable element being two fold: Not only were the color pigments free of varying degrees of oil absorption—since each pigment has its own rate of absorption; but also, that the black drying oil used in the forming of the pictorial vehicle—the tempering element for the color globules, is equitably balanced in each paint formation, lending an equal siccative and optical charge to each of the paint preparations.

Using a counter proposal to bolster Ruben's directive concerning grinding of color in "spirit of turpentine," there is an early 17th Century directive (cited in our First Key with reference to water-washing oil) where painters are advised to employ purified linseed oil for the grinding of "White and Blues."[3] This brings us to consider—why those specific pigments?

The reason is relatively simple. White lead, ultramarine and all other blues are structurally hardened when combined with leaded oils and mastic varnish, be it fixed oil or spirit of turpentine based. An effect which is advantageously offset by the compounding of those pigments with raw oil, due to its free fatty acid content. This process clearly favors walnut oil, the fatter of the two primary oils. Reducing in degree the restrictive binding of the pigments when rendered into paint form with any of the various Italian pictorial vehicles and those which form the differing strengths of 17th Century Flemish and Dutch pictorial vehicles, all of which employed in their body both leaded oils and mastic varnish.

Thus, it is by singling out such a small number of colors to be ground in raw oil that we are led to question—what then was the element employed for the grinding and compacting of the other colors? The answer, of course, is found in the directive of Rubens' and his proposal for "spirit of turpentine," in actuality, a grinding element used for compacting pigments into a non-malleable form, then to be brought to a ductile, tractable state by immixture of a black drying oil tempered Venetian pictorial vehicle.

While, no doubt, we will have our critics regarding our interpretation of Ruben's directive, consider how simply it is stated, a black and white proposal, the likes of which is seldom found in other extant proposals concerning the pictorial practices employed by the masters. As an example, it is the Talley's *Portrait Painting in England*, where with respect to the technique of Sebastiano Bombelli (1635—1724), there is reference concerning the preparation of what was termed Bombelli's "oil", a designated structure which is quickly followed in the same directive by referring to that "oil" as a "White Jelly" (pp. 326—327). Obviously this is a serious contradiction in terms –oil is a liquid and saturating, whereas a jelly is colloidal and fixed in structure, acting to surround rather then saturate a pigment, lending reflectivity and brilliance instead of a paste-like, non-reflective, density. An error of such significance to even lead one to question the term 'White Jelly," especially in the absence of the (elsewhere noted) "caveat"—"when you keep it long"—time obviously being at least one of the factors causing the jelly to become white.

The above concerns having been stated, let us consider the preparation of colors with the exception of "blues" which, as white lead, are to be compacted with a raw oil into a tight globule which is then tempered to paint form by the addition of an approximate equal amount of the Venetian pictorial vehicle.

## Directive VI

___

INGREDIENTS
>    Color pigments
>    Spirit of turpentine
>    Venetian pictorial vehicle

In rendering the color pigments into paint form, each in turn, place a determined pile of dry pigment on the grinding stone and taking some spirit of turpentine with a palette knife, immix the two ingredients in a grinding motion, adding, as needed, additional turpentine with the knife. The objective being to achieve a tightly compacted, non-fluid, globule of color. Immediately following the compounding of the color globule, thoroughly immix with the knife, by judgment of eye, an approximate equal amount of Venetian pictorial vehicle. When duly immixed, each paint preparation is then to be placed on the palette along with the white lead paint. Thereafter, add a portion of the Venetian pictorial vehicle itself, to be used during the course of the painting for increased transparency, translucency and to aid in the spreading of the paints.

---

## The Essential Oil of Venice Turpentine and the 16th Century Venetians

Since the "essential oil of Venice turpentine" was virtually indispensable to the technique of certain 17th Century Flemish and Dutch painters, we shall revisit this discussion in our Fifth Key directives.

Respecting the use of the diluent by the 16th Century Venetian painters, it functioned primarily in the process referred to in the Observations of Anthony van Dyck as *la maniera lavata*, employed for the washing-in of the paints and line defining. This mode of rendering is readily evidenced in Giorgione's *Christ Carrying the Cross*, Venice, Scuola di San Rocco.

As to how much the diluent functioned in successive sittings, it would have been far less than that used in the first sitting. It should be noted that owing to the densely pigmented and fat quality of the white lead paint and the transparent pictorial vehicle, the use of the diluent would be obscured, melded, as it were, with the fat paint structure.

## Directive VII

---

INGREDIENTS
   Venice turpentine
   Spirit of turpentine

Place a given liquid measure of the thickest Venice turpentine in a bottle or jar, adding four or five parts liquid measure of spirit of turpentine. Cap well and place the receptacle in the hot water-bath, swirling the ingredients from time to time until the contents are thoroughly immixed. Allow the contents to cool and reserve for use.

---

## *The* Optical Prime *of Panel*

For the first time in the pictorial technique of oil painting the *optical prime* structure employed by the 16th Century Venetians was leaner in construction than the pictorial vehicle and paint preparations to be worked over it. However, due to the fact that all the ingredients involve in the Venetian palette preparations were fat-laden, the lineage between the dry *optical prime* coat and the palette preparations was relatively close, limiting the tactile advantage. It was through the strong "active lead" content of the *oglio cotto*, coupled with the "lead saturated" oxygen inducing strength of the black drying oil and rapid setting of the mastic resin present in the *liquid varnish*, that provided the necessary siccative grasp so as to allow Giorgione and his Venetian brethren to paint directly from nature—"shading with the colder or warmer tints as the living object might demand." Offering degrees of painterly freedom over those of earlier techniques, allowing a measure, though not the absolute letter of *alla prima* response.

## *Directive VIII*

---

INGREDIENTS
Portion of the Venetian lead-wax medium
Spirit of turpentine

Place the Venetian medium on the mixing stone or palette and immix with the knife a sufficient amount of turpentine, a bit at a time, to soften the heavy medium. Then, spread the mixture thinly and evenly over the glue isolated white gesso ground of panel, adding turpentine with the brush if needed; preserving the egg shell-like texture of the gesso ground.

The resultant amber toned, low-level prime coat will dry within 6 to 8 hours, the tone noted when first spread dissipating to a near colorless film.

Although the prime coat may appear to be meager quality, it is sufficiently cohesive to support the vehicle-laden paints, preventing their absorption into the underlying ground, while offering liaison attraction.

---

## Sixteenth Century Venetian Grounds and the Optical Prime of Canvas, Oil and Pigment Grounds of Canvas

It is seldom that such relevant information such as the 16th Century Venetian preparation of canvas emanates from as creditable source as Giorgio Vasari. What we might wish is that he would have been equally as diligent about identifying the make-up of what he termed "the composition or priming," the final layer of the canvas preparation. The layer which we have termed the *optical prime*, that transparent film composed of dry burnt umber tinted *Venetian medium*. A most sophisticated prime over which the greatest Venetian masters of the 16th Century created works that to this day continue to excite through color and quality lay persons and artists alike, save for certain works rudely cleaned and over painted.

## Directive IX

---

INGREDIENTS

    Soft jelly size (see Pre-Key directive)
    White lead pigment
    Venetian black drying oil
    Venetian medium

Dry burnt umber pigment

*Step 1—Size*: Using a large flat brush or sponge, spread one or two coats of, as Vasari said, "smooth" or "soft size," scraping off any excess with a palette knife or spatula. It is recommended that when employing two coats of size, the first coat should be sanded, prior to the application of the second coat.

Step 2—*Ground*: Grind with the knife a sufficiently pliable paste composed of black oil and white lead. Spread the paste with a knife or spatula over the sized canvas, scraping the excess paste from one area and applying the scraping to another, until the canvas is sufficiently nourished.

Step 3—*Isolation*: When thoroughly dry, sand the ground and isolate with, as Vasari advised, "one or two more coats of soft size."

Step 4—*Optical Prime*: Then, in a unique procedure, a transparent *optical prime* coat of dry burnt umber tinted *Venetian medium* is to be knife scraped over the size ground and the whole allowed to dry several days before use. Such primed canvases may be stored and kept for years—constantly improving with age.

The primary function of the prime coat, what Vasari termed "composition or priming," is to offer in kind to the *optical prime* of panel, a compatible, liaison attractor of the materially related pictorial vehicle and oleaginous paint preparations. The tinting of the prime is to tone the cold white lead ground over which it is spread, as well as add optical variation through the contrast of the darker, *Venetian medium* trapped in the *valleys* of the canvas weave and the lighter toned *hills* from which the tined medium has been thinly scraped.

This illuminating canvas preparation is so superior to the dark, solid-toned, light depressing gray and red bolus ground-prime introduced by Palma Giovane (1544—1628) late in the 17th Century that it is difficult to understand why Venetian painters would have abandoned its use. It was not until variations were made in the 17th Century to the 16th Century Venetian medium and pictorial technique by, we propose, Domenico Feti (1589—1624) that solid-toned grounds or ground-primes were made acceptable. Variation which, regrettably, time will not permit me to pursue, save for my belief that the "new" Venetian technique would have incorporated in some fashion means and methods inherent n the 17th Century Flemish technique.

---

## Weak-Gesso Grounds of Canvas

For better understanding of the analytical reasoning concerning the gesso grounds of canvas, it is best to review the text contained in the Fourth Key, regarding Volpato's 17th Century manuscript, *The Mode to be Observed in Painting*.

Regarding the weak gesso ground and *optical prime* of canvas, except for the involvement of gesso, all other preparations and procedures are identical with Steps 1, 3, and 4, given in the preceding Key Directive IX, *Oil and Pigment Grounds of Canvas* and need but to be followed in the forthcoming directive in their respective order. Requiring that we consider only *Step 2*, dealing with the preparation and application of the weak-gesso ground.

## Directive X

---

INGREDIENTS
Weak glue-water
Whiting or Gypsum

Step 1. (see: Key Directive IX)
Step 2. Place into the upper section of a double boiler containing hot, weak-glue water, a ratio proportion of ½ to ¾ oz. whiting or gypsum to each fluid oz. of weak-glue water. Stir the ingredients and using a wide bristle brush quickly and thinly paint or scrub a coat of the weak-gesso over the sized canvas; and, when dry, sand or pumice the gesso ground.
Step 3. (see: Key Directive IX)
Step 4. (see: Key Directive IX)

No preparation can be simpler than the optical primed, glue isolated, weak-gesso ground of canvas. It was employed on the smallest as well as the largest of canvases and, I would suggest, was employed far more often then is generally thought.

# *Fifth Key Directives*
## *Jan 'Velvet' Bruegel and the 17th Century Flemish*

### *The Elder Jan Bruegel, Flemish Lumiere*

While I have, perhaps, involved myself in a romance of invention, I feel bound to once again stress the point that the great 17th Century Flemish painters and their Dutch counterparts owed a debt of gratitude to the Elder Jan Bruegel for the invention and communication of what must be recognized as the most technically rewarding pictorial system ever to have been employed by the "masters of past times."

An ultra-sophisticated, materially infallible technical system, generously handed by Jan to the painters of Flanders and Holland, as it is said "on a silver platter."

It was for the reason of generosity that the great still-life painter, Frans Snyders (1579—1654), while not a student of Jan's but of Jan's brother, Pieter Bruegel the Younger, (1564—1638), sometime in 1607, nursed Jan back to health during a long period of a serious illness, an acknowledged debt or better, homage, paid by Frans to the inventor of the 17th Century Flemish technique. The technique which allowed the younger master to develop a style richly akin to that of Peter

Paul Rubens who, obviously feeling no sense of diminished station, acted "over a period of twelve years from 1610 on" as secretary to Jan, "whose fluency in Italian," as it was written, "fell far short of his own." In a letter written by Jan himself to Fredrigo Cardinal Borromeo on February 11, 1622, Jan noted "My secretary Rubens is in France, otherwise I should have written. The Queen Mother of the King has built a palace, and desires to ornament it with pictures by Rubens," "probably the main reason" as Magurn wrote "for the termination of this unique partnership."[1]

Perhaps the greatest homage and respect paid by Rubens was in allowing Jan the use of his studio "for the rest of his life... regardless of whether they were engaged in the same enterprise or concentrating on separate projects." It was the fact of Rubens generous, highly ethical, morally straight and sterling character that led the Elder Jan to unselfishly praise "Rubens genius" and "gloried in his great success," referring to Rubens in a letter written to "Cardinal Borromeo in 1624," as "fortune's favorite" further noting, " to such an extent that he has received more honors and riches than any other artist of our time, and no artist in our history has more deserved them."[2]

When we consider Jan and Rubens, these "best of friends" and most conscientious of collaborators, who have given us so many magnificent works, one must agree with Edwards when he suggested, "The relationship of the two men was so close that it is worthy of further examination"—a task equally as worthy of collaboration between the best of scholars.

While the acts of respect paid by artists to Jan are indicative of something he has done to earn their respect, there were no lack of public honors. He was appointed Dean of the Antwerp Guild of St. Luke, and in addition, he was acclaimed Dean of the Antwerp Society of Romanists, consisting of those painters who had traveled to Italy to study the works of the ancients as well as the master painters of the 16th Century. Even more lucrative, in 1609, Jan was appointed as Court Painter to the Archducal pair Isabella and Albert, a position which granted him exemption from paying certain taxes and allowed him to accept as many students as he wished.

Whether or not all of Jan's patrons understood the reason that other painters so admired this master of bright, jewel-like colors and small well articulated forms, is difficult to say. What can be said, is if we are correct in identifying the Elder Jan Bruegel as the inventor of the 17th Century Flemish pictorial system, that which assured artists such as Rubens, Van Dyck, Jordeans, Rembrandt and Vermeer the ability to forge their dynamic and diverse means by which to best express themselves; then, as with Maroger's assignment of Antonello da Messina as an "inventor," our similar assignment of the Elder Jan Bruegel, will assure that justice has been done and truth well served.

## The Black Drying Oil of Anthony van Dyck

With respect to directives, the various types and strengths of black drying oils take precedent over other elements involved in the 17th Century technique. It is these lead-saturated, non-polymerized oils that, when combined with a turpentine based mastic varnish triggers suspension, thereby forming the Flemish medium. And, when used as the tempering vehicle for that medium, forms the pictorial vehicle by which to render the paint forms. Preparation which call for the intake of oxygen that directly influences the stroke of brush, thereby, offering varying degrees of wet-into-wet superimposition of the paints. In short, if the lead-saturation of the black drying oil is insufficient, all painterly response and optical rewards granted through the medium and its related pictorial vehicle will suffer in direct accord with that insufficiency.

As to the actual preparation of the various types and strengths of black oil, the first, the 1:16 ratio strength of the litharge saturated oil is known by way of the De Mayerne Ms., the oil which Maroger dubbed the "black oil of Giorgione." The preparation of which has been cited and fully discussed in the Fourth Key and its Key Directives section (see: Key Directive II).

Regarding the second type of black drying oil, it is a white lead saturated oil, proportioned respectively in a 1 ½ :16 and a 2:16 white lead to oil ratio. Both oils are directly connected with Anthony van Dyck by way of Eastlake and the salvaged document which we have termed the *English Document*. Siccative wise the lesser ratio strength oil produces a considerably softer oil than the stronger of the two oils. Quality wise, both of these oils vary greatly from oils which have been litharge saturated: the white lead oils being less tensive and lighter in color and body; lending to the medium which they help to form a certain softness and buoyancy that cannot be achieved through the use of litharge. A consciously designed reward which van Dyck obviously preferred.

In regard to Giorgione's litharge-saturated black drying oil, the proportion was based on a 1:16 litharge to oil ratio. As earlier noted the given amount of ½ oz. of litharge to 8 oz. of oil, recorded in the De Mayerne manuscript by way of M. Sallé, being the maximum amount of oil to be prepared at one time; arrived to in accord with the circumference of the pot and perforated heating area of the underlying heat source, requiring a total 2 hour cooking time.

Based on what we believe to be a known factor and relating it to van Dyck's white lead saturated black oils, the so-called "better" proportion of 2:16 white lead to oil—double the amount of lead dryer as used in the preparation of Giorgione's black drying oil, would require a 1 inch depth of oil to be cooked over a total period of 4 hours. Whereas the weaker or softer oil, proportioned 1 ½ :16 white lead to oil ratio would require an approximate depth of ¾ inch, to be cooked for a total of 3 ½ hours.

It is important to note that in the *English Document*, when it is stated that of the two strengths of drying oils, the 2:16 ration strength is "better," reference is being made to an increased response of *siccative grasp*, a tactile reward inherent in the black drying oil tempered pictorial vehicle and its related paint preparation.

It is the cooking of that "better" proportioned oil that will be considered in the following directive.

Lest there be confusion between methods, it should be noted that unlike the "black oil of Giorgione," where there are two separate and differing heat ranges, one for the 'incorporation' of the lead and the other the 'lead-saturation' of the oil, van Dyck's drying oil is prepared in a steadily increasing range of heat. The two periods occur as a consequence of reaching certain degrees of temperature. The 'incorporation period' begins in the early stages of the heating process and culminates when reaching 185° C, while the 'saturation period' begins at that degree and continues, hopefully, without significant heat rise, throughout the remainder of the four hour cooking.

## Directive I

MATERIALS

   2 parts, by weight, finely powered, reagent grade white lead
   16 parts, by weight, linseed or walnut oil

When poured into the cooking vessel, the oil should measure not appreciably more or less than 1 inch in depth. The vessel is then set over the heat source. After a few minutes a slow undulating or churning action is noticed in the body of the oil. And, within the first few minutes of the heating, the white lead is to be added by degrees, sprinkling and distributing it evenly over the surface of the oil, taking care not to add too large an amount of lead at a time. And, never, from beginning to the end of the cooking period should the oil be stirred.

Although the white lead pigment generally falls to the bottom of the oil, at times, due to the fineness of the particles, a small amount of lead may float on the surface of the oil. This is remedied by gently touching the particles with the tip of the palette knife, which will be sufficient to coax the settling of the lead particles.

Once the white lead has been added to the oil, requiring but a minute or so, the timing of the cooking should then begin.

In the early stages of the cooking due to the hydrate content common to white lead, a spume is formed, gathering over the surface of the oil in greater or lesser amounts depending on the rate of heat acceleration.

In time, the small bubbles which form the spume, gives way to ever enlarging bubbles which burst and reform and, in time, dissipate. If the depth of the pot is insufficient and the bubbles become excessively large, they may be controlled by gently touching and bursting them with the tip of the palette knife.

Within the first hour of cooking the spume and bubbles will completely dissipate and once the oil appears black and smooth, the degree should then be taken, bearing in mind that by the end of the first hour the oil must be no less than 185°C and for the remaining 3 hours, preferably not to exceed 200°C.

At the end of the respective cooking time the black oil is to be removed from the heat and, when cooled below 100°C, is then to be decanted into a bottle or jar and well capped.

The oil is then to be monitored for signs of the transparent, finely particularized lead beginning to re-solidify and group. This grouping may appear much like a curdle, or a solid, brownish tan-toned mass. A process which generally occurs within six to eight hours after decanting the oil. At that time, the black oil is then to be re-decanted by straining it into another bottle through several layers of gauze or cheesecloth placed in a funnel. By this straining, most of the lead pigment is removed from the body of the oil and the remaining lead then settles out of the oil by "repose," appearing as a tan-toned deposit.

The oil should then be kept for use. Such an oil has a peak life of approximately one month. Thereafter, any remaining oil may be used in the preparation of canvas as the grinding element for the *ground coat* and the *ground prime.*

---

## *Another Process*

If one chooses, at the end of the cooking, the black oil may be removed from the heat source and a lid placed on the cooking vessel. After allowing the vessel to stand over night the oil is then to be strained in the process above given, the bottle of black oil then to be well capped and allowed to "repose." Very often, due to the resting of the oil, before decanting, there will be no accumulated residue, all having been removed through the initial straining process.

## *Seventeenth Century Flemish Varnish*

Although the development of turpentine based mastic varnish is to be credited to Leonardo da Vinci, the two strengths of that 16th Century prototype are associated more with the 17th Century Flemish school of painting and specifically dealt with in our reconstructed methods and materials employed in the techniques of Anthony van Dyck and Peter Paul Rubens.

Chronologically, the varnish strength employed by Van Dyck must be considered first, owing to its confirmed 17th Century relationship to that particular master through Maroger's quoting of a 17th Century source which he claimed to have emanated from De Mayerne, although obviously not from the pages generally accepted as the De Mayerne Manuscript. That such a source of information did exist, I have no doubt; whether it is in some manner connected with De Mayerne, I cannot say. We do know that the same proportions for Van Dyck's mastic varnish was salvaged by Eastlake from "a collection of memorandum containing successive accounts of painters who practiced in England from the time of van Dyck to that of Kneller"—the collection which we refer to as the *English Document*.

Regarding the proportions of Van Dyck's mastic varnish both sources propose, by weight, one part mastic resin dissolved in two parts spirit of turpentine. Quality wise, such a varnish is best thought of as soft, a characteristic reflecting the combination of that varnish with either of the two strengths of van Dyck's white lead-saturated black drying oils, forming his preferred structure of Flemish medium, the base source for the rendering of his "airy style."

The second varnish strength to be considered, which I have assigned to Rubens, is so placed because it is a product of our own design—an empirical resolve, reasoned through painterly logic, pictorial needs, tactile response and optical values. We propose the ratio strength to be equal parts, by weight of mastic resin to spirit of turpentine. Such a resin strength produces a highly vitreous and reasonably heavy bodied varnish requiring, when compared to the soft mastic varnish employed by Van Dyck, a greater amount of time for the fine, secondary insoluble debris to settle from the varnish.

In kind with the preparation of Leonardo's Mastic Picture Varnish (see: Third Key Directive IV), all strengths of such varnish are made in the same manner.

The mastic tears or crystals are to be well pulverized and combined with spirit of turpentine in a heat proof glass container. The ingredients are then to be gently stirred, the container well capped and rested in a pot of boiling water, preferably on a trivet or some other device so as to prevent direct contact of the glass container with the ever heating bottom of the cooking vessel. With occasional gentle swirlings, the varnish is to be cooked until the mastic is completely dissolved save, that is, for the heavy bodied, insoluble debris. The container may then be removed from the boiling water and rested until the fine, light bodied insoluble debris deposits and the varnish becomes as clear as crystal. The varnish may then be re-decanted into a glass bottle, well-capped, and kept in an area where sunlight might play upon it even if but at brief intervals. Such varnish preparations may be kept for years and are actually improved with age.

## The Seventeenth Century Flemish Medium

Based on the principle of lead-resin suspension, the Flemish medium, an epoxy-like structure, is an amalgamation of a thoroughly lead-saturated black drying oil and spirit of turpentine based mastic varnish. It is a variable structure, the degree of its suspension being related to both the lead-saturated strength of the black drying oil and the resin strength of the mastic varnish. In kind with the 15th and 16th Century Italian mediums which spurred its reasoning, the more sophisticated Flemish medium is, as the 16th Century Venetian medium, a concentrate, to be used as the *optical prime* structure and, when oleously adjusted, to act as the pictorial vehicle and binder of the paints.

Composed of two parts mastic varnish set in solution with but one part black drying oil, the Flemish medium was designed to avoid fat-saturation both in the means by which the mastic resin was transported into the black drying oil—via the essential oil of turpentine and by the superior amount of the lean mastic varnish contained within its body. In addition, this relatively lean and suspended medium was also designed to quickly *set* and *control* the necessary vehicle input of additional black oil. A resulting oleoresinous compound, triggered by the catalyst black drying oil to offer maximum rewards of superimposition of the paints, wet-into-wet. In kind with the basic medium structure itself, those rewards were also realized in varying degrees according to the lead- saturation strength of the drying oil and the resin strength of the varnish—the stronger those two elements, the more rewarding the *alla prima* response of the black oil extended pictorial vehicle.

In the actual preparation of the Flemish medium, it is for the individual artist to decide the strength and type of black oil and mastic varnish most suited their particular needs. Although all Flemish mediums are prepared in the same manner, in the following directive the proportions of the two most important structures, those mediums employed by Anthony van Dyck, and Peter Paul Rubens will be considered.

Once again, as with evidence of Van Dyck's drying oils and mastic varnish, evidence of the proportions and method of preparing the medium employed by Van Dyck stems primarily from Eastlake and our so named *English Document.* Whereas the medium which we herein propose for Peter Paul Rubens, as was the proposed strength for this mastic varnish of our own reasoning, aided by what we hold to be known quantity respecting the type and strength of black drying oil employed by that master, and the extant 17th Century evidence regarding Van Dyck's Flemish medium structure—which as Maroger proposed must have been "essentially the same as that of Rubens."

## *Directive II*

### *The Medium of Anthony van Dyck*
MATERIALS

    1 part by volume measure, of either a 1 ½ :16 or 2:16 white lead-saturated black drying oil
    2 parts, by volume measure, Van Dyck's 1:2, mastic resin to spirit of turpentine varnish

### *The Medium of Peter Paul Rubens*
MATERIALS

    1 part, by volume measure, Giorgione's 1:16 litharge-saturated black drying oil
    2 parts, by volume measure, Rubens 1:1, mastic resin to spirit of turpentine varnish

Using the ingredients in either of the above formulas, combine the respective black oil and mastic varnish into a heat tempered jar. Stir the ingredients well and cap the jar. Depending on conditions, the mixture may or may not gel though usually, in the case of Rubens strong ingredients, a jelly will occur. The jar is then to rest in a pot of boiling water. It should be noted that the water must extend above the contents of the jar during the course of heating. It the water should evaporate below the level of the ingredients, additional boiling water should be added.

After a reasonable length of time, the jar should be taken from the boiling water and keeping the jar capped, the ingredients should be swirled and the contents examined near a light. If any portion of jelly is noticed to remain in the mixture, the jar must be returned to the boiling water until the contents are completely liquidized. The jar may then be removed from the boiling water and while still capped, wiped dry. The jar is then to be uncapped and the rich amber fluid decanted into a wide mouth container, well-capped and rested to allow the contents to congeal into a jellified form.

Regarding the characteristics of the Flemish mediums they directly reflect, as earlier noted, the character of the two formulative ingredients. Whereas Van Dyck's medium was soft and of low-vitrification, Rubens medium was densely cohesive, highly vitreous and enameling. How many variation there were of the Flemish mediums and their base ingredients, we cannot know. That there were a variety of adjustments, perhaps even the architectonic structure of the medium itself, we have no doubt; the decision to be made by the individual painter, determined by the material needs in accord with aesthetic desires and dictates of the inner-eye pictorial visions.

---

## The Flemish Pictorial Vehicle

In kind with the various schools of oil painting that came before them, the 17th Century Flemish painters were aware of the necessity for a well calculated play between oil and resin. Since they understood that mastic resin enhanced the quality of oil, so they also knew that oil was the protector of that resin. Thus, with respect to the large varnish proportions of their medium, there were no fears concerning longevity since, in the black drying oil extension of that medium—used to form the pictorial vehicle, protectively for that vulnerable element was guarantied.

In addition, since the input of black drying oil was quickly set into solution via the lean compounding of the Flemish medium, the resulting pictorial vehicle, let us say 1/3 part black drying oil to 1 part Flemish medium—the ratio proportion used for the alla prima sketches, studies and the first sitting, "dead-coloring"— while sufficiently oleous was, nevertheless, advantaged by a low fat-saturation. An advantage which manifested itself through a greatly improved response of siccative—grasp—the means by which a painter may achieve a true, highly finished *alla prima* rendering.

You will recall, that with respect to the above mentioned dead coloring and the suggested 1/3 : 1 black drying oil to Flemish medium pictorial vehicle ratio, it was but the first stage of three pictorial vehicle stages or structures and related paint preparations used in the execution of works to "be finished in every detail". Each preparation to be up-graded by and additional 1/3 measure of the black drying oil to Flemish medium. As was the proportion of the first stage, "dead coloring" structure increased by 1/3 the amount of black oil over the structure of the transparent, striated, pure Flemish medium *optical prime* of panel or the somewhat more oleaginous, solid-toned *ground prime* of canvas. Thus leading us to consider the remaining two pictorial vehicle structures and their related paint preparations, each structure to be worked over a successive, dry underlying paint film. The ratio proportion of the second stage, "modeling" or epidermal vehicle being 2/3 : 1 black drying oil to Flemish medium: and the third stage, a glaze vehicle, necessarily being composed of equal parts of black drying oil to Flemish medium.

It was this ordered, oleaginous upgrading of the pictorial vehicles and related paint forms employed by Rubens which, by the well calculated mode of rendering, lent a virtually effortless degree of finish to his work, those "to be finished in every detail" without the need for insipid, soft-blender "sweetening" of the paint, a system so effortless it led Maroger to believe that all of Rubens' works were executed *alla prima*, without considered method or repaint.

## Rubens' Sun-thickened Oil Varnish

While we have dealt with the varnishes to be used in the preparation of the Flemish medium, there is yet another varnish to be considered, primarily because of the artist who recommended the varnish and even offered a directive for its preparation. It is through De Mayerne that the authoritative words of Peter Paul Rubens regarding a truly protective superficial varnish structure are noted.

Referring to the failings of a Venice turpentine surface varnish, Rubens stated: "Turpentine [Venice turpentine being meant] in time becomes arid (as the essential oil of turpentine or the petroleum evaporates), and is not proof against water. The best varnish, resisting water, is made with drying oil, much thickened in the sun on litharge, without boiling at all."[3]

Before discussing the above directive, two important points must be made. First, since fine pigment particulates were not necessary and density of litharge structure was actually advantageous, Rubens probably intended the use of a fused, flake litharge rather than the soft, finely divided, roasted white lead pigment such as was necessary for the preparation of black drying oil. Had Rubens intended the latter, he most likely would have used the term "litharge of gold." Second, Rubens' sun-thickened, litharge enforced drying oil was designed to act in accord with yet another element, necessary to *set* and *cohesively spread* the viscous fluid.

Turning to the preparation of this thickened oil, litharge is to be ground in water and formed into mounds or globules which, when thoroughly dry, are then equitably dispersed in a ceramic or glass tray. The oil, to be reasoned in an amount that would not be excessively deep, is then poured over the litharge and the tray covered with a sheet of glass, which should be slightly elevated above the edge of the tray in order to allow for the circulation of air. The whole then was placed in the sun.

Much depending on the heat of the sun's rays, the oil will thicken and, depending on the length of time it is exposed to the sun, will become more and more siccatively charged as well as becoming lighter in color. For the intended purpose of such an oil, it would be best brought to the consistency of heavy syrup.

Since all fixed oils, whether thick or thin, cannot of themselves be spread in a continuous, cohesive film without *creeping* and *puddling*, there must have been a means by which the above described drying oil was set and fixed from flow. This having been considered and our insistence that there were no free oils employed in the master schools of painting (save for the transitional technique of Leonardo da Vinci), the following preparation is proposed. To one part, volume measure, of Rubens strong, Flemish medium structure placed on the stone, an equal one part measure of the litharge enforced sun-thickened drying oil was added and immixed with the knife. Owing to the pale color of the thickened oil, the dark amber tone of Rubens' medium was made significantly lighter in tone. While, via the principle of lead-resin suspension—the essential reason for the exposure of the oil to the dry globules of litharge—the soft, oleaginous compound remains fixed from flow, set in a softened, suspended structure.

A preparation of this nature can be thinly brush spread with brush additives of spirit of turpentine, into a continuous, cohesive film. The amber tone noted when first spread, dissipated shortly thereafter to naught but a warm tonal whisper. Such a varnish coating dries within a reasonable time frame; leaving the film virtually unperceivable, save for the high, effective luster. While we have no doubt that Rubens employed such a varnish preparation, it would have rarely been employed, due to the fact that his paints would generally have dried with a high glossy, enamel-like finish, an intrinsic quality which is preferable to the use of a superficial varnish.

That we are fortunate to have access to Rubens directive we most certainly agree. However, it was this source of evidence which prompted certain writers to incorrectly speculate that such a oil was employed by Rubens as a vehicle for painting. Nothing could be further from the truth, for while this sun-thickened oil is a drying oil, it is not lead-saturated—the only possible means by which that could occur being by cooking oil and lead at a reasonably high degree of heat for an extended time period. Only by such means could an oil be combined with Rubens strong and richly vitreous Flemish medium, sufficient enough to rapidly call oxygen into the paint film granting, thereby, siccative-grasp necessary to insure *alla prima* rendering of the paints, an absolute must with respect to the 17th Century Flemish and Dutch pictorial techniques.

# Source Notes

## Foreword

1. Jacques Maroger, *The Secret Formulas and Techniques of the Masters* (London and New York: Studio Publications Inc., 1948), p.13. Hereafter in notes, Maroger.
2. Ibid., p.31.
3. *The Strasburg Manuscript*, translated by Viola and Rosamund Borradaile (London; Alec Tiranti, 1966), p.55.

## Introduction

1. David Rosen, Preservation Versus Restoration (Magazine of Art, November, 1941), p.2.
2. *Emile Renders, "Cracks in Flemish Painting"* (The Burlington Magazine, Vol. LII, 1928), p. 65. Had Renders based his suggestion on the remark made by Albrecht Dürer in his diary entry of July 1521, during a visit to Brussels, wherein he states, "I paid 2 st. to the lad, Bartholomaeus by name, who rubbed the colours for me." He was referring to the finishing of the frame for the "King's portrait" and not to the oleaginous paint film which formed the portrait (see: William Martin Conway's *The Writings of Albrecht Dürer, p.125. ck. Bibliography*).
3. Dr. Theodore Turquet De Mayerne (first physician to Charles I of England) was the author of the manuscript now in the British Museum entitled "Pictoria Sculptoria et quae subalternarum artium."

## Book One: First Key

1. Giorgio Vasari, *Lives of the Most Eminent Painters, Sculptors, and Architects*, 5 vols. Trans. Mrs. Jonathan Foster (London: Henry G. Bohn, 1855) vol II pp. 56-58. Hereafter in notes, Vasari, *Lives*.

2. Sir Charles Lock Eastlake, *Materials for a History of Oil Painting* 2 vol. (London: Longman, Brown, Green and Longman, 1847-1868), vol. I, p.253. Reprint, Dover, 1960. Hereafter in notes, Eastlake I, II.

3. Theophilus, *An Essay Upon Various Arts*, trans. Robert Hendrie (London: John Murray, 1847) p.27.

4. Ibid. pp.31, 33.

5. Elizabeth Gilmore Holt, *A Documentary History of Art* 2 vol. (New York: Doubleday Anchor book, 1957), vol. I, pp.199, 200.

6. Filarete, *Treatise on Architecture*, trans. John R. Spencer (New Haven and London: Yale University Press, 1965) vol. I p.311 Hereafter in notes, Filarete, I.

7. Eastlake I, p. 16.

8. Ibid. pp.327, 328. Since linseed is the only oil mentioned suggests the directive is directly linked with Rogier van der Weyden and his 1450 Italian sojourn.

9. Mary P. Merrifield, *Original Treatises*, dating from the XII[th] to the XVIII[th] Centuries, 2 vol. (London: Murray, 1849) vol. I, p. 232. rpt. Dover, 1960. Hereafter in notes, Merrifield.

10. Wolfgang Stechow, *Northern Renaissance Art 1400 – 1600 (New Jersey: Prentice Hall, Inc., 1966) p. 66, n. 42. Hereafter in notes, Northern Renaissance.*

11. Filarete I, p.311.

12. Eastlake I, pp.224, 225.

13. Northern Renaissance Art, p.66.

14. Erwin Panofsky, *Early Netherlandish Painting, its Origins and Character*, 2 vol. (Cambridge: Harvard University, 1966) vol. I p.185.

15. Filarete I, p.311.

## Book One: Second Key

1. Vasari II, p. 62.
2. Maroger, p. 49.
3. Eastlake I, p. 199.
4. Giorgio Vigni, *All the Paintings of Antonello Da Messina*, trans. Anthony Firmin O'Sullivan (New York: Hawthorn Books, Inc., Date unknown) pp.27, 28. Hereafter in notes Vigni.
5. Maroger, p.47.
6. M.J.F.L. Merimee, *The Art of Painting in Oil, and in Fresco*, trans. W.B. Sarsfield Talyor (London: Whittaker and Co., 1839), pp.32, 33.
7. Ibid. pp.61, 62.
8. Maroger, p.52,
9. Ibid. p.154.
10. Anthony W. Robbins, *The Paintings of Antonello Da Messina*, (Connoisseur, March 1975) p.187.
11. Pliny, *Natural History*, 10 vol. trans. H. Rackham, M.A. (Massachusetts: Harvard University Press, 1952) vol. IX p.333.
12. Kirk-Othmer, *Encyclopedia of Chemical Technology*: Second completely revised edition (Information concerning publisher and date unknown) vol. 7. p.272.
13. Martin Davies, *Rogier van der Weyden*, (London: Phaidon, 1972) p.212.
14. Vasari, II, p.225.
15. Ibid. pp.313, 314.
16. Vasari incorrectly believed Perugino to have employed the Eyckian technique. Thus, when he wrote "it was but in his time that the practice of painting well in oil first commences" he was obliquely informing us that he knew there had been an earlier, less well practiced system of oil painting; refuting the belief usually put forward, the Van Eyck invented the first use of oil within the pictorial practices.
17. Vasari, II, p.61.
18. Vigni, vol. 14, p.16.

19. Harry B. Wehle and Margarette Salinger, *A Catalogue of Early Flemish, Dutch and German Paintings*, (New York: The Metropolitan Museum of Art, 1947) p.180.
20. Ibid. p.181.
21. Maroger, p.48.

## *Book One: Third Key*

1. Maroger, p.57.
2. Eastlake, vol. II, p.112.
3. *Codex Atlanticus* composed between 1483 to 1518.
4. *The Literary Works of Leonardo da Vinci*, 2 vol. compiled and edited by Jean Paul Richter, 2nd. ed. Jean Paul Richter and Irma A. Richter (London, New York, Toronto: Oxford University Press, 1939), vol. I, p.363, #364. Hereafter in notes Lit, Works L.d.V.
5. op cit.
6. Maroger, pp.157, 159.
7. Ibid. p.62.
8. Lit. Works, L. d. V. vol. I p.362, #628.
9. Ibid. p. 360, #618, and p.362, #628.
10. Rutherford J. Gettens and George L. Stout, *Painting Materials a Short Encyclopedia* (New York: D. Van Nostrand Co., Inc., 1942) pp.72, 214, 215. Hereafter in notes, Get. and ST. Ptg. MAT.
11. Vasari, Lives II, p.388.
12. Lit. Works L. d. V., vol. I, p.360, #618.
13. Ibid. p.362, #628.
14. *The Writings of Albrecht Dürer*: Trans. and edited by William Martin Conway (New York: Philosophical Library, 1958), pp.69, 70. There are certain contradictions to be found in Dürer's letter of August 26, 1509, written to Jacob Heller, regarding the famed Heller Alter piece. Concerning on instance, Dürer states "If it is kept clean I know it will remain bright and fresh 500 years." Yet elsewhere, he notes that when he checks on the painting after "one, two, or three years time, if the painting is properly dry, it must be taken down and I will varnish over anew with some

excellent varnish, which no one else can make: it will then last 100 years longer...." Hereafter in notes, Dürer's Writings.

It should be obvious to any painter that a work which might not be properly dry after one, two, or three years, will have accumulated so much dust and grime that it would be beyond proper repair. In other words Dürer was exaggerating a condition in order to impress a technically ignorant client: A not too uncommon practice employed, regrettably, by some artists.

It is by that ruse that I base my belief that the varnish which Dürer proposed as a coating capable of extending the visual appearance of the painting for an additional 100 years was but the simple mastic picture varnish available to many painters of his time; particularly those painters who has traveled to Italy.

If I am wrong in my proposal and Dürer actually had invented a new and secret varnish, then, my apology to that great German master.

15. Eastlake, II, p. 121.


## Book One: Fourth Key

1. Vasari, II, p.395.
2. Vasari, V pp.382, 383.
3. Maroger, pp.68, 160.
4. Maroger, p.98.
5. Maroger, pp.160 – 162.
6. Maroger, p.98.
7. Eastlake, I fn. p.529.
8. Eastlake, I pp.527, 528.
9. Giorgio Vasari, *Vasari on Technique*, trans. Louisa S, Maclehose, edited with introduction and notes by Professor G. Baldwin Brown (New York: reprint Dover, 1960) pp.236, 237.
10. Merrifield II, p.730.
11. Maroger, pp.66, 67.

## Book One: Fifth Key

1. Maroger, p.93.
2. Maroger, p.95.
3. Gertrude Winkelmann-Rhein, *The Paintings and Drawings of Jan "Flower" Bruegel* (New York: Harry Abrams, Inc.) p.81.
4. Eugene Fromentin, *The Masters of Past Time,* (London: Phaidon Press Ltd, 1948) p.86.
5. Maroger, p.98. Maroger is incorrect in crediting the recordings of this observation to De Mayerne. However, its sophisticated wording suggest it was taken from a creditable source which, at this time, we have been unable to trace and identify. It is my belief that the transcriber of this directive was mistaken when using the phrase "slightly warned with white lead" and that the communicant of the directive actually said "slowly warmed with white lead", as far more meaningful terminology with respect to the preparation of Van Dyck's white lead saturated drying oil.
6. Eastlake, I pp.307, 308. Let it be noted that we accept Eastlake's quoted "modern manuscript without a name" without engaging in the problem of origin. It is, in our opinion, reflective of Anthony van Dyck's technique and has provided us with sufficient information so as to enable realization of rewarding empirical resolve concerning one of the most plaguing questions of this research: Namely, the preparation of the basic 17th Century Flemish painting medium and the realization of the pictorial methods employed by the painters of both Flanders and Holland. Satisfying, thereby, our painterly curiosity.
7. Ibid., p.530.
8. Maroger, p.95.
9. Mansfield Kirby Talley, *Portrait Painting in England: Studies in the Technical Literature Before 1700* (London: Published privately by the Paul Mellon Centre for Studies in British art, 1981) p.328. Hereafter in Notes, Talley.

10. Ibid. p.326.
11. *Bailey's Industrial Oil and Fat Products,* ed. Daniel Swern (New York, Interscience Publishers, a Division of John Wiley and Sons) p.539. Hereafter in notes, Bailey.
12. Maroger, pp.95, 101, 165.
13. Ibid., p.103.
14. Eastlake I, pp.527, 528.
15. Lionel H. Cust, *Anthony van Dyck, and Historical Study of His Life and Work* (London: Bell, 1900) pp.179, 180. Hereafter in notes, Cust.
16. Maroger, p.409.
17. Carel van Mander, *Dutch and Flemish Painters*, Trans. by Constant Van de Wall (New York, McFarlane, 1936) p.60, notes pp.451, 452.
18. Eastlake I, pp.491-493.
19. Peter Paul Rubens, *Letters* ed. by Ruth Magurn (Cambridge: Harvard University Press, 1955) p.70 letter # 37, note p.144. Hereafter in notes, Rubens Letters.
20. Maroger, p.116.
21. Talley, pp.150-151.
22. Ibid. pp.316, 329.

## Book One: The Dutch Addendum

1. Rubens *Letters*, pp.53, 54, letter #21.
2. Maroger, p.168.
3. *The Paintings of Rembrandt*, ed. by A. Bredius (Great Britain: Phaidon 2 vol.) vol I, p.8.
4. *The Complete Paintings of Rembrandt*, Intro. by Gregory Martin with notes and catalogue by Paolo Lecaidano (New York: Harry N. Abrams) p.10.
5. Maroger, p.168.
6. Frithjof van Thienen, *Jan Vermeer of Delft* (New York: Harper and Brothers, 1949) p.14.
7. Charles Holmes, *Old Masters and Modern Art*, (New York: Harcourt Brace) pp.139, 140.

8. R. H. Wilenski, *Dutch Painting* (New York: The Beechhurst Press) p.66.

## Book One: Random Thoughts
1. Cust, p. 182.
2. Madeleine Hour, *Secrets of the Great Masters: A Study in Artistic Techniques* (New York: G. P. Putnam's Sons, 1964) p.28.

## Book Two: Materials and Pre-Key Directives
1. Charles R. Martens, *Technology of Paints, Varnishes and Lacquers* (New York: Reinhold Book Corporation (n.d.). p.28.
2. Eastlake I, p.531.
3. W. Weber, *Artists' Pigments* (New York: D. van Nostrand, 1923) p.121.
4. Gettens and Stout, p.129.
5. Daniel V. Thompson, *The Practice of Tempera Painting* (New Haven: Yale University Press, 1936. rept. Dover, 1962) p.39. Hereafter in notes, Thompson Tem. Ptg.
6. Ibid. 17-34 note p.39.

## Book Two: First Key Observations and Directives
1. Arthur P. Laurie, *The Painter's Methods and Materials: The Handling of Pigments in Oil, Tempera, Water-colour and in Mural Painting* (Philadelphia: Lippincott, 1926). p.128.
2. Eastlake I, pp.326-341.
3. Ibid. pp.327-332.
4. Dürer's Writings. p.106, 114.

## Book Two: Second Key Observations and Directives
1. Northern Renaissance Art. p.66.


## Book Two: Fourth Key Observations and Directives
1. North Renaissance Art. p.53.
2. Bailey, p.510.
3. Eastlake I, p.329.


## Book Two: Fifth Key Observations and Directives
1. Rubens Letters. pp.5 and 447-448.
2. Samuel Edwards, *Peter Paul Rubens* (New York: David McKay Co., Inc., 1973). pp.147-148.
3. Eastlake I, p.520.

# Bibliography

Alberti, Leone Battista. *On Painting*. Trans. By J. R. Spencer. (New Haven: Yale Univ. 1966).

Andrews, Keith. *Adam Elsheirmer, Paintings – Drawings – Prints*. (New York1: Rizzoli, 1977).

Alpers, Svetlana. *The Making of Rubens*. (New Haven and London: Yale University Press, 1995).

Bachoffner, George H. *Chemistry as Applied to Fine Arts*. (London: J. Carpenter, 1837).

*Bailey's Industrial Oil and Fat Products*. Ed. Daniel Swern. (New York: Interscience Publishers, a Division of John Wiley and Sons.

Baldass, Ludwig. *Jan van Eyck*. (New York: Phaidon, 1952).

Brown, Christopher. *Making and Meaning Rubens Landscapes*. (London: National Gallery Publication, 1997).

Burroughs, Alan. *Art Criticism from a Laboratory*. (Boston: Little, Brown and Company, 1938).

Cawse, John. *The Art of Painting – Portraits, Landscapes, Animals, Draperies, Satins, etc. in Oil Colours*. (London: Rudolph Ackermann, 1840).

Chatelet, Albert. *Van Eyck*. Trans. Murtha Baca. (New York: Woodbury: American Edition, Garron's Educational Series, Inc., 1980).

Constable, W. E. *The Painter's Workshop*. (London: Oxford, 1954).

Conway, Martin. *The Van Eycks and Their Followers*. (New York: E. P. Dutton and Co., 1921).

Cust, Lionel. *Anthony van Eyck, an Historical Study of His Life and Works*. (London: Bell, 1900).

Davis, Martin. *Rogier van der Weyden*. (London: Phaidon, 1972).

Denis, Valentine. *All the Paintings of Jan van Eyck*. (New York: Hawthorn Books, Inc., 1961).

*Dürer, Albrecht, The Writings of*, Trans. and edited by William Martin Conway. (New York: Philosophical Library, 1958).

Engass, Robert and Brown, Jonathan. *Italy and Spain 1600—1750; Sources and Documents*. (New Jersey: Prentice Hall, 1970).

Eastlake, Sr. Charles Lock. *Materials for a History of oil Painting*. 2 vol. (London: Longman, Brown, Green and Longman, 1847 – 1868. Reprint, Dover, 1960).

Edwards, Samuel. *Peter Paul Rubens*. (New York: David McKay Co. Inc., 1973).

Elst, Baron van der. *The Last Flowering of the Middle Ages*. (New York: Doubleday, 1944).

Filarete. *Treatise on Architecture*. Trans. J. R. Spencer, 2 vol. (New Haven and London: Yale University Press, 1965).

Fromentin, Eugene. *The Masters of Past Time*. (London: Phaidon Press, 1948).

Gettens, Rutherford J. and Stout, George L. *Painting Materials: A Short Encyclopedia*. (New York: D. Van Nostrand Co., Inc., 1942).

Harley, R. D. *Artists' Pigments c. 1600 – 1835*. (New York: American Elsevier Pub. Co., Inc., 1970).

Held, Julius S. *Rubens in America*. (New York: Pantheon, 1947).

Held, Julius S. *Rubens Selected Drawings*, 2 vol. (London: Phaidon, 1959).

Held, Julius S. *The Oil Sketches of Peter Paul Rubens*, 2 vol, (Princeton, New Jersey: University Press, 1980).

Held, Julius S. *Rubens and His Circle*. (Princeton, New Jersey: University Press, 1982).

Holmes, Charles. *Old Masters and Modern Art*. (New York: Harcourt Brace).

Holmes, Charles. *Notes on the Science of Picture-Making*. (New York: Frederick A. Stokes Company

Holt, Elizabeth Gilmore. *A Documentary History of Art*. 2 vol. (New York: Doubleday Anchor Book, 1957).

Hurst, George H. *Painters' Colours, Oils, and Varnishes: A Practical Manual*. (London: Charles Griffin and Co. Limited).

Hour, Madeleine. *Secrets of the Great Masters: A Study in Artistic Techniques*. (New York): G. P. Putnam's Sons, 1964).

Irwin, Keith Gordon. *The Romance of Weights and Measures* (Bew Yorj: Viking Press (n.d.).

Jaffe, Michael. *Rubens and Italy*. ( New York: Cornell University Press, 1977).

Kirk-Othmer. *Encyclopedia of Chemical Technology*, Second Completely Revised Edition. vol. 7. (Information concerning publisher and date unknown).

Klein, Robert and Zerner, Henri. *Italian Art 1500 – 1600: Sources and Documents*. (New Jersey: Prentice Hall, 1966).

Laurie, Arthur P. *The Materials of the Painter's Craft in Europe and Egypt From Earliest Times to the End of the XVIIth Century*. (Philadelphia: Lippincott, 1926).

Laurie, Arthur P. *The Painter's Methods and Materials; The Handling of Pigments in Oils, Tempera, Water-colour and in Mural Painting.* (Philadelphia: Lippincott, 1926).

Laurie, Arthur P. *The Technique of the Great Painters.* (London: Carroll, 1949).

Mander, Carel van. *Dutch and Flemish Painters.* Trans. Constant Van de Wall. (New York: McFarlane, 1936).

Maroger, Jacques. *The Secret Formulas and Techniques of the Masters.* (London and New York: Studio Publications Inc., 1948).

Martens, Charles R. ed. *Technology of Paints, Varnishes and Lacquers.* (New York: Reinhold Book Corporation (n.d.).

Merimee, M. J. F. L. *The Art of Painting in Oil, and in Fresco.* Trans. W. B. Sarsfield Talyor (London: Whittaker and Co., 1839).

Merrifield, Mary P. *Original Treatises, Dating From the XIIth to XVIIth Centuries on the Arts of Painting in Oil, Miniature, Mosaic, and on Glass.* 2 vol. (London: Murray, 1849),

Panofsky, Erwin. *Early Netherlandish Painting, Its Origins and Character.* 2 vol. (Cambridge: Harvard University Press, 1954).

Philips, Lottie Brand. *The Ghent Alterpiece and the Art of Jan van Eyck.* (Princeton, University Press. 1971).

Pliny, the Elder. *Natural History.* 10 vol., Trans. H. Rackham. (Cambridge: Harvard University Press, 1938 – 1962).

Puyvelde, Leo van. *The Sketches of Rubens.* (London: Kegan Paul, Trench, Trubner and Co. Ltd., 1947).

Puyvelde, Leo van and Thierry van Puyvelde. *Flemish Painting the Art of Rubens and van Dyck.* Trans. Alan Kendall. (New York: McGraw Hill, 1970).

Rubens, Peter Paul. *Letters*. ed. Ruth Magurn. (Cambridge: Harvard University Press, 1955).

Stechow, Wolfgang. *Northern Renaissance Art, 1400 – 1600: Sources and Documents*. (New Jersey: Prentice Hall, 1966).

Stevenson, Robert A. M. *Rubens, Paintings and Drawings*. (London: Phaidon, 1939).

Stillman, John Maxson. *History of Early Chemistry*. (Canada: General Publishing Co., Ltd.,1924. reprint Dover, 1960).

*Strasburg Manuscript*. Trans. V. and R. Borradaile. (London: Alec Tiranti, 1966).

Tally, Mansfield Kirby. *Portrait Painting in England: Studies in the Technical Literature Before 1700*. (London: Published privately by the Paul Mellon Centre for Studies in British Art, 1981).

Theophilus. *An Essay Upon Various Arts*. Trans. Robert Hendrie. (London: John Murray, 1847).

Theophilus. *On Divers Arts, the Treatise of Theophilus*. Trans, John G. Hawthorne and Cyril Stanley Smith. (Chicago: University Press, 1963).

Thienen, Frithjof van. *Jan Verneer of Delft*. (New York: Harper and Brothers, 1949).

Thompson, Daniel V. *The Materials and Medieval Painting*. (New Haven: Yale University Press, 1936. reprint Dover, 1956).

Thompson, Daniel V. *The Practice of Temper Painting*. (New Haven: Yale University, 1936. reprint Dover, 1962).

Thompson, Daniel V. *Il Libro dell'Arte: The Craftsman's Handbook of Cenino d'Andrea Cennini*. (New Haven: Yale University Press, 1933. reprint Dover, 1960).

Toch, Maximilian. *The Chemistry and Technology of Paintings*. 3rd ed. (New York: D. van Nostrand, 1925).

Vasari, Georgio. *Lives of the Most Eminent Painters, Sculptors, and Architects*. 5 vols. Trans. Mrs. Jonathon Foster (London: Henry G. Bohn, 1855).

Vasari, Georgio. *Vasari on Technique*. Trans. Louisa S. Maclehose (New York: reprint, 1960).

Vigni, Giorgio. *All the Paintings of Antonello Da Messina*. Trans. Anthony Formin O'Sullivan (New York: Hawthorn Books, Inc., 1963).

Waetzoldt, Wilhelm. *Dürer and His Times*. (New York: Phaidon, 1950).

Weber, F. W. *Artist Pigments*. (New York: D, van Nostrand, 1923).

Wild, Angenitus M. de. *The Scientific Examination of Pictures: an Investigation of the Pigments Used by the Dutch and Flemish Masters*. Trans. L. C. Jackson (London: Bell, 1929).

Wilenski, Reginald H. *Dutch Painting*. (London: Faber, 1955).

Wilenski, Reginald H. *Flemish Painters 1430 – 1830*. 2 vol. (New York, Viking Press, 1960).

Winkelmann-Rhein, Gertrude. *The Paintings and Drawings of Jan "Flower" Bruegel*. Trans. Leonard Mins. (New York: Abrams, 1968).

Zeri, Federico. "Giovanni Da Asola," "The Holy Family with SS, John the Baptist and Jerome." *Italian Paintings in the Walters Art Gallery* (Baltimore, Maryland: Published by the Trustees (1976).

# Magazines, Journals, Bulletins, etc.

Ainsworth, Maryan W. *"Workshop Practice in early Netherlandish Painting: An Inside View." From Van Eyck to Bruegel* (New York) Metropolitan Museum of Art (1998). pp. 205-211.

Barbera, Gioacchino. "The Life and Work of Antonello da Messina, Sicily's Renaissance Master." (New York) Metropolitan Museum of Art. (2005). pp. 17-30.

Baudouin, Frans. "Two Oil Sketches by Rubens." *The Connoisseur*, vol. 194, no. 782. (April 1977). pp. 261-265.

Bijl, Martin. "*The Meagre Company* and Frans's Hals Working Method." Frans Hals—(London) Royal Academy of Arts. (1989). pp. 103-108.

Bortolaso, Giovanna. "Titian's Technique"—"A Study of Various Works from the Period 1542-1576." *Titian: Prince of Painters.* (Venice) Marsilio Editori (June, 1990). pp. 385-387.

Bowron, Edgar Peters. "Oil and Tempera Mediums and Their Identification." *A View from the Laboratory.* Apollo, vol. C, no. 53. (November 1974). pp. 34-41.

Brachett, Thomas. trans. C.P. Casparis. "A Distinctive Aspect in the Painting Technique of the 'Ginevra de' Benci' and of Leonardo's Early Works." (Washington, D. C.) National Gallery of Art, Report and Studies in the History of Art (1969). pp. 85-102.

Brockwell, Maurice W. "The Ghent Alterpiece: the Inscription Obliterated" and "Hubert van Eyck: the Hubertist Bubble Finally Deflated." *Burlington Magazine* n.d. p. 99; pp. 111, 136.

Buck, Richard W. "Rubens-The Gerbier Family: Examination and Treatment." (Washington, D. C.) National Gallery of Art: Studies in the History of Art (1973). pp. 32-53.

Bull, David and Plesters, Joyce. "The Feast of the Gods, Conservation, Examination, and Interpretation." (Washington, D. C.) National Gallery of Art: Studies in History of Are.40. (1990). pp. 21-50.

Butler, Marigene H. "Appendix; An Investigation of the Technique and Materials used by Jan Steen." Bulletin, Philadelphia Museum of Art (1983). pp. 44-52.

Butler, Marigene H. "An Investigation of the Philadelphia Saint Francis Receiving the Stigmata." Jan van Eyck: *Two Paintings of Saint Francis Receiving the Stigmata.* Philadelphia Museum of Art (1997). pp. 28-46.

Charlton, John. "Rubens and the Ceiling Painting." The Banqueting House, Whitehall, London (1964). pp. 48-49.

Christensen, Carol; Palmer, Michael; Swicklik, Michael. "Van Dyck's Painting Technique, His Writings and Three Paintings in the National Art Gallery." *Anthony Van Dyck*, National Gallery of Art (1990-1991). pp. 45-52.

Cormans, Paul. "Van Eyck in the Laboratory" Burlington Magazine, n.d.

De Mayerne Ms. Xerox (From Ernest Berger's *Beitrage*).

Desneux, Jules. "Underdrawings and Pentimenti in the Pictures of Jan van Eyck." (no pertinent information regarding source of date).

Fassina, Vasco; Mattenini, Mauro; Moles, Arcangelo. "A Study of the Binders of Seven Painting by Titian in Venice." *Titian Prince of Painters* (Venice) Marsilio Editori (June, 1990). pp. 388-400.

Feller Robert. "Rubens: Technical Examination of the Pigments and Paint Layers." (Washington, D. C.) National Gallery of Art: Studies in the History of Art (1973). pp. 54-74.

Feller, Robert. "Dammar and Mastic Varnishes—Hardness and Change in Weight Upon Drying." Studies in Conversation, III (1958). pp. 162-174.

Gluck, H. "The Dilemma of the Painter and Conservator in the Synthetic Age." The Museums Journal, LIV. (1954). pp. 149-158.

Gombrich E. H. "Dark varnishes: Variations of the Theme of Pliny." The Burlington Magazine, CIV. (1962). pp. 51-55.

Groen, Karin and Hendricks, Ella. "Frans Hals: A Technical Examination." (London) Royal Academy of Arts. pp. 109-123.

Held, Julius S. "Van Dyck's Oil Sketches:" "Catalogue of Oil Sketches." Anthony van Dyck: National Gallery of Art (Washington, D. C.) (1990-1991). pp. 326-329; pp. 330-336.

Huyghe, Bene. "In the light of Vermeer." *Five Centuries of Paintings: In the Light of Vermeer.* (The Hague) Jubilee-Exhibition Mauritshuis 1816-1966 (1966). Pages unnumbered.

Keisch, Brenard. "X-ray Diffraction and the Lead White." (Washington, D. C.) Studies in the History of Art, National Gallery of Art (1971-1972). pp. 121-133.

Kuhn, Hermann. "A Study of the Pigments and the Grounds Used by Jan Vermeer" (Washington D. C.) Reports and Studies in the History of Art, National Gallery of Art (1968). pp. 155-175.

Kurz, Otto. "Varnishes, Tinted Varnishes, and Patina." The Burlington Magazine CIV. (February, 1962). pp. 56-59.

Lazzarini, Lorenzo. "Titian's Technique" – "A Study of Various Works from the Period 1510-1542." *Titian: Prince of Painters* (Venice). Marsilio Editori (June, 1990). pp. 378-384.

Lewman, Larry. "A Portrait of Maroger." (Baltimore, Maryland) WMAR television script, mimeograph. (1991).

Lowenthal, Anne Walter. "Wtewael's Moses and Dutch Mannerism." (Washington, D. C.) Studies in the History of Art, National Gllery of Art (1974). pp. 124-141.

Martin, Gregory. "The Marriage of Giovanni Arnolfini and Giovanna Cenami;" "A Man in a Turban;" Portrait of a Young Man;" Portrait of Susanna Lunden (nee Fourment) (?); "A Lion Hunt;" "The Birth of Venus;" "Paris Awards the Golden Apple to Venus (The Judgment of Paris);" and "Appendix II" – "The Grounds for Pictures by or Associated with Rubens" (Joyce Plesters). (London) *The Flemish School*, circa 1600-1900. The National Gallery MCMIXX. pp. 33-34; 34-35; 35; 174-176; 182-185; 188-191; 213-215; 289-290.

Narodny, Leo. "Microscopic Examination of Thin Section of the Old Masters." Unpublished-typewritten. (River road, Norwalk Conn.). (1980's). pp. 1-3.

Packard, Elizabeth C. G. "A Problem in Technical Research; The Walters "St. Francis" – A Contribution to El Greco Studies." (Baltimore, Maryland) The Journal of Walters Art Gallery, XXIII (1960). pp. 49-71.

Plesters, Joyce. "Dark Varnishes-some further comments" *The Burlington Magazine*, CIV. (1963). pp. 452-460.

Plesters, Joyce. "Cross-sections and Chemical Analysis of Paint Samples" Studies in Conversation, XII (1956). pp. 110-157.

Plesters, Joyce. see: Martin, Gregory, Appendix II: "The Grounds for Pictures by or Associated with Rubens."

Plesters, Joyce and Lazzarini, Lorenzo. "Preliminary Obsevations on the Technique and Materials of Tintoretto." *Painting Methods and Materials.* (London) Scientific Department, National Gallery. (Wording document). pp. 153-179.

Pouthas, Charles H. "Discovery of the Secret of the Van Eyck's" (pamphlet – n.d.) no. of pages, 7.

Rees Jones, Stephen. "The Cleaning Controversy: Further Comments." *The Burlington Magazine,* CV (1962). pp. 97-98.

Rosen, David. "Preservation Versus Restoration." *Magazine of Art* (1941). pp. 2-15.

Shapley, Fern Rusk. "Titian's Venus with a Mirror." (Washington, D. C.). Studies in the History of Art, National Gallery (1971-1972). pp. 93-105.

Spicer, Joaneath. "A Beggar Attributed to Jacques Bellange." (Baltimore, Maryland). The Walters, bulletin (1991). pp. 2-3.

Walker, John. "Ginevra de' Benci by Leonardo da Vinci." (Washington, D. C.). Report and Studies in the History of Art, National Gallery of Art (1967). pp. 1-22.

Van De Graff, J. A. "The Interpretation of Old Painting Recipes." The Burlington Magazine, CIV. (1962). pp. 471-475.

Wehle, Harry B. "Antonello da Messina," "Portrait of a Young Man;" "Christ Crowned with Thorns;" "Giorgione or Titian;" "Portrait of a Man;" "Titian;" "Portrait of Alfonso d'Este, Duke of Ferrara;" "Tintoretto;" "The Finding of Moses;" "Doge Alvise Mocenigo Presented to the Redeemer;" "Feti;" "The Good Samaritan;" "Velazquez;" "Christ and the Pilgrims of Emmaus;" A Catalogue of Italian, Spanish, and Byzantine Paintings (New York). The Metropolitan Museum of Art (1940). pp. 174-176; 188-189; 192-193; 198-199, 200; 256; 236-238.

Wehle, Henry B. and Salinger, Margaretta, "Hubert van Eyck," "The Crucifixion and the Last Judgment;" "Jan van Eyck and Helpers;" "The Annunciation;" "Petrus Christus;" "Portrait of a Carthusian;" "Joos van Gent;" "The Adoration of the Magi;" "Hieronymus Bosch;" "The Adoration of the Magi;" "Pieter Bruegel the Elder;" "The Harvesters (July);" "Albert Dürer;" "Salvator Mundi," (New York) A Catalogue of Early Flemish, Dutch and German Paintings. The Metropolitan Museum of Art (1947). pp. 1-9; 12-15; 17-18; 53-55; 120-122; 156-158; 179-181.

*About the Author*

After Frank Redelius was discharged from the United States Marine Corps, during which he experienced 34 days of combat during the invasion of Iwo Jima, he began his artistic career. He enrolled in the Maryland Institute College of Art in Baltimore, Maryland. There he came under the tutelage and influence of Jacques Maroger, author of *The Secret Formulas and Techniques of the Old Masters*. When he finished his postgraduate studies, he graduated with honors in 1950-51 and became Maroger's principal technical assistant. Redelius continued to work with Maroger until the evening of Maroger's death in 1962 when he and Madame Maroger heard him draw his last breath.

It was then that Redelius—at Maroger's request—continued the search for the body of truth surrounding the techniques of the masters from the 15th through the 17th Centuries. As Redelius researched and experimented he began to question and reevaluate some of the theories, principles, and practices described in *The Secret Formulas*. This book, *The Master Keys*, is the result of 35 years of work to advance Maroger's research and to prepare the way for future discoveries.

# Index of Painters

Altdorfer, Albrecht: 41, 172
Apelles: 31-32, 133
Bassano, Jacopo: 74, 77
Bellini, Giovanni: 39, 54, 69-70
Bloemaert, Abraham: 81, 123
Bombelli, Sebastiano: 94-95, 194
Bosch, Hieronymus: 154
Botticelli, Sandro: 36
Bouts, Dirk: 26
Bril, Paul: 80
Bruegel, Jan: 79-82, 96, 103, 105, 114, 123, 134-135, 186,
        201-203
Bruegel, Pieter (Elder): 12, 41, 401, 166, 171-173
Bruegel, Pieter (Younger): 201
Campin, Robert: 26
Christus, Petrus: 26
Cranach, Lucas: 26
Da Castelfranco, Giorgione: 53-57, 61-71, 75-76, 86, 88--91,
        100, 117, 127, 134-135, 159, 166, 175, 182-191, 196,
        203-205
Da Messina, Antonello: 1, 7, 27-47, 50, 52-53 ,64-65, 76,
        104, 132, 134, 154-155, 159, 166-167, 169, 171-172,
        174-178, 182-184, 203
Da Vinci, Leonardo: 42-55, 64-65, 67, 69, 72, 76 , 133, 145,
        155-160, 166, 172, 176-180, 183, 185, 190-191, 201-
        208, 214
David, Gerard: 41, 172
De Hollander, Jan: 104
De Hooch, Pieter: 126, 128

Dei Barbari, Jacopo: 41, 166
Della Francesca, Piero: 37
Descamps, J.B.: 110-111
Dufy, Raoul: 137
Dürer, Albrecht: 12, 40-41, 52, 159, 172
Elsheimer, Adam: 80, 123, 129
Fabritius, Carel: 126
Feti, Domenico: 198
Fromentin, Eugene: 83
Giovane, Palma: 198
Gossaert, Jan: 41
Grunewald, Mathias: 41
Hals, Frans: 122, 127, 133
Hondecoeter, Melchior: 122
Jansen, Cornelius: 84
Kneller, Godfrey: 207
Lastman, Pieter: 81, 122-123
Lely, Peter: 94, 120
Marsh, Reginald: 149
Memling, Hans: 26
Metsu, Gabriel: 128
Perugino, Pietro: 37
Pino, Paolo: 173
Pollaiuolo, Antonio: 36
Pollaiuolo, Piero: 36
Pordenone, Giovanni: 117
Rubens, Peter Paul: 58, 66, 69, 79-83, 88-89, 96-103, 106-
       115, 122-123, 129, 133, 135, 142, 180, 190, 192-193,
       201-203, 207-214
Ruisdael, Jacob: 122
Snyders, Frans: 201
Steen, Jan: 126
Ter Borch, Gerard: 126, 128
Tintoretto, Jocopo Robusti: 189
Titian: 69, 72, 104-105, 117, 124, 133, 189
Utewael, Joachim: 123
Van Balen, Hendrik: 89

Van der Goes, Hugo: 26
Van der Weyden, Rogier: 7, 10, 15, 26, 36, 155
Van Dyck, Anthony: 58, 83-101, 103, 105-107, 109, 115-116,
        120-122, 124, 127, 129-130, 133, 142, 190, 195, 203-
        205, 207-211
Van Eyck, Jan: 1-22, 25-26, 28, 30-31, 33-37, 40-42, 45, 49-
        50, 76-77, 179, 182, 184, 191
Van Helst, Bartholomeus: 122
Van Leyden, Lucas: 12, 41
Van Mander, Carel: 13, 20, 23, 104, 153, 170-171
Van Rijn, Rembrandt: 122-123, 142, 190, 203
Van Veen, Otto: 81
Vasari, Giorgio: 1-4, 6, 8, 15, 19, 25, 27, 37-39, 48, 54, 71-
        76, 149, 180, 197-198
Vermeer, Jan: 126-131, 190
Veronese, Paolo: 70, 189
Vivarini, Alvise: 39